The Definitive Book of

BODY LANGUAGE

Why not use Allan Pease as guest speaker for your next conference or seminar?

Allan and Barbara Pease are the most successful relationship authors in the business. They have written a total of 16 bestsellers - Including 9 number ones - and give seminars in up to 30 countries each year. Their books are available in over 100 countries, are translated into 53 languages and have sold over 25 million copies. They appear regularly in the media worldwide and their work has been the subject of 9 television series, a stage play in Paris and Amsterdam and a number one box office movie which attracted a combined audience of over 100 million.

Their company, Pease International Ltd, produces videos, training courses and seminars for business and governments worldwide. Their monthly relationship column had over 20 million readers in 25 countries. They have 6 children and 7 grandkids and are based in Australia and the UK.

Also by Allan & Barbara Pease:

DVD Programs
Body Language Series
Silent Signals Series
How To Be A People Magnet
The Best Of Body Language
How To Develop Powerful
Communication Skills - Managing the
Differences Between Men & Women

Audio Programs
The Definitive Book Of Body Language
Why Men Don't Listen & Women Can't
 Read Maps
Why Men Don't Have A Clue & Women
 Always Need More Shoes
How To Make Appointments By
 Telephone
Questions Are The Answers
It's Not What You Say

Books
The Definitive Book Of Body Language
Why Men Don't Listen & Women Can't
 Read Maps
Why Men Don't Have A Clue & Women
 Always Need More Shoes!
Why Men Want Sex & Women Need
 Love
Easy Peasey - People Skills For Life
Questions Are The Answers
Why He's So Last Minute & She's Got It
 All Wrapped Up
Why Men Can Only Do One Thing At A
 Time & Women Never Stop Talking
How Compatible Are You? - Your
 Relationship Quiz Book
Talk Language
Write Language
Body Language in the Workplace
The Body Language of Love

www.PeaseInternational.com

The Definitive Book of

BODY LANGUAGE

Allan & Barbara Pease

*This book is dedicated to all people
who have good eyesight but who cannot see.*

PEASE INTERNATIONAL
www.peaseinternational.com

This edition published in 2012 by
Pease International Pty Ltd
Phone: +61-7-5445 5600
Fax: +61-7-5445 5688
Email: info@peaseinternational.com
Web: www.peaseinternational.com
Facebook Fan Page: www.facebook.com/AllanandBarbaraPease

Published in Great Britain by Orion Publishing Group
Distributed in Australia and New Zealand by HarperCollins Publishers Pty Ltd
Distributed in Asia by Pansing Distribution

Art direction by Santamaria www.santamaria.co.uk
Illustrations by Piero and John Hepworth

Printed in Australia by Griffin Press

The publisher and authors wish to thank the following for permission to reproduce images: Alpha, Aquarius Library, Ardea, Associated Press, Brigeman Art Library, Camera Press, Corbis UK, Empics, Getty, Getty Hulton, Getty/Rubberball Productions, Getty/Time Life, John Frost Newspaper Collection, The Kobal Collection, LP Pictures, Nature, NHPA, PA Photos, Picture Bank, Powerstock/Banana Stock, Powerstock/Mauritius, Reuters, Rex Features and Scala Archives

Paperback 1 92081607 0
Hardback 1 92081610 0

www.peaseinternational.com
www.pease.tv

CONTENTS

12. Mirroring – How We Build Rapport 250

13. The Secret Signals of Cigarettes, Glasses and Make-up 265

14. How the Body Points to Where the Mind Wants to Go 279

ACKNOWLEDGEMENTS

These are some of the people who have directly or indirectly contributed to this book, whether they knew it or not:

Dr John Tickel, Dr Dennis Waitley, Dr Andre Davril, Professor Phillip Hunsaker, Trevor Dolby, Armin Gontermann, Lothar Menne, Ray & Ruth Pease, Malcolm Edwards, Ian Marshall, Laura Meehan, Ron & Toby Hale, Darryl Whitby, Susan Lamb, Sadaaki Hayashsi, Deb Mehrtens, Deb Hinckesman, Doreen Carroll, Steve Wright, Derryn Hinch, Dana Reeves, Ronnie Corbett, Vanessa Feltz, Esther Rantzen, Jonathan Coleman, Trish Goddard, Kerri-Anne Kennerley, Bert Newton, Roger Moore, Lenny Henry, Ray Martin, Mike Walsh, Don Lane, Ian Lesley, Anne Diamond, Gerry & Sherry Meadows, Stan Zermarnik, Darrel Somers, Andres Kepes, Leon Byner, Bob Geldof, Vladimir Putin, Andy McNab, John Howard, Nick & Katherine Greiner, Bryce Courtney, Tony & Cherie Blair, Greg & Kathy Owen, Lindy Chamberlain, Mike Stoller, Gerry & Kathy Bradbeer, Ty & Patti Boyd, Mark Victor Hansen, Brian Tracy, Kerry Packer, Ian Botham, Helen Richards, Tony Greig, Simon Townsend, Diana Spencer, Princes William and Harry, Prince Charles, Dr Desmond Morris, Princess Anne, David & Jan Goodwin, Iven Frangi, Victoria Singer, John Nevin, Richard Otton, Raoul Boielle, Matthew Braund, Doug Constable, George Deveraux, Rob Edmonds, Gerry Hatton, John Hepworth, Bob Heussler, Gay Huber, Ian McKillop, Delia Mills, Pamela Anderson, Wayne Mugridge, Peter Opie, David Rose, Alan White, Rob Winch, Ron Tacchi, Barry Markoff, Christine Maher, Sallie & Geoff Burch, John Fenton, Norman & Glenda Leonard

and
Dorie Simmonds, whose encouragement and enthusiasm
drove us to write this book.

Introduction

By a man's fingernails, by his coat-sleeve, by his boots, by his trouser-knees, by the calluses of his forefinger and thumb, by his expression, by his shirt-cuffs, by his movements — by each of these things a man's calling is plainly revealed. That all united should fail to enlighten the competent enquirer in any case is almost inconceivable.
SHERLOCK HOLMES, 1892

As a young boy, I was always aware that what people said was not always what they meant or were feeling and that it was possible to get others to do what I wanted if I read their real feelings and responded appropriately to their needs. At the age of eleven, I began my sales career selling rubber sponges door-to-door after school to make pocket money and quickly worked out how to tell if someone was likely to buy from me or not. When I knocked on a door, if someone told me to go away but their hands were open and they showed their palms, I knew it was safe to persist with my presentation because, despite how dismissive they may have sounded, they weren't aggressive. If someone told me to go away in a soft voice but used a pointed finger or closed hand, I knew it was time to leave. I loved being a salesperson and was excellent at it. As a teenager, I became a pots and pans salesperson, selling at night, and my ability to read people earnt me enough money to buy my first piece of property. Selling gave me the opportunity to meet people and study them at close range and to evaluate whether they would buy or not, simply by watching their body language. This skill also proved a bonanza for meeting girls in discos. I could nearly always predict who would say 'yes' to a dance with me and who wouldn't.

1

I joined the life insurance business at the age of twenty, and went on to break several sales records for the firm I worked for, becoming the youngest person to sell over a million dollars' worth of business in my first year. This achievement qualified me for the prestigious Million Dollar Round Table in the USA. As a young man I was fortunate that the techniques I'd learned as a boy in reading body language while selling pots and pans could be transferred to this new area, and was directly related to the success I could have in any venture involving people.

All Things Are Not What They Seem

The ability to work out what is really happening with a person is simple - not easy, but simple. It's about matching what you see and hear in the environment in which it all happens and drawing probable conclusions. Most people, however, only see the things they think they are seeing.

Here's a story to demonstrate the point:

Two men were walking through the woods when they came across a big deep hole.

'Wow ... that looks deep,' says one. 'Let's toss a few pebbles in and see how deep it is.'

They threw in a few pebbles and waited, but there was no sound.

'Gee – that is a *really* deep hole. Let's throw one of these big rocks in. That should make a noise.'

They picked up two football-sized rocks and tossed them into the hole and waited, but still they heard nothing.

'There's a railway sleeper over here in the weeds,' said one. 'If we toss that in, it's *definitely* going to make some noise.'

They dragged the heavy sleeper over to the hole and heaved it in, but not a sound came from the hole.

Suddenly, out of the nearby woods, a goat appeared, running like the wind. It rushed towards the two men and ran right between them, running as fast as its legs could go. Then it leaped into the air and disappeared into the hole. The two men stood there, astonished at what they'd just seen.

Out of the woods came a farmer who said, 'Hey! Did you guys see my goat?'

'You bet we did! It was the craziest thing we've ever seen! It came running like the wind out of the woods and jumped into that hole!'

'Nah,' says the farmer. 'That couldn't have been my goat. My goat was chained to a railway sleeper!'

How Well Do You Know the Back of Your Hand?

Sometimes we say we know something 'like the back of our hand' but experiments prove that less than 5% of people can identify the back of their hands from a photograph. The results of a simple experiment we conducted for a television programme showed that most people are generally not good at reading body language signals either. We set up a large mirror at the end of a long hotel lobby, giving the illusion that, as you entered the hotel, there was a long corridor going through the hotel and out the back of the lobby. We hung large plants from the ceiling to a distance of 5 feet above the floor so that, as each person entered the lobby, it looked as if another person was entering at the same time from the other end. The 'other person' was not readily recognisable because the plants covered their face, but you could clearly see their body and movement. Each guest observed the other 'guest' for five to six seconds before turning left to the reception desk. When asked if they had recognised the other 'guest', 85% of men answered 'no'. Most men had failed to recognise themselves in a mirror, one saying, 'You mean that fat, ugly guy?' Unsurprisingly, 58% of the women said it was a mirror and 30% said the other 'guest' looked 'familiar'.

*Most men and nearly half of all women
don't know what they look like from the neck down.*

How Well Can You Spot Body Language Contradictions?

People everywhere have developed a fascination with the body language of politicians because everyone knows that politicians sometimes pretend to believe in something that they don't believe in, or infer that they are someone other than who they really are. Politicians spend much of their time ducking, dodging, avoiding, pretending, lying, hiding their emotions and feelings, using smokescreens or mirrors and waving to imaginary friends in the crowd. But we instinctively know that they will eventually be tripped up by contradictory body language signals, so we love to watch them closely, in anticipation of catching them out.

*What signal alerts you that a politician is lying?
His lips are moving.*

For another television show, we conducted an experiment with the co-operation of a local tourist bureau. Tourists entered the bureau to ask for information about local sightseeing and other tourist attractions. They were directed to a counter where they spoke with a tourism officer, a man with blond hair, a moustache, wearing a white shirt and tie. After a few minutes discussing possible itineraries, the man bent down out of sight below the counter to get some brochures. Then, another man with a clean-shaven face, dark hair and wearing a blue shirt appeared from beneath the counter holding the brochures. He continued the discussion from exactly where the first man had left off. Remarkably, around half the tourists failed to notice the change and men were twice as likely as women to completely miss the change, not only in body language but in the appearance of a completely new person! Unless you have an innate ability or have learned to read body language, the chances are you're missing most of it too. This book will show you what you've been missing.

How We Wrote This Book

Barbara and I have written *The Definitive Book of Body Language* using my original book, *Body Language*, as our base. Not only have we considerably expanded on that one, we have also introduced research from new scientific disciplines, such as evolutionary biology and evolutionary psychology as well as technologies such as Magnetic Resonance Imaging (MRI), which shows what happens in the brain. We have written it in a style that means it can be opened and read on almost any page at random. We've kept the content mainly to the movement of the body, expressions and gestures, because these are the things you need to learn to get the most out of every face-to-face encounter. *The Definitive Book of Body Language* will make you more aware of your own non-verbal cues and signals, and will show you how to use them to communicate effectively and how to get the reactions you want.

This book isolates and examines each component of body language and gesture in simple terms to make it accessible to you. Few gestures are made in isolation of others however, so we have also, at the same time, tried to avoid oversimplifying things.

There will always be those who throw up their hands in horror and claim that the study of body language is just another means by which scientific knowledge can be used to exploit or dominate others by reading their secrets or thoughts. We feel however, that this book seeks to give you greater insight into communication with your fellow humans, so that you can have a deeper understanding of other people and, therefore, of yourself. Understanding how something works makes living with it easier, whereas ignorance and lack of understanding promote fear and superstition and make us more critical of others. A birdwatcher doesn't study birds so that he can shoot them down and keep them as trophies. In the same way, the knowledge and skills in body language serve to make every encounter with another person an exciting experience.

For the purpose of simplicity, and unless otherwise stated, the use of 'he' or 'him' will apply equally to both genders.

Your Body Language Dictionary

The original book was intended as a working manual for sales people, managers, negotiators and executives, but this one can be used for any aspect of your life, be it at home, on a date or at work. *The Definitive Book of Body Language* is the result of over 30 years of our cumulative knowledge and involvement in this field and we give you the basic 'vocabulary' you need to read attitudes and emotions. This book will give you answers to some of the most puzzling questions you've ever had about why people use some of the behaviours they do, and it will change forever your own behaviour. It will seem as if you've always been in a dark room and, while you could always feel the furnishings, the wall hangings and the door, you've never actually seen what they look like. This book will be like turning on the lights to see what was always there. But now, you'll know exactly what things are, where they are and what to do about them.

Allan Pease

Chapter 1

UNDERSTANDING THE BASICS

This is 'good' to Westerners, 'one' to Italians,
'five' to Japanese and 'up yours' to the Greeks

Everyone knows someone who can walk into a room full of people and, within minutes, give an accurate description about the relationships between those people and what they are feeling. The ability to read a person's attitudes and thoughts by their behaviour was the original communication system used by humans before spoken language evolved.

Before radio was invented, most communication was done in writing through books, letters and newspapers, which meant that ugly politicians and poor speakers, such as Abraham Lincoln, could be successful if they persisted long enough and wrote good print copy. The radio era gave openings to people who had a good command of the spoken word, like Winston Churchill, who spoke wonderfully but may have struggled to achieve as much in today's more visual era.

Today's politicians understand that politics is about image and appearance and most high-profile politicians now have personal body language consultants to help them come across as being sincere, caring and honest, especially when they're not.

It seems almost incredible that, over the thousands of years of our evolution, body language has been actively studied on any scale only since the 1960s and that most of the public has become aware of its existence only since our book *Body Language* was published in 1978. Yet most people believe that speech is still our main form of communication. Speech has been part of our communication repertoire only in recent times in evolutionary terms, and is mainly used to convey facts and data. Speech probably first developed between 2 million and 500,000 years ago, during which time our brain tripled its size. Before then, body language and sounds made in the throat were the main forms of conveying emotions and feelings, and that is still the case today. But because we focus on the words people speak, most of us are largely uninformed about body language, let alone its importance in our lives.

Our spoken language, however, recognises how important body language is to our communication. Here are just a few of the phrases we use –

Get it off your chest. Keep a stiff upper lip.
Stay at arm's length. Keep your chin up.
Shoulder a burden. Face up to it.
Put your best foot forward. Kiss my butt.

Some of these phrases are hard to swallow, but you've got to give us a big hand because there are some real eye-openers here. As a rule of thumb, we can keep them coming hand over fist until you either buckle at the knees or turn your back on the whole idea. Hopefully, you'll be sufficiently touched by these phrases to lean towards the concept.

In the Beginning...

Silent movie actors like Charlie Chaplin were the pioneers of body language skills, as this was the only means of communication available on the screen. Each actor's skill was classed as good or bad by the extent to which he could use gestures and body signals to communicate to the audience. When talking films became popular and less emphasis was placed on the non-verbal aspects of acting, many silent movie actors faded into obscurity and only those with good verbal and non-verbal skills survived.

As far as the academic study of body language goes, perhaps the most influential pre-twentieth-century work was Charles Darwin's *The Expression of the Emotions in Man and Animals*, published in 1872, but this work tended to be read mainly by academics. However, it spawned the modern studies of facial expressions and body language, and many of Darwin's ideas and observations have since been validated by researchers around the world. Since that time, researchers have noted and recorded almost a million non-verbal cues and signals. Albert Mehrabian, a pioneer researcher of body language in the 1950s, found that the total impact of a message is about 7% verbal (words only) and 38% vocal (including tone of voice, inflection and other sounds) and 55% non-verbal.

It's how you looked when you said it, not what you actually said.

Anthropologist Ray Birdwhistell pioneered the original study of non-verbal communication – what he called 'kinesics'. Birdwhistell made some similar estimates of the amount of non-verbal communication that takes place between humans. He estimated that the average person actually speaks words for a total of about ten or eleven minutes a day and that the average sentence takes only about 2.5 seconds. Birdwhistell also estimated we can make and recognise around 250,000 facial expressions.

Like Mehrabian, he found that the verbal component of a face-to-face conversation is less than 35% and that over 65% of communication is done non-verbally. Our analysis of thousands of recorded sales interviews and negotiations during the 1970s and 1980s showed that, in business encounters, body language accounts for between 60 and 80% of the impact made around a negotiating table and that people form 60 to 80% of their initial opinion about a new person in less than four minutes. Studies also show that when negotiating over the telephone, the person with the stronger argument usually wins, but this is not so true when negotiating face-to-face, because overall we make our final decisions more on what we see than what we hear.

Why It's Not What You Say

Despite what it may be politically correct to believe, when we meet people for the first time we quickly make judgements about their friendliness, dominance and potential as a sexual partner – and their eyes are *not* the first place we look.

Most researchers now agree that words are used primarily for conveying information, while body language is used for negotiating interpersonal attitudes and in some cases is used as a substitute for verbal messages. For example, a woman can give a man a 'look to kill' and will convey a very clear message to him without opening her mouth.

Regardless of culture, words and movements occur together with such predictability that Birdwhistell was the first to claim that a well-trained person should be able to tell what movement a person is making by listening to their voice. Birdwhistell even learned how to tell what language a person was speaking, simply by watching their gestures.

Many people find difficulty in accepting that humans are still biologically animals. We are a species of primate – *Homo sapiens* – a hairless ape that has learned to walk on two limbs and has a clever, advanced brain. But like any other species, we are still dominated by biological rules that control our actions, reactions, body language and gestures. The fascinating thing is that the human animal is rarely aware that its postures, movements and gestures can tell one story while its voice may be telling another.

How Body Language Reveals Emotions and Thoughts

Body language is an outward reflection of a person's emotional condition. Each gesture or movement can be a valuable key to an emotion a person may be feeling at the time. For example, a man who is self-conscious about gaining weight may tug at the fold of skin under his chin; the woman who is aware of extra pounds on her thighs may smooth her dress down; the person who is feeling fearful or defensive might fold their arms or cross their legs or both; and a man talking with a large-breasted woman may consciously avoid staring at her breasts while, at the same time, unconsciously use groping gestures with his hands.

Prince Charles finds a bosom buddy

The key to reading body language is being able to understand a person's emotional condition while listening to what they are saying and noting the circumstances under which they are saying it. This allows you to separate fact from fiction and reality from fantasy. In recent times, we humans have had an obsession with the spoken word and our ability to be conversationalists. Most people, however, are remarkably unaware of body language signals and their impact, despite the fact that we now know that most of the messages in any face-to-face conversation are revealed through body signals. For example, France's President Chirac, USA's President Ronald Reagan and Australia's Prime Minister Bob Hawke all used their hands to reveal the relative sizes of issues in their mind. Bob Hawke once defended pay increases for politicians by comparing their salaries to corporate executive salaries. He claimed that executive salaries had risen by a huge amount and that proposed politicians' increases were relatively smaller. Each time he mentioned politicians' incomes, he held his hands a yard (1m) apart. When he mentioned executive salaries, however, he held them only a foot (30cm) apart. His hand distances revealed that he felt politicians were getting a much better deal than he was prepared to admit.

President Jacques Chirac – measuring the size
of an issue or simply boasting about his love life?

Why Women are More Perceptive

When we say someone is 'perceptive' or 'intuitive' about people, we are unknowingly referring to their ability to read another person's body language and to compare these cues with verbal signals. In other words, when we say that we have a 'hunch' or 'gut feeling' that someone has told us a lie, we usually mean that their body language and their spoken words don't agree. This is also what speakers call audience awareness, or relating to a group. For example, if an audience were sitting back in their seats with their chins down and arms crossed on their chest, a 'perceptive' speaker would get a hunch or feeling that his delivery was not going across well. He would realise that he needed to take a different approach to gain audience involvement. Likewise, a speaker who was not 'perceptive' would blunder on regardless.

....

Being 'perceptive' means being able to spot the contradictions between someone's words and their body language.

....

Overall, women are far more perceptive than men, and this has given rise to what is commonly referred to as 'women's intuition'. Women have an innate ability to pick up and decipher non-verbal signals, as well as having an accurate eye for small details. This is why few husbands can lie to their wives and get away with it and why, conversely, most women can pull the wool over a man's eyes without his realising it.

Research by psychologists at Harvard University showed how women are far more alert to body language than men. They showed short films, with the sound turned off, of a man and woman communicating, and the participants were asked to decode what was happening by reading the couple's expressions. The research showed that women read the situation accurately 87% of the time while the men scored only 42% accuracy. Men in 'nurturing' occupations, such as artistic types, acting and nursing, did nearly as well as the women; gay men also scored well. Female intuition is particularly evident in women who have raised children. For the first few years, the mother relies almost solely on the non-verbal channel to communicate with the child and this is why women are often more perceptive negotiators than men because they practise reading signals early.

What Brain Scans Show

Most women have the brain organisation to out-communicate any man on the planet. Magnetic Resonance Imaging brain scans (MRI) clearly show why women have far greater capacity for communicating with and evaluating people than men do. Women have between fourteen and sixteen areas of the brain to evaluate others' behaviour versus a man's four to six areas. This explains how a woman can attend a dinner party and rapidly work out the state of the relationships of other couples at the party – who's had an argument, who likes who and so on. It also explains why, from a woman's standpoint, men don't seem to talk much and, from a man's standpoint, women never seem to shut up.

As we showed in *Why Men Don't Listen & Women Can't Read Maps* (Orion), the female brain is organised for multitracking – the average woman can juggle between two and four unrelated topics at the same time. She can watch a television programme while talking on the telephone plus listen to a second conversation behind her, while drinking a cup of coffee. She can talk about several unrelated topics in the one conversation and uses five vocal tones to change the subject or emphasise points. Unfortunately, most men can only identify three of these tones. As a result, men often lose the plot when women are trying to communicate with them.

Studies show that a person who relies on hard visual evidence face to face about the behaviour of another person is more likely to make more accurate judgements about that person than someone who relies solely on their gut feeling.

The evidence is in the person's body language and, while women can do it subconsciously, anyone can teach themselves consciously to read the signals. That's what this book is about.

How Fortune-Tellers Know So Much

If you've ever visited a fortune teller you probably came away amazed at the things they knew about you – things no one else could possibly have known – so it must be ESP, right? Research into the fortune-telling business shows that operators use a technique known as 'cold reading' which can produce an accuracy of around 80% when 'reading' a person you've never met. While it can appear to be magical to naïve and vulnerable people, it is simply a process based on the careful observation of body language signals plus an understanding of human nature and a knowledge of probability statistics. It's a technique practised by psychics, tarot card readers, astrologists and palm readers to gather information about a 'client'. Many 'cold readers' are largely unaware of their abilities to read non-verbal signals and so also become convinced that they really must have 'psychic' abilities. This all adds to a convincing performance, bolstered by the fact that people who regularly visit 'psychics' go with positive expectations of the outcome. Throw in a set of tarot cards, a crystal ball or two and a bit of theatre, and the stage is perfectly set for a body-language-reading session that can convince even the most hardened sceptic that strange, magical forces must be at work. It all boils down to the reader's ability to decode a person's reactions to statements made and to questions asked, and by information gathered from simple observation about a person's appearance. Most 'psychics' are female because, as women, as discussed previously, they have the extra brain wiring to allow them to read the body signals of babies and to read others' emotional condition.

....

The fortune-teller gazed into her crystal ball and then started laughing uncontrollably. So John punched her on the nose. It was the first time he'd ever struck a happy medium.

....

To demonstrate the point, here now is a psychic reading for you personally. Imagine you've come to a dimly lit, smoke-filled room where a jewel-encrusted psychic wearing a turban is seated at a low, moon-shaped table with a crystal ball:

> I'm glad you've come to this session and I can see you have things that are troubling you because I am receiving strong signals from you. I sense that the things you really want out of life sometimes seem unrealistic and you often wonder whether you can achieve them. I also sense that at times you are friendly, social and outgoing to others, but that at other times you are withdrawn, reserved and cautious. You take pride in being an independent thinker but also know not to accept what you see and hear from others, without proof. You like change and variety but become restless if controlled by restrictions and routine. You want to share your innermost feelings with those closest to you but have found it unwise to be too open and revealing. A man in your life with the initial 'S' is exerting a strong influence over you right now and a woman who is born in November will contact you in the next month with an exciting offer. While you appear disciplined and controlled on the outside, you tend to be concerned and worried on the inside and at times you wonder whether or not you have made the right choice or decision.

So how did we go? Did we read you accurately? Studies show that the information in this 'reading' is more than 80% accurate for any person reading it. Throw in an excellent ability to read body language postures, facial expressions and a person's other twitches and movements, plus dim lighting, weird music and a stick of incense, and we guarantee you can even amaze the dog! We won't encourage you to become a fortune-teller but you'll soon be able to read others as accurately as they do.

Inborn, Genetic or Learned Culturally?

When you cross your arms on your chest, do you cross left over right or right over left? Most people cannot confidently describe which way they do this until they try it. Cross your arms on your chest right now and then try to quickly reverse the position. Where one way feels comfortable, the other feels completely wrong. Evidence suggests that this may well be a genetic gesture that cannot be changed.

Seven out of ten people cross their left arm over their right.

Much debate and research has been done to discover whether non-verbal signals are inborn, learned, genetically transferred or acquired in some other way. Evidence has been collected from observation of blind people (who could not have learned non-verbal signals through a visual channel), from observing the gestural behaviour of many different cultures around the world and from studying the behaviour of our nearest anthropological relatives, the apes and monkeys.

The conclusions of this research indicate that some gestures fall into each category. For example, most primate babies are born with the immediate ability to suck, showing that this is either inborn or genetic. The German scientist Eibl-Eibesfeldt found that the smiling expressions of children born deaf and blind occur independently of learning or copying, which means that these must also be inborn gestures. Ekman, Friesen and Sorenson supported some of Darwin's original beliefs about inborn gestures when they studied the facial expressions of people from five widely different cultures. They found that each culture used the same basic facial gestures to show emotion, which led them to the conclusion that these gestures must also be inborn.

> *Cultural differences are many but the basic body language signals are the same everywhere.*

Debate still exists as to whether some gestures are culturally learned, and become habitual, or are genetic. For example, most men put on a coat right arm first; most women put it on left arm first. This shows that men use their left brain hemisphere for this action while women use the right hemisphere. When a man passes a woman in a crowded street, he usually turns his body towards her as he passes; she instinctively turns her body away from him to protect her breasts. Is this an inborn female reaction or has she learned to do this by unconsciously watching other females?

Some Basic Origins

Most of the basic communication signals are the same all over the world. When people are happy they smile; when they are sad or angry they frown or scowl. Nodding the head is almost universally used to indicate 'yes' or affirmation. It appears to be a form of head lowering and is probably an inborn gesture because it's also used by people born blind. Shaking the head from side to side to indicate 'no' or negation is also universal and appears to be a gesture learned in infancy. When a baby has had enough milk, it turns its head from side to side to reject its mother's breast. When the young child has had enough to eat, he shakes his head from side to side to stop any attempt to spoon-feed him and, in this way, he quickly learns to use the head shaking gesture to show disagreement or a negative attitude.

*The head-shaking gesture signals 'no'
and owes its origin to breastfeeding.*

The evolutionary origin of some gestures can be traced to our primitive animal past. Smiling, for example, is a threat gesture for most carnivorous animals, but for primates it is done in conjunction with non-threatening gestures to show submission.

Baring the teeth and nostril flaring are derived from the act of attacking and are primitive signals used by other primates. Sneering is used by animals to warn others that, if necessary, they'll use their teeth to attack or defend. For humans, this gesture still appears even though humans won't usually attack with their teeth.

Human and animal sneering – you wouldn't want to go
on a date with either of these two

Nostril flaring allows more air to oxygenate the body in preparation for fight or flight and, in the primate world, it tells others that back-up support is needed to deal with an imminent threat. In the human world, sneering is caused by anger, irritation, when a person feels under physical or emotional threat or feels that something is not right.

Universal Gestures

The *Shoulder Shrug* is also a good example of a universal gesture that is used to show that a person doesn't know or doesn't understand what you are saying. It's a multiple gesture that has three main parts: exposed palms to show nothing is being concealed in the hands, hunched shoulders to protect the throat from attack and raised brow which is a universal, submissive greeting.

The Shoulder Shrug shows submission

Just as verbal language differs from culture to culture, so some body language signals can also differ. Whereas one gesture may be common in a particular culture and have a clear interpretation, it may be meaningless in another culture or even have a completely different meaning. Cultural differences will be covered later, in Chapter 5.

Three Rules for Accurate Reading

What you see and hear in any situation does not necessarily reflect the real attitudes people may actually have. You need to follow three basic rules to get things right.

Rule 1. Read Gestures in Clusters

One of the most serious errors a novice in body language can make is to interpret a solitary gesture in isolation of other gestures or circumstances. For example, scratching the head can mean a number of things – sweating, uncertainty, dandruff, fleas, forgetfulness or lying - depending on the other gestures that occur at the same time. Like any spoken language, body language has words, sentences and punctuation. Each gesture is like a single word and one word may have several different meanings. For example, in English, the word 'dressing' has at least ten meanings including the act of putting on clothing, a sauce for food, stuffing for a fowl, an application for a wound, fertiliser and grooming for a horse.

It's only when you put a word into a sentence with other words that you can fully understand its meaning. Gestures come in 'sentences' called clusters and invariably reveal the truth about a person's feelings or attitudes. A body language cluster, just like a verbal sentence, needs at least three words in it before you can accurately define each of the words. The 'perceptive' person is the one who can read the body language sentences and accurately match them against the person's verbal sentences.

Scratching the head can mean uncertainty
but it's also a sign of dandruff.

So always look at gesture clusters for a correct reading. Each of us has one or more repetitive gestures that simply reveal we are either bored or feeling under pressure. Continual hair touching or twirling is a common example of this but, in isolation of other gestures, it's likely to mean the person is feeling uncertain or anxious. People stroke their hair or head because that's how their mother comforted them when they were children.

To demonstrate the point about clusters, here's a common

Critical Evaluation gesture cluster someone might use when they are unimpressed with what they are hearing:

You're losing points with this man

The main Critical Evaluation signal is the hand-to-face gesture, with the index finger pointing up the cheek while another finger covers the mouth and the thumb supports the chin. Further evidence that this listener is having critical thoughts about what he hears is supported by the legs being tightly crossed and the arm crossing the body (defensive) while the head and chin are down (negative/hostile). This body language 'sentence' says something like, 'I don't like what you're saying', 'I disagree' or 'I'm holding back negative feelings'.

Hillary Clinton uses this cluster when she's not convinced

Rule 2. Look for Congruence

Research shows that non-verbal signals carry about five times as much impact as the verbal channel and that, when the two are incongruent people – especially women - rely on the non-verbal message and disregard the verbal content.

If you, as the speaker, were to ask the listener shown above to give his opinion about something you've said and he replied that he disagreed with you, his body language signals would be congruent with his verbal sentences, that is, they would match. If, however, he said he *agreed* with what you said, he would more likely be lying because his words and gestures would be incongruent.

When a person's words and body language are in conflict, women ignore what is said.

If you saw a politician standing behind a lectern speaking confidently but with his arms tightly folded across his chest (defensive) and chin down (critical/hostile), while telling his audience how receptive and open he is to the ideas of young people, would you be convinced? What if he attempted to convince you of his warm, caring approach while giving short, sharp karate chops to the lectern? Sigmund Freud once reported that while a patient was verbally expressing happiness with her marriage, she was unconsciously slipping her wedding ring on and off her finger. Freud was aware of the significance of this unconscious gesture and was not surprised when marriage problems began to surface.

Observation of gesture clusters and congruence of the verbal and body language channels are the keys to accurately interpreting attitudes through body language.

Rule 3. Read Gestures in Context

All gestures should be considered in the context in which they occur. If, for example, someone was sitting at a bus terminal with his arms and legs tightly crossed and chin down and it was a cold winter's day, it would most likely mean that he was cold, not defensive. If, however, the person used the same gestures while you were sitting across a table from him trying to sell him an idea, product or service, it could be correctly interpreted as meaning that the person was feeling negative or rejecting your offer.

Cold, not defensive

Throughout this book all body language gestures will be considered in context and, where possible, gesture clusters will be examined.

Why It Can be Easy to Misread

Someone who has a soft or limp handshake – especially a man – is likely to be accused of having a weak character and the next chapter on handshake techniques will explore the reason behind this. But if someone has arthritis in their hands it is likely that they will also use a soft handshake to avoid the pain of a strong one. Similarly, artists, musicians, surgeons and those whose occupation is delicate and involves use of their hands generally prefer not to shake hands, but, if they are forced into it, they may use a 'dead fish' handshake to protect their hands.

Someone who wears ill-fitting or tight clothing may be unable to use certain gestures, and this can affect their use of body language. For example, obese people can't cross their legs. Women who wear short skirts will sit with their legs tightly crossed for protection, but this results in them looking less approachable and less likely to be asked to dance at a nightclub. These circumstances apply to the minority of people, but it is important to consider what effect a person's physical restrictions or disabilities may have on their body movement.

Why Kids are Easier to Read

Older people are harder to read than younger ones because they have less muscle tone in the face.

The speed of some gestures and how obvious they look to others is also related to the age of the individual. For example, if a five-year-old child tells a lie, he's likely to immediately cover his mouth with one or both hands.

The child telling a lie

The act of covering the mouth can alert a parent to the lie and this mouth-covering gesture will likely continue throughout the person's lifetime, usually only varying in the speed at which it's done. When a teenager tells a lie, the hand is brought to the mouth in a similar way to the five-year-old, but instead of the obvious hand-slapping gesture over the mouth, the fingers rub lightly around it.

The teenager telling a lie

The original mouth-covering gesture becomes even faster in adulthood. When an adult tells a lie, it's as if his brain instructs his hand to cover his mouth in an attempt to block the deceitful words, just as it did for the five-year-old and the teenager. But, at the last moment, the hand is pulled away from the face and a nose touch gesture results. This is simply an adult's version of the mouth-covering gesture that was used in childhood.

Bill Clinton answering questions about
Monica Lewinsky in front of the Grand Jury

This shows how, as people get older, their gestures become more subtle and less obvious and is why it's often more difficult to read the gestures of a fifty-year-old than those of a five-year-old.

Can You Fake it?

We are regularly asked, 'Can you fake body language?' The general answer to this question is 'no', because of the lack of congruence that is likely to occur between the main gestures, the body's micro-signals and the spoken words. For example, open palms are associated with honesty but when the faker holds his palms out and smiles at you as he tells a lie, his micro-gestures give him away. His pupils may contract, one eyebrow may lift or the corner of his mouth may twitch, and these signals contradict the open palm gesture and the sincere smile. The result is that the receivers, especially women, tend not to believe what they hear.

> *Body language is easier to fake with men than with women because, overall, men aren't good readers of body language.*

True-Life Story: The Lying Job Applicant

We were interviewing a man who was explaining why he had quit his last job. He told us that there had been insufficient future opportunity available to him and that it was a hard decision to leave as he got on well with all the staff there. A female interviewer said she had an 'intuitive feeling' that the applicant was lying and that he had negative feelings about his former boss, despite the applicant's continual praising of his boss. During a review of the interview on slow-motion video, we noticed that each time the applicant mentioned his former boss a split-second sneer appeared on the left side of his face. Often these contradictory signals will flash across a person's face in a fraction of a second and are missed by an untrained observer. We telephoned his former boss and discovered the applicant had been fired for dealing drugs to other staff members. As confidently as this applicant had tried to fake his body language, his contradictory micro-gestures gave the game away to our female interviewer.

The key here is being able to separate the real gestures from fake ones so a genuine person can be distinguished from a liar or impostor. Signals like pupil dilation, sweating and blushing cannot be consciously faked but exposing the palms to try to appear honest is easily learned.

....

Fakers can only pretend for a short period of time.

....

There are, however, some cases in which body language is deliberately faked to gain certain advantages. Take, for example, the Miss World or Miss Universe contest, in which each contestant uses studiously learned body movements to give the impression of warmth and sincerity. To the extent that each contestant can convey these signals, she will score points from the judges. But even the expert contestants can only fake body language for a short period of time and eventually the body will show contradictory signals that are independent of conscious actions. Many politicians are experts in faking body language in order to get the voters to believe what they are saying, and politicians who can successfully do this – such as John F Kennedy and Adolf Hitler – are said to have 'charisma'.

In summary, it is difficult to fake body language for a long period of time but, as we will discuss, it's important to learn how to use positive body language to communicate with others and to eliminate negative body language that may give out the wrong message. This can make it more comfortable to be with others and make you more acceptable to them, which is one of the aims of this book.

How to Become a Great Reader

Set aside at least fifteen minutes a day to study the body language of other people, as well as acquiring a conscious awareness of your own gestures. A good reading ground is anywhere that people meet and interact. An airport is a particularly good place for observing the entire spectrum of human gestures as people openly express eagerness, anger, sorrow, happiness, impatience and many other emotions through body language. Social functions, business meetings and parties are also excellent. When you become proficient at the art of reading body language, you can go to a party, sit in a corner all evening and have an exciting time just watching other people's body language rituals.

Modern humans are worse at reading body signals than their ancestors because we are now distracted by words.

Television also offers an excellent way of learning. Turn down the sound and try to understand what is happening by first watching the picture. By turning the sound up every few minutes, you will be able to check how accurate your nonverbal readings are and, before long, it will be possible to watch an entire programme without any sound and understand what is happening, just as deaf people do.

Learning to read body language signals not only makes you more acutely aware of how others try to dominate and manipulate, it brings the realisation that others are also doing the same to us and, most importantly, it teaches us to be more sensitive to other people's feelings and emotions.

We have now witnessed the emergence of a new kind of

social scientist – the Body Language Watcher. Just as the bird-watcher loves watching birds and their behaviour, so the Body Language Watcher delights in watching the non-verbal cues and signals of human beings. He watches them at social functions, at beaches, on television, at the office or anywhere that people interact. He's a student of behaviour who wants to learn about the actions of his fellow humans so that he may ultimately learn more about himself and how he can improve his relationships with others.

···

What's the difference between an observer and a stalker?
A clipboard and pen.

···

Chapter 2

THE POWER IS IN YOUR HANDS

How the Palms and Handshakes are used to control

In ancient times, open palms were used to show
that no weapons were being concealed

It was Adam's first day on the job with his new PR company and he wanted to make a good impression on everyone. As he was introduced to colleague after colleague, he shook their hands enthusiastically and gave everyone a broad smile. Adam stood 6 foot 3 inches (1.9m) tall and was good looking, well dressed and certainly looked like a successful PR man. He always gave a firm handshake, just the way his father had taught him when he was young. So firm in fact, that it drew blood on the ring fingers of two female colleagues and left several others feeling injured. Other men competed with Adam's handshake – that's what men do. The women, however, suffered in silence and soon were whispering, 'Stay away from that new guy Adam – he's a bruiser!' The men never brought it up – but the women simply avoided Adam. And half the firm's bosses were women.

Here's a handy thought – whether you are heavy-handed or high-handed, engage in sleight-of-hand to avoid a hand-to-mouth existence, you might have to show your hand sometimes to gain the upper hand. Don't get caught red-handed, or try to wash your hands of a mistake, because if you bite the hand that feeds you, things could get out of hand.

The hands have been the most important tools in human evolution and there are more connections between the brain and the hands than between any other body parts. Few people ever consider how their hands behave or the way they shake hands when they meet someone. Yet those first five to seven pumps establish whether dominance, submission or power plays will take place. Throughout history, the open palm has been associated with truth, honesty, allegiance and submission. Many oaths are still taken with the palm of the hand over the heart, and the palm is held in the air when somebody is giving evidence in a court of law; the Bible is held in the left hand and the right palm held up for the members of the court to view. One of the most valuable clues to discovering whether someone is being open and honest – or not – is to watch for palm displays. Just as a dog will expose its throat to show submission or surrender to the victor, humans use their palms to display in a similar way to show that they are unarmed and therefore not a threat.

....

Submissive dogs reveal their throats.
Humans show their palms.

....

How to Detect Openness

When people want to be open or honest, they will often hold one or both palms out to the other person and say something like, 'I didn't do it!', 'I'm sorry if I upset you' or 'I'm telling you the truth'. When someone begins to open up or be truthful, they will likely expose all or part of their palms to the other person. Like most body language signals, this is a completely unconscious gesture, one that gives you an 'intuitive' feeling or hunch that the other person is telling the truth.

'Trust me – I'm a doctor'

The palms are intentionally used everywhere
to infer an open, honest approach

33

When children are lying or concealing something, they'll often hide their palms behind the back. Similarly, a man who wants to conceal his whereabouts after a night out with the boys might hide his palms in his pockets, or in an arms-crossed position, when he tries to explain to his partner where he was. However, the hidden palms may give her an intuitive feeling that he is not telling the truth. A woman who is trying to hide something will try to avoid the subject or talk about a range of unrelated topics while doing various other activities at the same time.

When men lie their body language can be obvious.
Women prefer to look busy as they lie.

Salespeople are taught to watch for a customer's exposed palms when he gives reasons or objections about why he can't

buy a product, because when someone is giving valid reasons, they usually show their palms. When people are being open in explaining their reasons they use their hands and flash their palms whereas someone who isn't telling the truth is likely to give the same verbal responses but conceal their hands.

Keeping their hands in their pockets is a favourite ploy of men who don't want to participate in a conversation. The palms were originally like the vocal cords of body language because they did more 'talking' than any other body part and putting them away was like keeping one's mouth shut.

Palms-in-Pockets: Prince William showing the media that he doesn't want to talk

Intentional Use of the Palms to Deceive

Some people ask, 'If I tell a lie and keep my palms visible, will people be more likely to believe me?' The answer is yes – and no. If you tell an outright lie with your palms exposed, you might still appear insincere to your listeners because many of the other gestures that should also be visible when displaying honesty are absent and the negative gestures used during lying will appear and will be incongruent with the open palms. Con artists and professional liars are people who have developed the special art of making their non-verbal signals complement their verbal lies. The more effectively the professional con artist can use the body language of honesty when telling a lie, the better he is at his job.

....

'Will you still love me when I'm old and grey?' she asked, palms visible. 'Not only will I love you,' he replied, 'I'll write to you.'

....

The Law of Cause and Effect

It's possible, however, to appear more open and credible by practising open palm gestures when communicating with others. Interestingly, as the open palm gestures become habitual, the tendency to tell untruths diminishes. Most people find it difficult to lie with their palms exposed because of the law of cause and effect. If a person is being open they'll expose their palms, but just having their palms exposed makes it difficult for the person to tell a convincing lie. This is because gestures and emotions are directly linked to each other. If you feel defensive, for example, you're likely to cross your arms across your chest. But if you simply cross your arms you'll begin to experience defensive feelings. And if you are talking with your palms exposed it puts even more pressure on the other person to be truthful too. In other words, open palms can help to suppress some of the false information others may tell and encourage them to be more open with you.

3 5

Palm Power

One of the least noticed, but most powerful, body signals is given by the human palm when giving someone directions or commands and in handshaking. When used in a certain way, *Palm Power* invests its user with the power of silent authority.

There are three main palm command gestures: the *Palm-Up* position, the *Palm-Down* position and the *Palm-Closed-Finger-Pointed* position. The differences of the three positions are shown in this example: let's say that you ask someone to pick up something and carry it to another location. We'll assume that you use the same tone of voice, the same words and facial expressions in each example, and that you change only the position of your palm.

The palm facing up is used as a submissive, non-threatening gesture, reminiscent of the pleading gesture of a street beggar and, from an evolutionary perspective, shows the person holds no weapons. The person being asked to move the item will not feel they are being pressured into it and are unlikely to feel threatened by your request. If you want someone to talk you can use the Palm-Up as a 'handover' gesture to let them know you expect them to talk and that you're ready to listen.

The Palm-Up gesture became modified over the centuries and gestures like the *Single-Palm-Raised-in-the-Air*, the *Palm-Over-the-Heart* and many other variations developed.

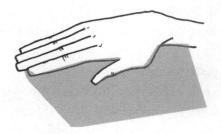

Palm up = non threatening   Palm down = authority

When the palm is turned to face downwards, you will project immediate authority. The other person will sense that you've given them an order to move the item and may begin to feel antagonistic towards you, depending on your relationship with him or the position you have with him in a work environment.

Turning your palm from facing upwards to facing downwards completely alters how others perceive you.

For example, if the other person was someone of equal status, he might resist a Palm-Down request and would be more likely to comply if you'd used the Palm-Up position. If the person is your subordinate, the Palm-Down gesture is seen as acceptable because you have the authority to use it.

The Nazi salute had the palm facing directly down and was the symbol of power and tyranny during the Third Reich. If Adolf Hitler had used his salute in the Palm-Up position no one would have taken him seriously – they would have laughed.

Adolf Hitler using one of history's most notable Palm-Down signals

When couples walk hand-in-hand the dominant partner, often the man, walks slightly in front with his hand in the above position, palm facing backwards while she has her palm facing forward. This simple little position immediately reveals to an observer who wears the loincloths in that family.

The Palm-Closed-Finger-Pointed is a fist where the pointed finger is used like a symbolic club with which the speaker figuratively beats his listeners into submission. Subconsciously, it evokes negative feelings in others because it precedes a right over-arm blow, a primal move most primates use in a physical attack.

Pointing finger = 'Do it or else!'

The Palm-Closed-Finger-Pointed gesture is one of the most annoying gestures anyone can use while speaking, particularly when it beats time to the speaker's words. In some countries such as Malaysia and the Philippines, finger pointing at a person is an insult as this gesture is only used to point at animals. Malaysians will use their thumb to point to people or to give directions.

Our Audience Experiment

We conducted an experiment with eight lecturers who were asked to use each of these three hand gestures during a series of ten-minute talks to a range of audiences and we later recorded the attitudes of the participants to each lecturer. We found that the lecturers who mostly used the Palm-Up position received 84% positive testimonials from their participants, which dropped to 52% when they delivered exactly the same presentation to another audience using mainly the Palm-Down position. The Finger-Pointed position recorded only 28% positive response and some participants had walked out during the lecture.

The pointing finger creates negative feelings in most listeners

Finger pointing not only registered the least amount of positive responses from the listeners; they could also recall less of what the speaker had said. If you are a habitual finger-pointer, try practising the palm-up and palm-down positions and you'll find that you can create a more relaxed atmosphere and have a more positive effect on others. Alternatively, if you squeeze your fingers against your thumb to make an 'OK' type of gesture and talk using this position, you'll come across as authoritative, but not aggressive. We taught this gesture to groups of speakers, politicians and business leaders and we measured the audience reactions. The audiences who listened to the speakers who used the fingertip-touch gestures described those speakers as 'thoughtful', 'goal-oriented' and 'focused'.

Squeezing the thumb against the fingertips avoids intimidating the audience

Speakers who used the finger-pointed position were described as 'aggressive', 'belligerent' and 'rude' and recorded the lowest amount of information retention by their audience. When the speaker pointed directly at the audience, the delegates became preoccupied with making personal judgements about the speaker rather than listening to his content.

An Analysis of Handshake Styles

Shaking hands is a relic of our ancient past. Whenever primitive tribes met under friendly conditions, they would hold their arms out with their palms exposed to show that no weapons were being held or concealed. In Roman times, the practice of carrying a concealed dagger in the sleeve was common so for protection the Romans developed the *Lower-Arm-Grasp* as a common greeting.

The Lower Arm Grasp – checking for concealed weapons – the original Roman method of greeting

The modern form of this ancient greeting ritual is the interlocking and shaking of the palms and was originally used in the nineteenth century to seal commercial transactions between men of equal status. It has become widespread only in the last hundred years or so and has always remained in the male domain until recent times. In most Western and European countries today it is performed both on initial greeting and on departure in all business contexts, and increasingly at parties and social events by both women and men.

> *The handshake evolved as a way men could cement a commercial deal with each other.*

Even in places such as Japan, where bowing is the traditional greeting, and Thailand, where they greet using the *Wai* – a gesture that looks similar to praying – the modern handshake is now widely seen. In most places, the hands are normally pumped five to seven times but in some countries, for example Germany, they pump two or three times with an additional hold time equal to an extra two pumps. The French are the biggest glad-handers, shaking on both greeting and departure and spending a considerable time each day shaking hands.

Who Should Reach First?

Although it is a generally accepted custom to shake hands when meeting a person for the first time, there are some circumstances in which it may not be appropriate for you to initiate a handshake. Considering that a handshake is a sign of trust and welcome, it is important to ask yourself several questions before you initiate the hand shake: Am I welcome? Is this person happy to meet me or am I forcing them into it? Salespeople are taught that if they initiate a handshake with a customer on whom they call unannounced or uninvited, it can produce a negative result as the buyer may not want to welcome them and feels forced to shake hands. Under these circumstances, salespeople are advised that it is better to wait for the other person to initiate the handshake and, if it is not forthcoming, use a small head-nod as the greeting. In some countries, shaking hands with a woman is still an uncertain practice (for example, in many Muslim countries it would be considered rude to do so; instead a small head-nod is acceptable), but it's now been found that women who initiate a firm handshake are rated – in most places – as more open-minded and make better first impressions.

How Dominance and Control Are Communicated

Considering what has already been said about the impact of the Palm-Up and Palm-Down gestures, let's explore their relevance in handshaking.

In Roman times, two leaders would meet and greet each other with what amounted to a standing version of modern arm wrestling. If one leader was stronger than the other, his hand would finish above the other's hand in what became known as the *Upper Hand* position.

Let's assume that you have just met someone for the first time and you greet each other with a handshake. One of three basic attitudes is subconsciously transmitted:

1. Dominance: 'He is trying to dominate me. I'd better be cautious.'
2. Submission: 'I can dominate this person. He'll do what I want.'
3. Equality: 'I feel comfortable with this person.'

These attitudes are sent and received without our being aware of them, but they can have an immediate impact on the outcome of any meeting. In the 1970s we documented the effect of these handshake techniques in our business skills classes and taught them as business strategies, which, with a little practice and application, can dramatically influence any face-to-face meeting, as you will see.

Dominance is transmitted by turning your hand (striped sleeve) so that your palm faces down in the handshake (see below). Your palm doesn't have to face directly down, but is the upper hand and communicates that you want to take control of the encounter.

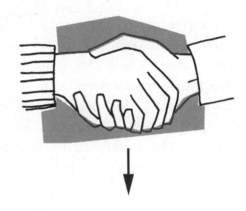

Taking control

Our study of 350 successful senior management executives (89% of whom were men) revealed that not only did almost all of the managers initiate the handshake, 88% of males and 31% of females also used the dominant handshake position. Power and control issues are generally less important to women, which probably accounts for why only one in three women attempted the Upper Hand ritual. We also found that some women will give men a soft handshake in some social contexts to imply submissiveness. This is a way of highlighting their femininity or implying that domination of her may be possible. In a business context, however, this approach can be disastrous for a woman because men will give attention to her feminine qualities and not take her seriously. Women who display high femininity in business meetings are not taken seriously by other business women or men, despite the fact that it's now fashionable or politically correct to say everyone is the same. This doesn't mean a woman in business needs to act in a masculine way; she simply needs to avoid signals of femaleness such as soft handshakes, short skirts and high heels if she wants equal credibility.

> *Women who show high feminine signals in a serious business meeting lose credibility.*

In 2001, William Chaplin at the University of Alabama conducted a study into handshakes and found that extroverted types use firm handshakes while shy, neurotic personalities don't. Chaplin also found that women who are open to new ideas used firm handshakes. Men used the same handshakes whether they were open to new ideas or not. So it makes good business sense for women to practise firmer handshaking, particularly with men.

The Submissive Handshake

The opposite of the dominant handshake is to offer your hand (striped sleeve) with your palm facing upwards (as below), symbolically giving the other person the upper hand, like a dog exposing its throat to a superior dog.

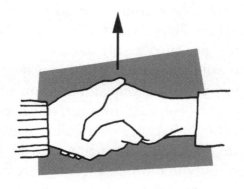

The submissive handshake

This can be effective if you want to give the other person control or allow him to feel that he is in charge of the situation if, for example, you were making an apology.

While the palm-up handshake can communicate a submissive attitude, there are sometimes other circumstances to consider. As we have seen, a person with arthritis in their hands will be forced to give you a limp handshake because of their condition and this makes it easy to turn their palm into the submissive position. People who use their hands in their profession, such as surgeons, artists and musicians, may also give a limp handshake, purely to protect their hands. The gesture clusters they use following their handshake will give further clues for your assessment of them – a submissive person will use more submissive gestures and a dominant person will use more assertive gestures.

How to Create Equality

When two dominant people shake hands, a symbolic power struggle takes place as each person attempts to turn the other's palm into the submissive position. The result is a vice-like handshake with both palms remaining in the vertical position and this creates a feeling of equality and mutual respect because neither is prepared to give in to the other.

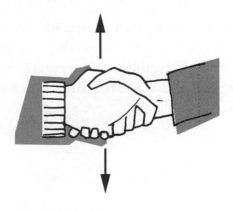

Communicating equality

How to Create Rapport

There are two key ingredients for creating rapport in a hand-shake. First, make sure that yours and the other person's palms are in the vertical position so that no one is dominant or sub-missive. Second, apply the same pressure you receive. This means that if, on a firmness scale of 1-10, your handshake registers a 7 but the other person is only a 5, you'll need to back off 20% in strength. If their grip is a 9 and yours is a 7, you'll need to increase your grip by 20%. If you were meeting a group of ten people, you'd probably need to make several adjustments of angle and intensity to create a feeling of rapport with everyone and to stay on an equal footing with each person. Also keep in mind that the average male hand can exert around twice the power of the average female hand, so allowances must be made for this. Evolution has allowed male hands to exert a grip of up to 100 pounds (45kg) for actions such as tearing, gripping, carrying, throwing and hammering.

Remember that the handshake evolved as a gesture to say hello or goodbye or to seal an agreement so it always needs to be warm, friendly and positive.

How to Disarm a Power Player

The *Palm-Down Thrust* is reminiscent of the Nazi salute and is the most aggressive of all handshakes because it gives the receiver little chance of establishing an equal relationship. This handshake is typical of the overbearing, dominant person who always initiates it, and their stiff arm with palm facing down-wards forces the receiver into the submissive position.

The Palm-Down Thrust

If you feel someone is giving a Palm-Down Thrust to you on purpose, here are several counters to it:

1. The Step-to-the-Right Technique

If you receive a dominant handshake from a power player – and it's mostly men who do it – it is not only difficult to turn his palm back up into an equal position, but it's obvious when you do it.

This technique involves first stepping forward with your left foot as you reach to shake hands. This takes a little practice, as stepping forward on the right foot is the natural position for 90% of people when shaking with the right hand.

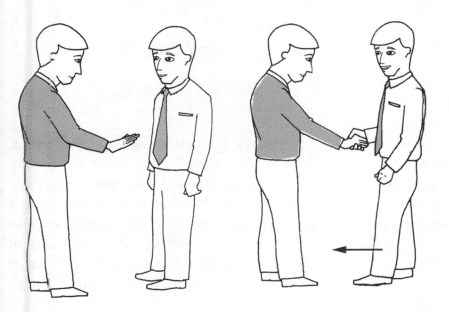

The power player attempts to control   Step forward on your left foot

Next, step forward with your right leg, moving across in front of the person and into his personal space. Finally, bring your left leg across to your right leg to complete the manoeuvre (see below), and shake the person's hand. This tactic allows you to straighten the handshake or even turn it over into the submissive position. It feels as if you're walking across in front of him and is the equivalent of winning an arm-wrestling bout. It also allows you to take control by invading his personal space.

Walk across in front with your right leg
and turn his palm up

Analyse your own approach to shaking hands and notice whether you step forward on your left or right foot when you extend your arm to shake hands. Most people are right footed and are therefore at a disadvantage when they receive a dominant handshake because they have little room to move and it allows the other person to dominate. Practise stepping into a handshake with your *left* foot and you will find that it is easier to deal with the power players who would try to control you.

2. The Hand-on-Top Technique

When a power player presents you with a Palm-Down Thrust, respond with your hand in the Palm-Up position then put your left hand over his right to form a *Double-Hander* and straighten the handshake.

The Double-Hander

This switches the power from him to you and is a much simpler way of dealing with the situation, and is much easier for women to use. If you feel the power player is purposefully trying to intimidate, and he does it regularly, grasp his hand on top and then shake it (as below). This can shock a power player so you need to be selective when using it and do it only as a last resort.

The last resort

The Cold, Clammy Handshake

No one likes receiving a handshake that feels like you've been handed four cold breakfast sausages. If we become tense when meeting strangers, blood diverts away from the cells below the outer layer of the skin on the hands – known as the dermis – and goes to the arm and leg muscles for 'fight or flight' preparation. The result is that our hands lose temperature and begin to sweat, making them feel cold and clammy and resulting in a handshake that feels like a wet salmon. Keep a handkerchief in a pocket or handbag so that you can dry your palms immediately before meeting someone important so you don't make a poor first impression. Alternatively, before a new meeting, simply visualise that you are holding your palms in front of an open fire. This visualisation technique is proven to raise the temperature of the average person's palm by 3–4 degrees.

Gaining the Left Side Advantage

When two leaders stand side by side for media photographs, they try to appear equal in physical size and dress code but the one who stands to the left of the picture is perceived by viewers to have a dominant edge over the other. This is because it is easier to gain the upper hand when they shake, making the one to the left of the photograph appear to be in control. This is obvious in the handshake that took place between John F Kennedy and Richard Nixon prior to their television debate in 1960. At that time the world was ignorant about body language but, on analysis, JFK appears to have had an intuitive understanding about how to use it. He made a practice of standing on the left-hand side of a photograph, and applying the Upper-Hand position was one of his favourite moves.

Gaining the Upper Hand –
JFK using the left-hand
side advantage to put
Richard Nixon into the
weaker-looking position

Their famous election debate revealed a remarkable testimony
to the power of body language. Polls showed that the majority
of Americans who listened to the debate on radio believed that
Nixon was the victor but the majority of those who watched it
on television believed Kennedy to be the clear winner. This
shows how Kennedy's persuasive body language made the difference and eventually won him the Presidency.

Standing on the left side of
shot gives Bill Clinton the
Upper Hand advantage over
Tony Blair

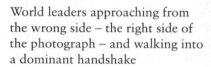
World leaders approaching from the wrong side – the right side of the photograph – and walking into a dominant handshake

When Men and Women Shake Hands

Even though women have had a strong presence in the work-force for several decades, many men and women still experience degrees of fumbling and embarrassment in male/female greetings. Most men report that they received some basic handshaking training from their fathers when they were boys, but few women report the same training. As adults, this can create uncomfortable situations when a man reaches first to shake a woman's hand but she may not see it – she's initially more intent on looking at his face. Feeling awkward with his hand suspended in mid-air, the man pulls it back hoping she didn't notice but as he does, she reaches for it and is also left with her hand dangling in a void. He reaches for her hand again and the result is a mish-mash of tangled fingers that look and feel like two eager squid in a love embrace.

Initial meetings between men and women can be thrown off by poor handshake technique.

If this ever happens to you, intentionally take the other person's right hand with your left, place it correctly into your right hand and say with a smile 'Let's try that again!' This can give you an enormous credibility boost with the other person, because it shows you care enough about meeting them to get the handshake right. If you are a woman in business, a wise strategy is to give notice to others that you intend to shake hands so as to not catch them off guard. Hold your hand out as early as possible to give clear notice of your intention to shake hands and this will avoid any fumbling.

The Double-Hander

A corporate favourite the world over, this is delivered with direct eye-contact, a candidly reassuring smile and a confident loud repetition of the receiver's first name, often accompanied by an earnest inquiry about the receiver's current state of health.

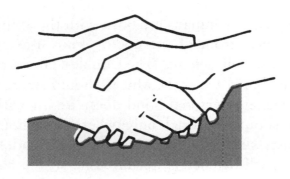

The Double-Hander

This handshake increases the amount of physical contact given by the initiator and gives control over the receiver by restricting his right hand. Sometimes called the 'politician's handshake', the initiator of the *Double-Hander* tries to give the impression he is trustworthy and honest, but when it's used on a person he's just met, it can have the reverse effect, leaving the receiver feeling suspicious about the initiator's intentions. The Double-Hander is like a miniature hug and is acceptable only in circumstances where a hug could also be acceptable.

'You're a lovable, memorable person – whoever you are...'

Ninety per cent of humans are born with the ability to throw the right arm in front of the body – known as an over-arm blow – for basic self-defence. The Double-Hander restricts this defence capability, which is why it should never be used in greetings where a personal bond doesn't exist with the other person. It should be used only where an emotional bond already exists, such as when meeting an old friend. In these circumstances, self-defence is not an issue so the handshake is perceived as genuine.

Yassar Arafat plants a Double-Hander on Tony Blair,
whose tight-lipped expression shows he's not impressed

Handshakes of Control

The intention of any two-handed handshake is to try to show
sincerity, trust or depth of feeling for the receiver. Two significant elements should be noticed. Firstly, the left hand is used
to communicate the depth of feeling the initiator wants to
convey and this is relative to the distance the initiator's left
hand is placed up the receiver's right arm. It's like an intention
to embrace and the initiator's left hand is used like a thermometer of intimacy – the further up the receiver's arm it's
placed, the more intimacy the initiator is attempting to show.
The initiator is both attempting to show an intimate connection with the receiver while, at the same time, attempting to
control their movement.

For example, the *Elbow Grasp* conveys more intimacy and
control than the *Wrist Hold*, and the *Shoulder Hold* conveys
more than the *Upper-Arm Grip*.

The Wrist Hold

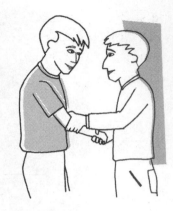

The Elbow Grasp

The Upper-Arm Grip

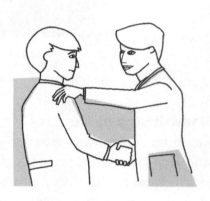

The Shoulder Hold

Secondly, the initiator's left hand is an invasion of the receiver's personal space. In general, the Wrist Hold and the Elbow Grasp are acceptable only where one person feels close to the other and in these cases the initiator's left hand enters only the outer edge of the receiver's personal space. The Shoulder Hold and Upper-Arm Grip show close intimacy and may even result in a hug ('personal space' will be covered more in Chapter 11). Unless the intimate feelings are mutual or the initiator doesn't have a good reason for using a double-handed handshake, the receiver will probably be suspicious and mistrust the initiator's intentions. In summary, if you don't have some sort of personal bond with the other person, don't use any Double-Hander. And if the person who gives you one doesn't have a personal connection with you, look for their hidden agenda.

> *Unless you and the other person have a personal or emotional bond, only use a single-handed handshake.*

It's common to see politicians greeting voters using double-handed handshakes and businesspeople doing it to clients without realising it can be business and political suicide, putting people offside.

The Blair–Bush Power Game

During the Iraq conflict in 2003, George W Bush and Tony Blair presented to the media the image of a powerful alliance that was 'united and equal', but close analysis of photographs shows strong power plays by George Bush.

Out-dressed and out-gunned: George Bush
putting the Upper Hand on Tony Blair

In the above picture, Bush leans in to deliver the Upper Hand from the left side of the photograph. Bush is dressed like an Armed Forces Commander-in-Chief and Blair is dressed like an English schoolboy meeting the headmaster. Bush has his feet firmly planted together on the ground and is using a Back Hold to control Blair. Bush regularly jockeys for the position left-of-picture, allowing him to be perceived as dominant and to look as if he were calling the shots.

The Solution

To avoid losing power if you inadvertently find yourself on the right-of-picture, extend your arm early as you approach from a distance as this forces the other person to face you straight on to shake hands. This lets you keep the handshake on an equal basis. If photos or video are being shot, always approach the other person so you occupy the left-of-picture position. At worst, use a Double-Hander to give yourself an equal footing.

The World's Eight Worst Handshakes

Here are eight of the world's most annoying and disliked handshakes and their variations. Avoid them at all times:

1. The Wet Fish
Credibility Rating: 1/10.
Few greetings are as uninviting as the *Wet Fish*, particularly when the hand is cold or clammy. The soft, placid feel of the Wet Fish makes it universally unpopular and most people associate it with weak character, mainly because of the ease with which the palm can be turned over. It is read by the receiver as a lack of commitment to the encounter, but there may be cultural or other implications – in some Asian and African cultures a limp handshake is the norm and a firm handshake can be seen as offensive. Also, one in twenty people

suffer from a condition called hyperhydrosis, which is a genetic condition that causes chronic sweating. It's wise to carry tissues or a handkerchief for mop-up strategies before any bout of handshaking.

The Wet Fish

The palms have more sweat glands than any other part of the body, which is why sweaty palms become so obvious. Surprisingly, many people who use the Wet Fish are unaware they do it so it's wise to ask your friends to comment on your handshake style before deciding what you'll use in future meetings.

2. The Vice
Credibility Rating: 4/10.
This quietly persuasive style is a favourite of men in business and reveals a desire to dominate and assume early control of the relationship or put people in their place. The palm is presented in the down position with one sharp downward pump followed by two or three vigorous return strokes and a grip that can even stop blood flow to the hand. Sometimes it will be used by a person who feels weak and fears they will be dominated by others.

The Vice

3. The Bone-Crusher

Credibility Rating: 0/10.

A second cousin to the *Vice*, the *Bone-Crusher* is the most feared of all handshakes as it leaves an indelible memory on the recipient's mind and fingers and impresses no one other than the initiator. The Bone-Crusher is the trademark of the overly aggressive personality who, without warning, seizes the early advantage and attempts to demoralise his opponent by grinding his knuckles to a smooth paste. If you are female, avoid wearing rings on your right hand in business encounters as the Bone-Crusher can draw blood and leave you to open your business dealings in a state of shock.

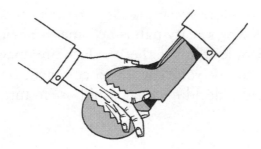

The Bone-Crusher

Unfortunately, there are no effective ways to counter it. If you believe someone has done it on purpose, you could bring it to everyone's attention by saying, 'Ouch! That really hurt my hand. Your grip is too strong.' This puts the advocate of the Bone-Crusher on notice not to repeat the behaviour.

4. The Finger-Tip Grab

Credibility Rating: 2/10.

A common occurrence in male–female greetings, the *Finger-Tip Grab* is a handshake that missed the mark and the user mistakenly grabs the other person's fingers. Even though the initiator may seem to have an enthusiastic attitude towards the receiver, he in fact lacks confidence in himself. In these circumstances, the main aim of the Finger-Tip Grab is to keep the receiver at a comfortable distance. The Finger-Tip Grab can also result from personal space differences between the people in the handshake. This could happen if one person's intimate space was two feet (60cm) and the other's was three feet (90cm), the latter stands further back during greeting so the hands don't connect properly.

The Finger-Tip Grab

If this happens to you, take the other person's right hand with your left and place it correctly in your right hand and say, with a smile 'Let's try that again!' and shake hands equally. This builds your credibility because you are telling the other person that you think they are important enough for you to get it right.

5. The Stiff-Arm Thrust
Credibility Rating: 3/10.
Like the Palm-Down Thrust, the *Stiff-Arm Thrust* tends to be used by aggressive types and its main purpose is to keep you at a distance and away from their personal space. It's also used by people raised in rural areas, who have larger personal space needs and want to protect their territory.

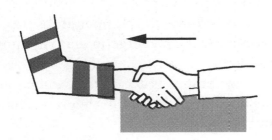

The Stiff-Arm Thrust

These people will even lean forward or balance on one foot to keep their distance when delivering a Stiff-Arm Thrust.

6. The Socket-Wrencher
Credibility Rating: 3/10.
A popular choice of power players and common cause of watering eyes and, in extreme cases, torn ligaments. This is the father of the *Bent-Arm-Pull-In*, and involves forcefully gripping the receiver's outstretched palm, then simultaneously applying a sharp reverse thrust, attempting to drag the receiver into the initiator's territory. This results in loss of balance and gets the relationship off on the wrong foot.

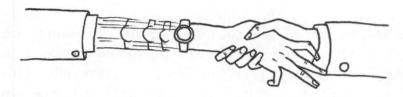

The Socket-Wrencher

Pulling the receiver into the initiator's territory can mean one of three things: first, the initiator is an insecure type who feels safe only within his own personal space; second, the initiator is from a culture that has smaller space needs; or third, he wants to control you by pulling you off balance. Either way, he wants the encounter to be on his terms.

7. The Pump Handle
Credibility Rating: 4/10.
With strong rural overtones, the pumper grabs the hand of the pumpee and commences an energetic and rhythmic series of rapid vertical strokes.

While up to seven pumps is acceptable, some pumpers continue to pump uncontrollably as if they are trying to draw water from the pumpee.

The Pump Handle

Occasionally, the pumper will cease pumping but continue to hold the receiver's hand to prevent their escape and, interestingly, few people try to pull their hand away. The act of being physically connected seems to weaken our resolve to retreat.

8. The Dutch Treat

Credibility Rating: 2/10.

Being somewhat vegetarian in approach, this handshake has its origins in the Netherlands, where a person can be accused of 'Geeft 'n hand als bosje worteljes' meaning 'Giving a handshake like a bunch of carrots'. It's a distant relative of the Wet Fish but stiffer and less clammy to the touch.

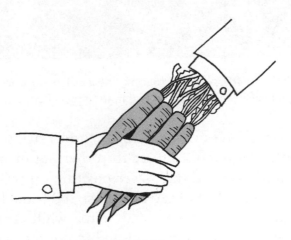

The Dutch Treat

It has been superseded in younger generations by *De Slappe Vaatdoek*, or *Sloppy Dishcloth*. This needs no further explanation.

The Arafat–Rabin Handshake

The photograph below shows the late Israeli Prime Minister, Yitzhak Rabin and Palestinian Chairman Yassar Arafat shaking hands at the White House in 1993 and it reveals several interesting attitudes. President Clinton is, in fact, the key figure in the shot because of his unobstructed centre position, extra height and *Arms-Spread-Open-Palms* gesture, reminiscent of a god presiding over his people. Clinton's *Half-Moon, Lips-Sucking* smile shows the emotional restraint he either felt or faked.

Yitzhak Rabin (left) holds his ground using a Stiff-Arm Thrust to resist being pulled forward as Yassar Arafat attempts a Bent-Arm-Pull-In

In this famous shot, both men keep their feet firmly planted on the ground and attempt to force the other out of his territory. Yitzhak Rabin assumed the power position on the left side of the picture and used a Stiff-Arm Thrust and leaned forward to keep Arafat out of his personal space while Yassar Arafat stood absolutely erect and attempted to counter with a Bent-Arm-Pull-In.

Summary

Few people have any idea how they come across to others in initial meetings, despite the fact that most of us are aware that the first few minutes of that meeting can make or break a relationship. Take the time to practise handshake styles with your friends and colleagues and you can quickly learn how to deliver a positive handshake every time. Keeping the palms held vertical and matching the other person's grip is usually perceived as a 10/10 handshake.

Chapter 3
THE MAGIC OF SMILES AND LAUGHTER

What makes this one of the
world's most irresistible icons?

Bob gazed across the room and locked eyes with an attractive brunette. She seemed to smile at him and, not being slow on the uptake, he swiftly crossed the room and began a conversation with her. She didn't seem to talk much but she was still smiling at him so he persisted. One of his female friends sauntered past and whispered, 'Forget it Bob...she thinks you're a jerk.' He was stunned. But she was still smiling at him! As with most men, Bob didn't understand the negative significance of the tight-lipped, no-teeth-visible female smile.

Children were often told by their grandmothers to 'put on a happy face', 'wear a big smile' and 'show your pearly whites' when meeting someone new because Grandma knew, on an intuitive level, it would produce a positive reaction in others.

The first recorded scientific studies into smiling were in the early part of the nineteenth century when French scientist Guillaume Duchenne de Boulogne used electrodiagnostics and electrical stimulation to distinguish between the smile of real enjoyment and other kinds of smiling. He analysed the heads of people executed by guillotine to study how the face muscles worked. He pulled face muscles from many different angles to catalogue and record which muscles caused which smiles. He discovered that smiles are controlled by two sets of muscles: the *zygomatic major* muscles, which run down the side of the face and connect to the corners of the mouth and the *orbicularis oculi*, which pull the eyes back. The zygomatic majors pull the mouth back to expose the teeth and enlarge the cheeks, while the orbicularis oculi make the eyes narrow and cause 'crow's feet'. These muscles are important to understand because the zygomatic majors are consciously controlled – in other words, they are used to produce false smiles of fake enjoyment to try to appear friendly or subordinate. The orbicularis oculi at the eyes act independently and reveal the true feelings of a genuine smile. So the first place to check the sincerity of a smile is to look for wrinkle lines beside the eyes.

A natural smile produces characteristic wrinkles around the eyes – insincere people smile only with their mouth.

In the enjoyment smile, not only are the lip corners pulled up, but the muscles around the eyes are contracted, while non-enjoyment smiles involve just the smiling lips.

Which smile is fake?
False smiles pull back only the mouth, real smiles pull
back both the mouth and eyes

Scientists can distinguish between genuine and fake smiles by using a coding system called the Facial Action Coding System (FACS), which was devised by Professor Paul Ekman of the University of California and Dr Wallace V Friesen of the University of Kentucky. Genuine smiles are generated by the unconscious brain, which means they are automatic. When you feel pleasure, signals pass through the part of your brain that processes emotion, making your mouth muscles move, your cheeks raise, your eyes crease up and your eyebrows dip slightly.

Photographers ask you to say 'Cheese' because this word pulls back the zygomatic major muscles. But the result is a false smile and an insincere looking photograph.

Lines around the eyes can also appear in intense fake smiles and the cheeks may bunch up, making it look as if the eyes are contracting and that the smile is genuine. But there are signs

68

that distinguish these smiles from genuine ones. When a smile is genuine, the fleshy part of the eye between the eyebrow and the eyelid – the eye cover fold – moves downwards and the end of the eyebrows dip slightly.

Smiling Is a Submission Signal

Smiling and laughing are universally considered to be signals that show a person is happy. We cry at birth, begin smiling at five weeks and laughing starts between the fourth and fifth months. Babies quickly learn that crying gets our attention – and that smiling keeps us there. Recent research with our closest primate cousins, the chimpanzees, has shown that smiling serves an even deeper, more primitive purpose.

To show they're aggressive, apes bare their lower fangs, warning that they can bite. Humans do exactly the same thing when they become aggressive by dropping or thrusting forward the lower lip because its main function is as a sheath to conceal the lower teeth. Chimpanzees have two types of smiles: one is an appeasement face, where one chimp shows submission to a dominant other. In this chimp smile – known as a 'fear face' – the lower jaw opens to expose the teeth and the corners of the mouth are pulled back and down, and this resembles the human smile.

A primate 'fear face' (left) and a primate 'play face'

The other is a 'play face' where the teeth are exposed, the corners of the mouth and the eyes are drawn upwards and vocal sounds are made, similar to that of human laughing. In both cases, these smiles are used as submission gestures. The first communicates 'I am not a threat because, as you can see, I'm fearful of you' and the other says 'I am not a threat because, as you can see, I'm just like a playful child'. This is the same face pulled by a chimpanzee that is anxious or fearful that it may be attacked or injured by others. The zygomatics pull the corners of the mouth back horizontally or downwards and the orbicularis eye muscles don't move. And it's the same nervous smile used by a person who steps onto a busy road and almost gets killed by a bus. Because it's a fear reaction, they smile and say, 'Gee...I almost got killed!'

In humans, smiling serves much the same purpose as with other primates. It tells another person you are non-threatening and asks them to accept you on a personal level. Lack of smiling explains why many dominant individuals, such as Vladimir Putin, James Cagney, Clint Eastwood, Margaret Thatcher and Charles Bronson, always seem to look grumpy or aggressive and are rarely seen smiling – they simply don't want to appear in any way submissive.

And research in courtrooms shows that an apology offered with a smile incurs a lesser penalty than an apology without one. So Grandma was right.

Happy, submissive or about to tear you limb from limb?

Why Smiling Is Contagious

The remarkable thing about a smile is that when you give it to someone, it causes them to reciprocate by returning the smile, even when you are both using fake smiles.

Professor Ulf Dimberg at Uppsala University, Sweden, conducted an experiment that revealed how your unconscious mind exerts direct control of your facial muscles. Using equipment that picks up electrical signals from muscle fibres, he measured the facial muscle activity on 120 volunteers while they were exposed to pictures of both happy and angry faces. They were told to make frowning, smiling or expressionless faces in response to what they saw. Sometimes the face they were told to attempt was the opposite of what they saw – meeting a smile with a frown, or a frown with a smile. The results showed that the volunteers did not have total control over their facial muscles. While it was easy to frown back at a picture of an angry man, it was much more difficult to pull a smile. Even though volunteers were trying consciously to control their natural reactions, the twitching in their facial muscles told a different story – they were *mirroring* the expressions they were seeing, even when they were trying not to.

Professor Ruth Campbell, from University College London, believes there is a 'mirror neuron' in the brain that triggers the part responsible for the recognition of faces and expressions and causes an instant mirroring reaction. In other words, whether we realise it or not, we automatically copy the facial expressions we see.

This is why regular smiling is important to have as a part of your body language repertoire, even when you don't feel like it, because smiling directly influences other people's attitudes and how they respond to you.

> *Science has proved that the more you smile, the more positive reactions others will give you.*

In over 30 years of studying the sales and negotiating process, we have found that smiling at the appropriate time, such as during the opening stages of a negotiating situation where people are sizing each other up, produces a positive response on both sides of the table that gives more successful outcomes and higher sales ratios.

How a Smile Tricks the Brain

The ability to decode smiles appears to be hardwired into the brain as an aid to survival. Because smiling is essentially a submission signal, ancestral men and women needed to be able to recognise whether an approaching stranger was friendly or aggressive, and those who failed to do this perished.

Do you recognise this actor?

When you look at the above photograph you'll probably identify actor Hugh Grant. When asked to describe his emotions in this shot, most people describe him as relaxed and happy because of his apparent smiling face. When the shot is turned the right way up, you get a completely different view of the emotional attitude conveyed.

We cut and pasted Grant's eyes and smile to produce a horrific-looking face but, as you can see, your brain can even identify a smile when a face is upside down. Not only can it do that, but the brain can separate the smile from every other part of the face. This illustrates the powerful effect a smile has on us.

Practising the Fake Smile

As we've said, most people can't consciously differentiate between a fake smile and a real one, and most of us are content if someone is simply smiling at us – regardless of whether it's real or false. Because smiling is such a disarming gesture, most people wrongly assume that it's a favourite of liars. Research by Paul Ekman showed that when people deliberately lie, most, especially men, smile *less* than they usually do. Ekman believes this is because liars realise that most people associate smiling with lying so they intentionally decrease their smiles. A liar's smile comes more quickly than a genuine smile and is held much longer, almost as if the liar is wearing a mask.

A false smile often appears stronger on one side of the face than the other, as both sides of the brain attempt to make it appear genuine. The half of the brain's cortex that specialises in facial expressions is in the right hemisphere and sends signals mainly to the left side of the body. As a result, false facial emotions are more pronounced on the left side of the face than the right. In a real smile, both brain hemispheres instruct each side of the face to act with symmetry.

When liars lie, the left side of the smile is
usually more pronounced than the right

Smugglers Smile Less

We were commissioned by Australian Customs, in 1986, to help create a programme to increase the number of seizures of illegal contraband and drugs being smuggled into Australia. Until that time, it had been assumed by law enforcement officers that liars increased their frequency of smiling when they were lying or under pressure. Our analysis of film of people who were intentionally told to lie showed the opposite – when the liars lied, they smiled less or not at all, regardless of culture. People who were innocent and telling the truth *increased* their smiling frequency when being honest. Because smiling is rooted in submission, the innocent people were attempting to appease their accusers while the professional liars were reducing their smiles and other body signals. It's the same as when a police car pulls up next to you at traffic lights – even though you haven't broken the law, the presence of the police is enough to make you feel guilty and start smiling. This highlights how fake smiling is controlled and should always be considered in the context of where it occurs.

Five Common Types of Smiles

What follows is a summary and an analysis of the common types of smiles that you're likely to see every day:

1. The Tight-Lipped Smile
The lips are stretched tight across the face to form a straight line and the teeth are concealed. It sends the message that the smiler has a secret or a withheld opinion or attitude that they will not be sharing with you. It's a favourite of women who don't want to reveal that they don't like someone and is usually clearly read by other women as a rejection signal. Most men are oblivious to it.

The Tight-Lipped Smile shows she has a
secret and won't be sharing it with you

For example, one woman might say of another woman, 'She's a very capable woman who knows what she wants', followed by a tight-lipped smile, rather than saying what she was really thinking: 'I think she's an aggressive, pushy bitch!' The *Tight-Lipped Smile* is also seen in magazine pictures of successful businessmen who are communicating 'I've got the secrets of success and you've got to try and guess what they are.' In these interviews, the men have a tendency to talk about principles of success but rarely do they reveal the exact details of how they succeeded. Conversely, Richard Branson is always seen sporting a wide toothy smile and is happy to explain the exact details of his success because he knows that most people won't do it anyway.

Tony and Cherie Blair were 'tight lipped'
about Cherie's last pregnancy

2. The Twisted Smile

This smile shows opposite emotions on each side of the face. In picture A below, the right brain raises the left side eyebrow, the left zygomatic muscles and left cheek to produce one type of smile on the left side of the face while the left brain pulls the same muscles downwards on the right side to produce an angry frown. When you place a mirror down the middle of illustration A, at an angle of 90 degrees to reflect each side of the face, you produce two completely different faces with opposite emotions. Mirroring the right side of the face reveals picture B, which has a cheesy grin, while mirroring the left side (picture C) reveals an angry frown.

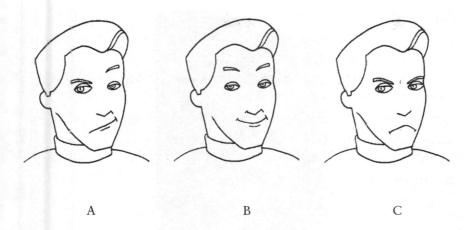

A   B   C

The *Twisted Smile* is peculiar to the Western world and can only be done deliberately which means it can send only one message – sarcasm.

3. The Drop-Jaw Smile

This is a practised smile where the lower jaw is simply dropped down to give the impression that the person is laughing or playful. This is a favourite of people such as The Joker in Batman, Bill Clinton and Hugh Grant, all of whom use it to engender happy reactions in their audiences or to win more votes.

Drop-Jaw smile with an attempt
to fake smiling eyes

A Drop-Jaw smile where only the jaw
is lowered to feign enjoyment

4. Sideways-Looking-Up Smile

With the head turned down and away while looking up with a
Tight-Lipped Smile, the smiler looks juvenile, playful and
secretive. This coy smile has been shown to be men's favourite
everywhere, because when a woman does it, it engenders
parental male feelings, making men want to protect and care
for females. This is one of the smiles Princess Diana used to
captivate the hearts of people everywhere.

Diana's Sideways-Looking-Up smile had a
powerful effect on both men and women

This smile made men want to protect her, and made women want to be like her. Not surprisingly, this smile is a regular in women's courtship repertoire for attracting men as it's read by men as seductive and is a powerful 'come-on' signal. This is the same smile now used by Prince William, which not only has the effect of winning people's affection, it also reminds them of Diana.

5. The George W Bush Grin

President George W Bush always has a permanent smirk on his face. Ray Birdwhistell found that smiling among middle-class people is most common in Atlanta, Louisville, Memphis, Nashville and most of Texas. Bush is a Texan and they smile more than most other Americans. As a result, in Texas, an unsmiling individual might be asked if he was 'angry about something', while in New York, the smiler might be asked, 'What's so funny?' President Jimmy Carter was also a South-erner who smiled all the time. This worried the Northerners who feared that he knew something they didn't.

*Smile constantly. Everyone will
wonder what you've been up to.*

Why Laughter Is the Best Medicine

As with smiling, when laughter is incorporated as a permanent part of who you are, it attracts friends, improves health and extends life. When we laugh, every organ in the body is affected in a positive way. Our breathing quickens, which exercises the diaphragm, neck, stomach, face and shoulders. Laughter increases the amount of oxygen in the blood, which not only helps healing and improves circulation, it also expands the blood vessels close to the skin's surface. This is why people go red in the face when they laugh. It can also lower the heart rate, dilate the arteries, stimulate the appetite and burn up calories.

Neurologist Henri Rubenstein found that one minute of solid laughter provides up to 45 minutes of subsequent relaxation. Professor William Fry at Stanford University reported that 100 laughs will give your body an aerobic workout equal to that of a ten-minute session on a rowing machine. Medically speaking, this is why a damn good laugh is damn good for you.

The older we become, the more serious we become about life. An adult laughs an average of 15 times a day; a preschooler laughs an average of 400 times.

Why You Should Take Laughter Seriously

Research shows that people who laugh or smile, even when they don't feel especially happy, make part of the 'happy zone' in the brain's left hemisphere surge with electrical activity. In one of his numerous studies on laughter, Richard Davidson, professor of psychology and psychiatry at the University of Wisconsin in Madison, hooked subjects up to EEG (electroencephalograph) machines, which measure brain wave activity, and showed them funny movies. Smiling made their happy zones click wildly. He proved that intentionally producing smiles and laughter moves brain activity towards spontaneous happiness.

Arnie Cann, professor of psychology at the University of North Carolina, discovered that humour has a positive impact in counteracting stress. Cann led an experiment with people who were showing early signs of depression. Two groups watched videos over a three-week period. The group that watched comedy videos showed more improvement in their symptoms than did a control group that watched non-humorous videos. He also found that people with ulcers frown more than people without ulcers. If you catch yourself frowning, practise putting your hand on your forehead when you talk, to train yourself out of it.

Why We Laugh and Talk, But Chimps Don't

Robert Provine, professor of psychology at the University of Maryland, Baltimore, found that human laughter is different from that of our primate cousins. Chimpanzee laughter sounds like panting, with only one sound made per outward or inward breath. It's this one-to-one ratio between breath cycle and vocalisation that makes it impossible for most primates to speak. When humans began walking upright, it freed the upper body from weight-bearing functions and allowed better breath control. As a result, humans can chop an exhalation and modulate it to produce language and laughter. Chimps can have linguistic concepts, but they can't physically make the sounds of language. Because we walk upright, humans have a huge range of freedom in the sounds we make, including speech and laughter.

How Humour Heals

Laughter stimulates the body's natural painkillers and 'feel good' enhancers, known as endorphins, helping relieve stress and heal the body. When Norman Cousins was diagnosed with the debilitating illness ankylospondylitis, the doctors told him they could no longer help him and that he would live in excruciating pain before he died. Cousins checked into a hotel room and hired every funny movie he could find: the Marx Brothers, *Airplane* and *The Three Stooges*, etc. He watched and re-watched them over and over, laughing as hard and loud as he could. After six months of this self-inflicted laughter therapy, the doctors were amazed to find that his illness had been completely cured – the disease was gone! This amazing outcome led to the publishing of Cousins' book, *Anatomy of an Illness*, and the start of massive research into the function of endorphins. Endorphins are chemicals released from the brain when you laugh. They have a similar chemical composition to morphine and heroin and have a tranquillising effect on the body, while building the immune system. This explains why happy people rarely get sick and miserable but complaining people often seem to be ill.

Laughing Till You Cry

Laughter and crying are closely linked from a psychological and physiological standpoint. Think of the last time someone told you a joke that made you buckle up with laughter and you could hardly control yourself. How did you feel afterwards? You felt a tingling sensation all over, right? Your brain released endorphins into your system that gave you what was once described as a 'natural high' and is the same experience that drug addicts get when they take dope. People who have trouble with laughing at the tough things in life often turn to drugs and alcohol to achieve the same feeling that endorphin-induced laughter produces. Alcohol loosens inhibitions and lets people laugh more, which releases endorphins. This is why most well-adjusted people laugh more when they drink alcohol, while unhappy people become even more despondent or even violent.

> *People drink alcohol and take drugs to try to feel how happy people feel normally.*

Paul Ekman found that one of the reasons we are attracted to smiling and laughing faces is because they can actually affect our autonomic nervous system. We smile when we see a smiling face and this releases endorphins into our system. If you are surrounded by miserable, unhappy people you are also likely to mirror their expressions and become morose or depressed.

> *Working in an unhappy environment is detrimental to your health.*

How Jokes Work

The basis of most jokes is that, at the punch line, something disastrous or painful happens to someone. In effect, the unexpected ending 'frightens' our brain, and we laugh with sounds similar to a chimp warning others of imminent danger. Even though we consciously know that the joke is not a *real* event, our laugh releases endorphins for self-anaesthesis as if the joke was a real event. If it *was* a real event, we may go into crying mode and the body would also release its endorphins. Crying is often an extension of a laughing bout and is why, in a serious emotional crisis, such as hearing about a death, a person who cannot mentally accept the death may begin laughing. When the reality hits, the laughter turns to crying.

The origin of human laughter is as a
primate warning signal

The Laughter Room

In the 1980s, several American hospitals introduced the concept of the 'Laughter Room'. Based on Norman Cousins' experiences and other laughter research by Dr Patch Adams, they allocated a room and filled it with joke books, comedy films and humorous tapes, and had regular visits from comedians and clowns. Patients were then exposed to 30- to 60-minute sessions each day. The result was impressive – a dramatic improvement in patient health and shorter average hospitalisation time per patient. The Laughter Rooms also showed a decrease in the number of painkillers required by those in pain, and patients became easier to deal with. So you could say that the medical profession now take their laughter seriously.

He who laughs, lasts.

Smiles and Laughter Are a Way of Bonding

Robert Provine found that laughing was more than 30 times as likely to occur in participants in a social situation than in a solitary setting. Laughter, he found, has less to do with jokes and funny stories and more to do with building relationships. He found that only 15% of our laughter has to do with jokes. In Provine's studies, participants were more likely to speak to themselves when alone than they were to laugh. Participants were videotaped watching a humorous video clip in three different situations: alone, with a same-sex stranger and with a same-sex friend.

Only 15% of our laughter has to do with jokes. Laughter has more to do with bonding.

Even though no differences existed between how funny the participants felt the video clip was, those who watched the amusing video clips alone laughed significantly less than did those who watched the video clip with another person present, whether it was a friend or a stranger. The frequency and time spent laughing·were significantly greater in both situations involving another person than when the participant was alone. Laughter occurred much more frequently during social inter-action. These results demonstrate that the more social a situation is, the more often people will laugh and the longer each laugh will last.

Humour Sells

Karen Machleit, professor of marketing at the University of Cincinnati's College of Business Administration, found that adding humour to advertisements increases sales. She found that humour makes it more likely that consumers will accept an advertiser's claims and increases source credibility, so that a funny ad with a famous person becomes even more readily accepted.

The Permanent Down-Mouth

The opposite to pulling up the corners of the mouth to show happiness is pulling both corners downward to show the *Down-Mouth* expression. This is done by the person who feels unhappy, despondent, depressed, angry or tense. Unfortu-nately, if a person holds these negative emotions throughout their lifetime, the corners of the mouth will set into a perma-nent down position.

In later life, this can give a person an appearance similar to a bulldog. Studies show that we stand further away from people who have this expression, give them less eye contact and avoid them when they are walking towards us. If you dis-cover that the Down-Mouth has crept into your repertoire, practise smiling regularly, which will not only help you avoid looking like an angry canine in later life, but will make you feel more positive. It will also help you avoid frightening little chil-dren and being thought of as a grumpy old cow.

The Down-Mouth expression can become a permanent
facial feature. Our intuition tells us to stay away from those
with a Down-Mouth expression.

Smiling Advice For Women

Research by Marvin Hecht and Marianne La France from
Boston University has revealed how subordinate people smile
more in the presence of dominant and superior people, in both
friendly and unfriendly situations, whereas superior people
will smile only around subordinate people in friendly situations.

This research shows that women smile far more than men in
both social and business situations, which can make a woman
appear to be subordinate or weak in an encounter with
unsmiling men. Some people claim that women's extra smiling
is the result of women historically being placed by men into
subordinate roles, but other research shows that by the age of
eight weeks, baby girls smile far more than baby boys, so it's
probably inborn as opposed to learned. The likely explanation
is that smiling fits neatly into women's evolutionary role as
pacifiers and nurturers. It doesn't mean a woman can't be as
authoritative as a man; but the extra smiling can make her
look less authoritative.

----

*Women's extra smiling is probably
hardwired into the brain.*

Social psychologist Dr Nancy Henley, at UCLA, described a woman's smile as 'her badge of appeasement' and it is often used to placate a more powerful male. Her research showed that, in social encounters, women smile 87% of the time versus 67% for men and that women are 26% more likely to return smiles from the opposite sex. An experiment using 15 photographs of women showing happy, sad and neutral faces were rated for attractiveness by 257 respondents. The women with the sad expressions were considered the least attractive. Pictures of unsmiling women were decoded as a sign of unhappiness while pictures of unsmiling men were seen as a sign of dominance. The lessons here are for women to smile less when dealing with dominant men in business or to mirror the amount of smiling that men do. And if men want to be more persuasive with women, they need to smile more in all contexts.

Laughter In Love

Robert Provine found that in courtship, it's also women who do most of the laughing and smiling, not men. Laughing in these contexts is used as a way of determining how success- fully a couple is likely to bond in a relationship. Simply put, the more he can make her laugh, the more attractive she will find him. This is because the ability to make others laugh is perceived as a dominant trait and women prefer dominant males, while males prefer subordinate females. Provine also found that a subordinate person will laugh to appease a supe- rior person and the superior person will make subordinates laugh – but without laughing himself – as a way of maintain- ing his superiority.

*Studies show that women laugh at men they're attracted to,
and men are attracted to women who laugh at them.*

This explains why having a sense of humour is near the top of women's priority list of what they look for in a man. When a woman says 'He's such a funny guy – we spent the whole night laughing together' she usually means that *she* spent the night laughing and he spent the night *making* her laugh.

*From a man's perspective, saying that a
woman has a good sense of humour doesn't mean
she tells jokes; it means she laughs at his jokes.*

On a deeper level, men seem to understand the attraction value of being humorous and spend much of their time with other men competing to tell the best joke to enhance their own status. Many men also become annoyed when one man dominates the joke-telling, especially when women are present and are also laughing. Men are likely to think the joke-teller is not only a jerk but he isn't particularly funny either, come to think of it – despite the fact he has all the women in fits of laughter. The point for men to understand is that humorous men look more attractive to most women. Fortunately, you can learn to be humorous.

How a woman sees a man: the picture on the left is how a woman perceives the man who doesn't make her laugh. The right hand picture is how she sees him when he *does* make her laugh

Summary

When you smile at another person they will almost always return the smile, which causes positive feelings in both you and them, because of cause and effect. Studies prove that most encounters will run more smoothly, last longer, have more positive outcomes and dramatically improve relationships when you make a point of regularly smiling and laughing to the point where it becomes a habit.

Evidence shows conclusively that smiles and laughter build the immune system, defend the body against illness and disease, medicate the body, sell ideas, teach better, attract more friends and extend life. Humour heals.

Chapter 4
ARM SIGNALS

Holding the hands over the crotch makes men
feel more secure when they feel threatened

Arm Barrier Signals

Hiding behind a barrier is a normal response we learn at an
early age to protect ourselves. As children, we hid behind solid
objects such as tables, chairs, furniture and mother's skirt
whenever we found ourselves in a threatening situation. As we
grew older, this hiding behaviour became more sophisticated
and by the age of about six, when it was unacceptable behaviour to hide behind solid objects, we learned to fold our arms
tightly across our chests whenever a threatening situation
arose. During our teens, we learned to make the crossed-arms
gesture less obvious by relaxing our arms a little and combin-
ing the gesture with crossed legs.

As we grow older, the arm-crossing gesture can evolve to the
point where we try to make it even less obvious to others. By

folding one or both arms across the chest, a barrier is formed that is an unconscious attempt to block out what we perceive as a threat or undesirable circumstances. The arms fold neatly across the heart and lungs regions to protect these vital organs from being injured, so it's likely that arm-crossing is inborn. Monkeys and chimps also do it to protect themselves from a frontal attack. One thing's certain: when a person has a nervous, negative or defensive attitude, it's very likely he will fold his arms firmly on his chest, showing that he feels threatened.

Why Crossed Arms Can be Detrimental

Research conducted in the United States into the *Crossed-Arms* gesture has shown some worrying results. A group of volunteers was asked to attend a series of lectures and each student was instructed to keep his legs uncrossed, arms unfolded and to take a casual, relaxed sitting position. At the end of the lectures each student was tested on his retention and knowledge of the subject matter and his attitude towards the lecturer was recorded. A second group of volunteers was put through the same process, but these volunteers were instructed to keep their arms tightly folded across their chests throughout the lectures. The results showed that the group with the folded arms had learned and retained 38% less than the group who kept its arms unfolded. The second group also had a more critical opinion of the lectures and of the lecturer.

When you fold your arms your credibility dramatically reduces.

We conducted these same tests in 1989 with 1500 delegates during 6 different lectures and recorded almost identical results. These tests reveal that, when a listener folds his arms, not only does he have more negative thoughts about the speaker, but he's also paying less attention to what's being said. It's for this reason that training centres should have chairs with arms to allow the attendees to leave their arms uncrossed.

Yes...But I'm Just 'Comfortable'

Some people claim that they habitually cross their arms because it's comfortable. Any gesture will feel comfortable when you have the corresponding attitude; that is, if you have a negative, defensive or nervous attitude, folded arms will feel comfortable. If you're having fun with your friends, folded arms will feel wrong.

Remember that with all body language, the meaning of the message is also in the receiver, as well as the sender. You may feel 'comfortable' with your arms crossed and your back and neck stiffened, but studies have shown that others' reactions to these gestures is negative. So the lesson here is clear – avoid crossing your arms under any circumstances unless your intention is to show others you don't agree or don't want to participate.

You may feel arm-crossing is simply comfortable but others will think you're not approachable.

Gender Differences

Men's arms rotate slightly inwards while women's arms rotate slightly outwards. These rotation differences have enabled men to aim and throw more accurately, while women's splayed elbows give them a wider, more stable position for carrying babies. One interesting difference is that women tend to keep their arms more open when they are around men they find attractive and are likely to fold their arms across their breasts around aggressive or unattractive men.

Inward rotating arms allow
men to throw accurately;
women's outward rotating
arms make for better carrying

Crossed-Arms-on-Chest

Both arms are folded together across the chest as an attempt to
put a barrier between the person and someone or something
they don't like. There are many arm-folding positions and
we'll discuss here the most common ones you're likely to see.
Crossed-Arms-on-Chest is universal and is decoded with the
same defensive or negative meaning almost everywhere. It is
commonly seen among strangers in public meetings, in queues
or cafeteria lines, elevators or anywhere that people feel uncertain or insecure.

Crossed-Arms-on-Chest:
he's not coming out and
you're not coming in

We attended a meeting of our local council where a debate was held on the cutting down of trees by developers. The developers sat to one side of the room and their opponents, the 'greenies', sat on the other. About half those attending sat with their arms crossed at the opening of the meeting and this increased to 90% of the 'greenies' when the developers addressed the audience, and almost 100% of the developers did it when the 'greenies' spoke. This shows how most people will take an arms-folded position when they disagree with what they're hearing. Many speakers fail to communicate their message to their audience because they haven't seen the crossed-arms position of their listeners. Experienced speakers know that this gesture means a good 'ice breaker' is needed to move their audience into a more receptive position that will change their attitude from negative to positive.

When you see someone take the arms-crossed position, it's reasonable to assume that you may have said something with which they disagree. It may be pointless continuing your line of argument even though the person could be verbally agreeing with you. The fact is that body language is more honest than words.

As long as someone holds an arms-folded position, a negative attitude will persist.

Your objective should be to try to work out why they crossed their arms and to try to move the person into a more receptive position. The attitude causes the gesture to occur and maintaining the gesture forces the attitude to remain.

Solution

A simple but effective way of breaking the arms-folded position is to give the listener something to hold or give them something to do. Giving them a pen, book, brochure, sample or written test forces them to unfold their arms and lean forward. This moves them into a more open position and, therefore, a more open attitude. Asking someone to lean forward to look at a visual presentation can also be an effective means of opening the arms-folded position. You could also lean forward with your palms up and say, 'I can see you have a question...what would you like to know?' or, 'What's your opinion?' You then sit or lean back to indicate that it's their turn to speak. By using your palms you non-verbally tell them that you would like them to be open and honest because that's what you're being.

'Why am I holding all these pens, pencils and brochures?' asked the customer, who began to look like a decorated Xmas tree. 'I'll come to that later,' said the negotiator.

Salespeople and negotiators are often taught that it's usually safer not to proceed with the presentation of a product or idea until the prospect's reason for folding his arms is uncovered. More often than not, buyers have hidden objections that most salespeople never discover because they missed seeing the buyer's arms-folded cluster, signalling that he was feeling negative about something.

Reinforced Arm-Crossing

If a person has clenched fists as well as a full arm-cross, this cluster, called *Fists-Clenched-Arm-Crossed*, shows hostility as well as defensiveness. If it's combined with a tight-lipped smile or clenched teeth and red face, a verbal or even physical attack could happen. A conciliatory approach is needed to discover what is causing it if the reason is not already apparent. This person has an aggressive, attacking attitude.

Fists-Clenched-Arms-
Crossed shows a hostile
attitude exists

Arm-Gripping

The *Double-Arm-Grip* is characterised by the person's hands tightly gripping their upper arms to reinforce themselves and avoid exposure of the front of the body. Sometimes the arms can be gripped so tight that the fingers and knuckles can turn white as blood circulation is cut off. It's a person's way of comforting himself with a form of self-hugging. Arm-gripping is commonly seen in doctors' and dentists' waiting rooms or with first-time air travellers who are waiting for lift-off. It shows a negative, restrained attitude.

The Double-Arm-Grip:
feeling insecure and not
buying what you're selling

In a courtroom, the claimant may be seen using a Fists-Clenched-Arm-Crossed pose while the defendant may have taken the Double-Arm-Grip position.

The Boss vs The Staff

Status can influence arm-folding gestures. A superior type can make his superiority felt by *not* folding his arms, saying, in effect, 'I'm not afraid, so I'll keep my body open and vulnerable.' Let's say, for example, that at a company social function, the general manager is introduced to several new employees. Having greeted them with a Palm-Down handshake, he stands back from them – a yard away (1 metre) – with his hands by his side or behind his back in the Prince Philip *Palm-in-Palm* position (superiority), or with one or both hands in his pocket (non-involvement). He rarely folds his arms across his chest so as not to show the slightest hint of nervousness.

Conversely, after shaking hands with the boss, the new employees may take full or partial arm-crossing positions because of their apprehension about being in the presence of the company's top person. Both the general manager and the new employees feel comfortable with their respective gesture clusters as each is signalling his status, relative to the other. But what happens when the general manager meets a young, up-and-coming male who is also a superior type and who may even signal that he is as important as the general manager? The likely outcome is that, after the two give each other a dominant handshake, the younger executive may take an arm-fold gesture with both thumbs pointing upwards.

Thumbs-Up: defensive, but he still thinks he's pretty cool

This gesture has the arms-crossed plus both thumbs up showing that he's feeling 'cool' and in control. As he talks, he gestures with his thumbs to emphasise points he is making. As we've already discussed, the thumbs-up gesture is a way of showing others we have a self-confident attitude and the folded arms still gives a feeling of protection.

Someone who is feeling defensive but also submissive at the same time will sit in a symmetrical position, which means one side of their body is a perfect mirror of the other. They display tense muscle tone and look as if they expect to be attacked, whereas a person who is feeling defensive and dominant will take an asymmetrical pose, that is, one side of the body doesn't mirror the other.

Getting the Thumbs-Up

When you're presenting your case to someone and the *Thumbs-Up-Arms-Crossed* appears towards the end of your presentation and is clustered with other positive gestures, it signals you can move comfortably into asking the person for a commitment. On the other hand, if at the close of the presentation the other person takes the *Fists-Clenched-Arms-Crossed* position and has a poker face, you can be inviting trouble by attempting to get a 'yes'. It would be better to ask questions to try to uncover the person's objections. When someone says 'no' to a proposal, it can become difficult to change their mind without looking as if you're aggressive. The ability to read body language allows you to 'see' a negative decision before it is verbalised and gives you time to take an alternative course of action.

When you can see a 'no' before it's said,
you can try a different approach.

People carrying weapons or wearing armour seldom use arm-cross gestures because their weapon or armour provides sufficient body protection. Police officers who wear guns, for example, rarely cross their arms unless they are standing guard and they normally use the fist-clenched position to communicate clearly that nobody is permitted to pass where they are standing.

Hugging Yourself

When we were children our parents or carers embraced or hugged us when we faced distressing or tense circumstances. As adults, we often attempt to recreate those same comforting feelings when we find ourselves in stressful situations. Rather than take a full arm-cross gesture, which can tell everyone we are fearful, women often substitute a subtler version – a *Partial-Arm-Cross*, where one arm swings across the body to hold or touch the other arm to form the barrier and it looks as if she is hugging herself. Partial arm barriers are often seen in meetings where a person may be a stranger to the group or is lacking in self-confidence. Any woman taking this position in a tense situation will usually claim she is just being 'comfortable'.

Holding herself like her mother held her when she was a child

Men use a partial arm barrier known as *Holding-Hands-With-Yourself*: it's commonly used by men who stand in front of a crowd to receive an award or give a speech. Also known as the *Broken Zipper Position* it makes a man feel secure because he can protect his 'crown jewels' and can avoid the consequences of receiving a nasty frontal blow.

The Broken
Zipper Position

It's the same position men take in a line at a soup kitchen or to receive social security benefits and reveals their dejected, vulnerable feelings. It recreates the feeling of having someone else hold your hand. Adolf Hitler used it regularly in public to mask the sexual inadequacy he felt because of having only one testicle.

It's possible that evolution shortened men's arms to allow them to take this protective position because when our closest primate cousins, the chimpanzees, assume the same position their hands cross at their knees.

Humans make a point of hiding the areas they think are their weakest or most vulnerable

How the Rich and Famous Reveal their Insecurity

People who are continually exposed to others, such as royalty, politicians, television personalities and movie stars, usually don't want their audiences to detect that they are nervous or unsure of themselves. They prefer to project a cool, calm, controlled attitude when on display, but their anxiety or apprehension leaks out in disguised forms of arm-crossing. As in all arm-cross gestures, one arm swings across in front of the body towards the other arm but instead of the arms crossing, one hand touches or holds on to a handbag, bracelet, watch, shirt cuff or object on or near their other arm. Once again the barrier is formed and the secure feeling is achieved.

Famous people are just as nervous in public as the rest of us

Men wearing cufflinks are often seen adjusting them as they cross a room or dance floor where they are in full view of others. The *Cuff-Link-Adjust* is the trademark of Prince Charles, who uses it to give himself a feeling of security any time he walks across an open space in full view of everyone.

Prince Charles' Cuff-Link-Adjust revealing his insecurities

You would think that after more than half a century of being scrutinised in public and being confronted by large crowds, royals, such as Prince Charles, would be resistant to nervous feelings but his small arm-crossing behaviours reveal that he feels just as insecure as you or I would feel in the same circumstances.

An anxious or self-conscious man will also be seen adjusting the band on his watch, checking the contents of his wallet, clasping or rubbing his hands together, playing with a button on his cuff or using any gesture that lets his arms cross in front of his body. A favourite of insecure businessmen is walking into a business meeting holding a briefcase or folder in front of the body. To the trained observer, these gestures are a giveaway because they achieve no real purpose except as an attempt to disguise nervousness. A good place to observe these gestures is anywhere that people walk past a group of onlookers, such as a man who crosses the dance floor to ask a woman to dance or someone who crosses a stage to receive an award.

Women's use of disguised arm barriers is less noticeable than men's because women can grasp onto things like handbags or purses if they become self-conscious or unsure of themselves. Royals like Princess Anne regularly clutch a bunch of flowers when walking in public and the *Flowers/Handbag-Clutch* is Queen Elizabeth's favourite. It's unlikely that she would be carrying lipstick, make-up, credit cards and theatre tickets in her handbag. Instead, she uses it as a type of security blanket when necessary and as a means of sending messages; royal watchers have recorded 12 signals she sends to her minders about when she wants to go, stop, leave or be rescued from someone who is boring her.

Handbag used to form a barrier

One of the most common versions of creating a subtle barrier is to hold a glass or cup with two hands. You need only one hand to hold a glass but two hands allows the insecure person to form an almost unnoticeable arm barrier. These types of gestures are used by almost everyone and few of us are aware that we're doing them.

Flower grasping shows self-consciousness

The Coffee Cup Barrier

Offering a refreshment during a negotiation is an excellent strategy for gauging how the other person is receiving your offer. Where a person places their cup immediately after they take a drink is a strong indicator of whether or not they are convinced or open to what you are saying. Someone who is feeling hesitant, unsure or negative about what they are hearing will place their cup to the opposite side of their body to form a single arm barrier. When they are accepting of what they are hearing they place the cup to the side of their body showing an open or accepting attitude.

The arm barrier says 'no'   She's now open to your ideas

Sitting with your elbows on the armrest of a chair is a position of power and conveys a strong, upright image. Humble, defeated individuals let the arms drop inside the arms of the chair, so avoid this at all times unless your goal is to appear defeated.

The Power of Touch

Touching a person with your left hand while shaking hands with your right hand can create a powerful result.

Researchers at the University of Minnesota conducted an experiment that became known as 'The Phone Booth Test'. They placed a coin on the ledge of a telephone booth then hid behind a tree and waited for an unsuspecting subject to walk in and find it. When this happened, one of the researchers would approach the subject and say, 'Did you happen to see my coin in that phone booth? I need it to make another call.' Only 23% of the subjects admitted they had found it and gave it back.

In the second part of the study, the coin was again placed in the phone booth but when the researchers approached the people who took it, they touched them lightly on the elbow for not longer than three seconds and inquired about the coin. This time, 68% admitted to having the coin, looked embarrassed and said things like, 'I was looking around to try to see who owned it...'

> *Skilful elbow-touching can give you up to three times the chance of getting what you want.*

There are three reasons this technique works: first, the elbow is considered a public space and is far away from intimate parts of the body; second, touching a stranger is not considered acceptable in most countries so it creates an impression; and third, a light, three-second elbow touch creates a momentary bond between two people. When we replicated this experiment for a television programme, we found the coin return rate varied from culture to culture depending on what the normal touch frequency was in a particular place. For example, with elbow touching, the coin was returned by 72% of Australians, 70% of English, 85% of Germans, 50% of French and 22% of Italians. This result shows how the elbow touch works better in places where frequent touching is *not* the cultural norm. We have recorded the touch frequencies between people in outdoor cafés in many of the countries we regularly visit and noted 220 touches an hour in Rome, 142 per hour in Paris, 25 touches an hour in Sydney, 4 per hour in New York and 0 per hour in London. This confirms that the more British or German your heritage, the less likely you are to touch others and, therefore, the more successful an elbow touch will be on you.

If you're of German or British origin,
you're an easier touch than everyone else.

Overall, we found that women were four times more likely to touch another woman than was a man to touch another man. In many places, touching a stranger *above* or *below* the elbow did not produce the same positive results as with directly touching the elbow and often received negative reactions. Touching for more than three seconds also received a negative response, with the person suddenly looking down at your hand to see what you are doing.

Touch their Hand Too

Another study involved librarians who, as they issued a book to a borrower, lightly brushed the hand of the person borrowing the book. Outside the library, the borrowers were surveyed and asked questions about their impressions of the service the library offered. Those who had been touched responded more favourably to all questions asked and were more likely to recall the name of the librarian. Studies conducted in British supermarkets where customers are lightly touched on the hand when they received their change show similar positive customer reactions. The same experiment has also been conducted in the USA with waitresses who derive much of their income from customer tips. The elbow-and-hand touching waitresses made 36% more tips from male diners than non-touching waitresses and male waiters increased their earnings by 22% regardless of which sex they touched.

When you next meet someone new and you shake hands, extend your left arm, give a light touch on their elbow or hand as you shake, repeat their name to confirm you heard it correctly, and watch their reaction. Not only does it make that person feel important, it lets you remember their name through repetition.

Elbow-and hand-touching – when done discreetly – grabs attention, reinforces a comment, underlines a concept, increases your influence over others, makes you more memorable and creates positive impressions on everyone.

Summary

It makes no difference how you look at it, any crossing of the arms in front of the body is seen as negative and the message is as much in the mind of the receiver as the sender. Even if you fold your arms because, for example, you have a backache, an observer will still unconsciously perceive you as closed to their ideas. Make a decision now to practise *not* crossing your arms and in the following chapters we will show you what to do to project a more positive, confident image.

Chapter 5
CULTURAL DIFFERENCES

How would a Brit, a German or an
American interpret this gesture?

Imagine this scene – you are inspecting a house with the possibility of purchasing it and you open a bathroom door to see a woman sitting naked in a bathtub. How would you expect the surprised woman to react? A British or American woman would cover her breasts with one hand and her genitals with the other, while a Swedish woman would cover only her genitals. A Muslim woman would cover her face, a Sumatran woman would cover her knees and a Samoan only her navel.

We Were Having Pizza at the Time

As we are writing this chapter, we are in Venice, Italy speaking at a conference on cultural differences. If we had never travelled to Italy, we would have been shocked by what we'd experienced. All cultures walk on the same side of the pavement as they drive on the road. This means if you're British, Australian, South African or a New Zealander, you drive and walk to the left. The consequence is that you'd find the Italians constantly bumping into you as you walk on the pavement because, as they approach and you step to your left, they step to their right. Wearing sunglasses in foreign countries is the single biggest cause of pavement collisions between cultures because no one can see the other person's gaze to know which way they intend to step. But it's a novel way of meeting new and interesting foreigners.

You'd also be stunned when you go to shake hands to say goodbye to an Italian but, instead, you get a kiss on both cheeks.

> *As I departed, the Italian man kissed me on both cheeks.*
> *I was tying my shoelaces at the time.*
> *WOODY ALLEN*

As you talk with local Italians, they seem to stand in your space, continually grabbing you, talking over the top of you, yelling in fact, and sounding angry about everything. But these things are a normal part of everyday friendly Italian communication. Not all things in all cultures mean the same things.

Take the Cultural Test

How aware are you of cultural differences in body language? Try this exercise – hold up your main hand to display the number five – do it now. Now change it to the number two. If you're Anglo-Saxon, there's a 96% chance you'll be holding up your middle and index fingers. If you're European, there's a 94% chance you'll be holding up your thumb and index finger. Europeans start counting with the number one on the thumb, two on the index finger, three on the middle finger, and so on. Anglo-Saxons count number one on the index finger, two on the middle finger and finish with five on the thumb.

Now look at the following hand signals and see how many different meanings you can assign to each one. For each correct answer, score one point and deduct one point for an incorrect answer. The answers are listed at the bottom of the page.

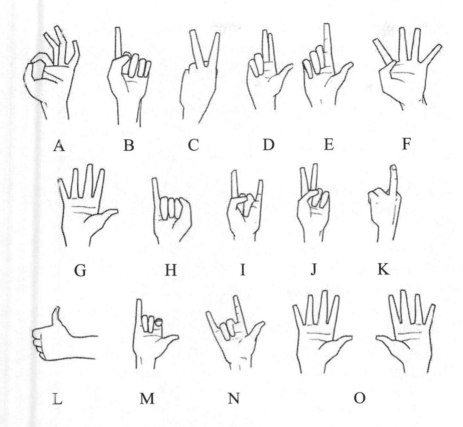

For each correct answer you got, allocate yourself one point.

A. Europe and North America: OK
   Mediterranean region, Russia, Brazil, Turkey:
   An orifice signal; sexual insult; gay man
   Tunisia, France, Belgium: Zero; worthless
   Japan: Money; coins

B. Western countries: One; Excuse me!; As God is my
   witness; No! (to children)

C. Britain, Australia, New Zealand, Malta: Up yours!
   USA: Two
   Germany: Victory
   France: Peace
   Ancient Rome: Julius Caesar ordering five beers

D. Europe: Three
   Catholic countries: A blessing

E. Europe: Two
   Britain, Australia, New Zealand: One
   USA: Waiter!
   Japan: An insult

F. Western countries: Four
   Japan: An insult

G. Western countries: Number 5
   Everywhere: Stop!
   Greece and Turkey: Go to hell!

H.Mediterranean: Small penis
   Bali: Bad
   Japan: Woman
   South America: Thin
   France: You can't fool me!

I. Mediterranean: Your wife is being unfaithful
   Malta and Italy: Protection against the Evil Eye (when pointed)
   South America: Protection against bad luck (when rotated)
   USA: Texas University Logo, Texas Longhorn Football Team

J. Greece Go to Hell!
   The West: Two

K.Ancient Rome: Up yours!
   USA: Sit on this! Screw you!

L. Europe: One
   Australia: Sit on this! (upward jerk)
   Widespread: Hitchhike; Good; OK

Greece: Up yours! (thrust forward)
Japan: Man; five

M. Hawaii: 'Hang loose'
  Holland: Do you want a drink?

N. USA: I love you

O. The West: Ten; I surrender
  Greece: Up Yours – twice!
  Widespread: I'm telling the truth

<u>What did you score?</u>
Over 30 points: You are a well-travelled, well-rounded, broad-thinking person who gets on well with everyone regardless of where they are from. People love you.
15–30 points: You have a basic awareness that others behave differently to you and, with dedicated practice, you can improve the understanding you currently have.
15 points or less: You think everyone thinks like you do. You should never be issued a passport or even be allowed out of the house. You have little concept that the rest of the world is different to you and you think that it's always the same time and season all over the world. You are probably an American.

Why We're All Becoming American

Due to the wide distribution of American television and movies, the younger generations of all cultures are developing a generic form of North American body language. For example, Australians in their sixties will identify the British *Two-Fingers-Up* gesture as an insult whereas an Australian teenager is more likely to read it as the number two and will recognise the American *Middle-Finger-Raised* as a main form of insult. Most countries now recognise the *Ring* gesture as meaning 'OK', even if it's not traditionally used locally. Young children in every country that has television now wear baseball caps backwards and shout 'Hasta la vista, baby', even if they don't understand Spanish.

American television is the prime reason cultural body language differences are disappearing.

The word 'toilet' is also slowly disappearing from the English language because North Americans, who are rugged pioneers and log splitters, are terrified to say it. North Americans will ask for the 'bathroom', which, in many parts of Europe, contains a bath. Or they ask for a 'rest room' and are taken to where there are lounge seats to relax. In England, a 'powder room' contains a mirror and washbasin, a 'little girls' room' is found in a kindergarten and 'comfort stations' are positioned on the motorways of Europe. And a North American who asks to 'wash up' is likely to be gleefully led to the kitchen, given a tea towel and invited to wash the dishes.

Cultural Basics are the Same Almost Everywhere

As discussed in Chapter 3, facial expressions and smiles register the same meanings to people almost everywhere. Paul Ekman of the University of California, San Francisco, showed photographs of the emotions of happiness, anger, fear, sadness, disgust and surprise to people in 21 different cultures and found that in *every* case, the majority in each country agreed about the pictures that showed happiness, sadness and disgust. There was agreement by the majority in 20 out of the 21 countries for the surprise expressions, for fear on 19 out of 21 agreed and for anger, 18 out of 21 agreed. The only significant cultural difference was with the Japanese who described the fear photograph as surprise.

Ekman also went to New Guinea to study the South Fore

culture and the Dani people of West Irian who had been isolated from the rest of the world. He recorded the same results, the exception being that, like the Japanese, these cultures could not distinguish fear from surprise.

He filmed these stone-age people enacting these same expressions and then showed them to Americans who correctly identified them all, proving that the meanings of smiling and facial expressions are universal.

The fact that expressions are inborn in humans was also demonstrated by Dr Linda Camras from DePaul University in Chicago. She measured Japanese and American infants' facial responses using the Facial Action Coding System (Oster & Rosenstein, 1991). This system allowed researchers to record, separate and catalogue infant facial expressions and they found that both Japanese and American infants displayed exactly the same emotional expressions.

So far in this book we have concentrated on body language that is generally common to most parts of the world. The biggest cultural differences exist mainly in relation to territorial space, eye contact, touch frequency and insult gestures. The regions that have the greatest number of different local signals are Arab countries, parts of Asia and Japan. Understanding cultural differences is too big a subject to be covered in one chapter so we'll stick to the basic things that you are likely to see abroad.

If a Saudi man holds another man's hand in
public it's a sign of mutual respect. But don't
do it in Australia, Texas or Liverpool, England

Greeting Differences

Handshaking differences can make for some embarrassing and humorous cultural encounters. British, Australian, New Zealander, German and American colleagues will usually shake hands on meeting, and again on departure. Most European cultures will shake hands with each other several times a day, and some French have been noted to shake hands for up to 30 minutes a day. Indian, Asian and Arabic cultures may continue to hold your hand when the handshake has ended. Germans and French give one or two firm pumps followed by a short hold, whereas Brits give three to five pumps compared with an American's five to seven pumps. This is hilarious to observe at international conferences where a range of different handshake pumping takes place between surprised delegates. To the Americans, the Germans, with their single pump, seem distant. To the Germans however, the Americans pump hands as if they are blowing up an airbed.

When it comes to greeting with a cheek kiss, the Scandinavians are happy with a single kiss, the French mostly prefer a double, while the Dutch, Belgians and Arabs go for a triple kiss. The Australians, New Zealanders and Americans are continually confused about greeting kisses and bump noses as they fumble their way through a single peck. The Brits either avoid kissing by standing back or will surprise you with a European double kiss. In his book *A View from the Summit*, Sir Edmund Hillary recounts that on reaching the peak of Everest, he faced Sherpa Tenzing Norgay and offered a proper, British, congratulatory handshake. But Norgay leaped forward and hugged and kissed him – the proper congratulations of Tibetans.

When One Culture Encounters Another

When Italians talk they keep their hands held high as a way of holding the floor in a conversation. What seems like affectionate arm touching during an Italian conversation is nothing more than a way of stopping the listener from raising his hands and taking the floor. To interrupt an Italian you must grab his hands in mid air and hold them down. As a comparison, the Germans and British look as if they are physically paralysed when they talk. They are daunted when trying to converse with Italians and French and rarely get an opportunity to speak. French use their forearms and hands when they talk, Italians use their entire arms and body, while the Brits and Germans stand at attention.

When it comes to doing international business, smart attire, excellent references and a good proposal can all become instantly unstuck by the smallest, most innocent gesture sinking the whole deal. Our research in 42 countries shows North Americans to be the least culturally sensitive people with the British coming in a close second. Considering that 86% of North Americans don't have a passport, it follows that they would be the most ignorant of international body language customs. Even George W Bush had to apply for a passport after becoming President of the United States so he could travel overseas. The Brits, however, do travel extensively but prefer everyone else to use British body signals, speak English and serve fish and chips. Most foreign cultures do not expect you to learn their language but are extremely impressed by the traveller who has taken the time to learn and use local body language customs. This tells them that you respect their culture.

The English Stiff-Upper-Lip

This gesture relates to pursing the lips to control the face so that facial expressions are reduced and as little emotion as possible is shown. This way the English can give the impression of being in complete emotional control. When Princes Philip, Charles, Harry and William walked behind the coffin of Diana in 1997, they each held the *Stiff-Upper-Lip* expression, which, to many in the non-British world, came across as unemotional about Diana's death.

Henry VIII was famous for pulling the *Lips-Pursed* expression. He had a small mouth and when he stiffened his upper lip for a portrait it looked even smaller. This habit led to a small mouth being a superiority signal among the English of the sixteenth century. The Lips-Pursed is an expression still used today by English people when they feel they are being intimidated by inferior people and this gesture is often accompanied by extended eye blinks.

Henry VIII popularised this gesture as a high-status signal because of his small mouth and modern Brits and Americans still use it

The Japanese

One area where handshakes, kissing and bear hugs have not become established is Japan, where such bodily contact is considered impolite. Japanese people bow on first meeting, the person with the highest status bowing the least and the one with the least status bowing the most. On first meeting, business cards are exchanged, each person assesses the other's status and appropriate bowing follows.

....

In Japan, make sure your shoes are spotlessly clean and in good condition. Every time a Japanese bows, he inspects them.

....

The Japanese way of listening to someone involves a repertoire of smiles, nods and polite noises, which have no direct equivalent in other languages. The idea is to encourage you to keep on talking but this is often misinterpreted by Westerners and Europeans as agreement. The *Head Nod* is an almost universal sign for 'yes', except for the Bulgarians who use the gesture to signify 'no', and the Japanese who use it for politeness. If you say something a Japanese doesn't agree with, he'll still say 'yes' – or *Hai* in Japanese – to keep you talking. A Japanese 'yes' usually means, 'yes, I heard you' and not 'yes, I agree'. For example, if you say to a Japanese person 'you don't agree, do you?' he will nod his head and say 'yes' even though he may not agree. In the Japanese context, it means 'Yes, you are correct – I don't agree.'

The Japanese are concerned with saving face and have developed a set of rules to prevent things going wrong so try to avoid saying no or asking questions when the answer might be no. The closest a Japanese will get to saying the word no is, 'It is very difficult,' or 'We will give this positive study' when they really mean, 'Let's forget the whole thing and go home.'

'You Dirty, Disgusting Pig!' – Nose Blowing

Europeans and Westerners blow their noses into a handkerchief or tissue while Asians and Japanese spit or snort. Each is appalled by what they see as the other's 'disgusting' behaviour. This dramatic cultural difference is the direct result of the spread of tuberculosis in past centuries. In Europe, tuberculosis was the AIDS of the era – a disease from which there was little hope of survival so governments instructed people to blow their nose to avoid further spreading the disease. This is why Westerners react so strongly to spitting – a spitting person could spread tuberculosis around, so people were as alarmed by that prospect as they would be if you could spread AIDS by spitting.

....

Modern nose-blowing is the result of a past epidemic of tuberculosis.

....

If tuberculosis had been a problem in Eastern countries, the cultural reaction would be the same as with Westerners. As a result, the Japanese are appalled when someone produces a handkerchief, blows their nose into it and puts it back in their pocket, purse or up their sleeve! Japanese are unimpressed at the English custom of men wearing a handkerchief in their jacket top pocket. This is the equivalent of proudly dangling a roll of toilet paper from the pocket, ready for action. Asians believe, correctly, that it is a healthier option to spit but it is a habit that is repulsive to Westerners and Europeans. This is why business meetings between Westerners and Europeans can fail when they've all got a cold. So don't feel upset by an Asian who spits or snorts and never blow your nose in front of a Japanese person.

The Three Most Common Cross-Cultural Gestures

Let's examine the cultural interpretations and implications of three common hand gestures, the *Ring*, the *Thumb-Up* and the *V-sign*.

1. The Ring
This gesture was popularised in the USA during the early nineteenth century by the newspapers that were starting a craze of using initials to shorten common phrases. There are many different views about what the initials 'OK' originally stood for, some believing it stood for 'all correct' which was regularly misspelled as 'oll korrect', while others say that it means the opposite of 'knock-out' that is, KO.

'OK' to a Westerner, 'money'
to a Japanese, 'zero' to
the French and insulting to
the Turks and Brazilians

Another popular theory is that it is an abbreviation of 'Old Kinderhook', from the birthplace of a nineteenth-century American president who used the initials as a campaign slogan. It's obvious that the ring itself represents the letter 'O' in the 'OK' signal. The 'OK' meaning is common to all English-speaking countries and its meaning is fast spreading everywhere due to American television and movies, but it has other origins and meanings in certain places. For example, in France and Belgium it also means 'zero' or 'nothing'. In a Paris restaurant one evening, the waiter showed us to our table and asked. 'Is the table OK?' We flashed him the OK signal and he responded, 'Well, if you don't like it here we'll find you another table...' He had interpreted the OK signal as meaning 'zero' or 'worthless' – in other words, he thought we had communicated that we didn't like the table.

Use the 'OK' gesture to tell a French person their cooking is wonderful and they'll probably throw you out.

In Japan it can mean 'money'; if you're doing business in Japan and you make this sign for 'OK' a Japanese may think you're asking them for a bribe. In some Mediterranean countries it's an orifice signal, often used to infer that a man is homosexual. Show a Greek man the OK signal and he may think you're inferring you or he is gay, while a Turk might think you're calling him an 'arsehole'. It's rare in Arab countries where it is used as either a threat signal or as an obscenity.

In the 1950s, before he became President, Richard Nixon visited Latin America on a goodwill tour to try to patch up strained relations with the locals. As he stepped out of his plane he showed the waiting crowds the American 'OK' signal and was stunned as they began booing and hissing at him. Being unaware of local body language customs, Nixon's OK signal had been read as 'You're all a bunch of arseholes.'

If you travel internationally, the safest rule is to always ask the locals to show you their insult signals to avoid any possible embarrassing circumstances.

2. The Thumb-Up

In places that have strong British influence, such as Australia, the USA, South Africa, Singapore and New Zealand, the *Thumb-Up* gesture has three meanings: it's commonly used by hitch-hikers who are thumbing a lift; it is an OK signal; and when the thumb is jerked sharply upwards it becomes an insult, meaning 'up yours' or 'sit on this'. In some countries, such as Greece, the thumb is thrust forward and its main meaning is 'get stuffed'!

Never hitch-hike in Greece.

As we have already demonstrated, when Europeans count from one to five, they use the *Thumb-Up* to mean 'one', the index finger becomes 'two', whereas most English-speaking people count 'one' on the index finger and 'two' on the middle finger. In this case the *Thumb-Up* will represent the number 'five'.

This can mean 'Good', 'One', 'Up yours' or 'Sit on this' depending where you live

Being the most powerful digit on the hand it is used as a sign of power and can be seen protruding from pockets, waistcoats and on lapels. The thumb is also used, in combination with other gestures, as a power and superiority signal or in situations where people try to get us 'under their thumb'. The thumb is referred to in this expression because of its physical power.

3. The V-Sign

This sign is common in Australia, New Zealand and Great Britain and carries an 'up yours' interpretation. Winston Churchill popularised the 'V for victory' sign during the Second World War, but his two-fingered version was done with the palm facing out, whereas the palm faces towards the speaker for the obscene insult version.

This can mean 'two' to an American, 'Victory' to a German and 'Up yours' in Britain

Its origin can be traced back centuries to the English archers who used these two fingers to fire their arrows. It was considered the ultimate degradation for a skilled archer to be captured and, rather than be executed, have his two shooting fingers removed. The two-fingered V sign quickly became used as a goading signal in battle by the British to show their enemies 'I've still got my shooting fingers.'

In parts of Europe, however, the palm-facing-in version still means 'victory' so an Englishman who uses it to tell a German 'up yours' could leave the German thinking he'd won a prize. This signal now also means the number two in some parts of Europe, and if the insulted European was a bartender, his response could be to give an Englishman, American or Australian two mugs of beer.

To Touch or Not to Touch?

Whether or not someone will be offended by being touched during conversation depends on their culture. For example, the French and Italians love to continually touch as they talk, while the British prefer not to touch at any time unless it's on a sports field in front of a large audience. Intimate embracing by British, Australian and New Zealand sportsmen is copied from South American and Continental sportsmen who embrace and kiss each other after a goal is scored and continue this intimate behaviour in the dressing rooms. The moment the Aussies, Brits and Kiwis leave the field, it reverts to the 'hands off – or else' policy.

British men will only touch each other on a sports field when someone scores a point or a goal and then it's a full embrace, kiss and the odd grope. But try it on in the pub and see what happens.

Dr Ken Cooper also studied touch frequencies in a number of countries and recorded the following results for touches per hour – Puerto Rico 180, Paris 110, Florida 2, London 0.

From our research and personal experience, here's a ready reckoner of places where it's acceptable to touch or not:

Don't touch	Do Touch
Germany	India
Japan	Turkey
England	France
USA & Canada	Italy
Australia	Greece
New Zealand	Spain

Estonia

Portugal

Northern Europe

Scandinavia

Middle East

Parts of Asia

Russia

How to Offend Other Cultures

When it comes to inadvertently offending other cultures, Americans usually take first prize. As mentioned, most Americans don't have a passport and believe the rest of the world thinks like them and wants to be like them. Here's a picture of George W Bush using the signature gesture of the Texas Longhorn football team, of which he is a supporter. The index finger and little finger represent the horns of the bull and this football gesture is recognised by most Americans.

Showing this American football gesture
is a jailable offence in Italy

In Italy, this gesture is known as the 'Cuckold' and is used to tell a man that other men are screwing his wife. In 1985, five Americans were arrested in Rome for jubilantly dancing and using this gesture outside the Vatican following the news of a major Longhorns win in the USA. Apparently the Pope was unimpressed.

Summary

People do business with people who make them feel comfortable and it comes down to sincerity and good manners. When entering a foreign country, concentrate on reducing the broadness of your body language until you have the opportunity to observe the locals. A simple way to learn and understand cultural body language differences is to record several foreign films and replay them with the sound off, but don't read the subtitles. Try to work out what is happening then watch again and read the subtitles to check your accuracy.

If you're not sure how to be polite in someone else's culture, ask the locals to show you how things are done.

Cultural misinterpretation of gestures can produce embarrassing results and a person's background should always be considered before jumping to conclusions about the meaning of his or her body language and gestures.

If you regularly travel internationally, we recommend Roger Axtell's *Gestures: Do's and Taboos of Body Language Around the World* (John Wiley & Sons). Axtell identified over 70,000 different physical signs and customs globally and shows you how to do business in most cultures.

Chapter 6

HAND AND THUMB GESTURES

Napoleon in his Study by Jacques-Louis David, 1812,
showing the French leader in his famous pose – did he really
have a peptic ulcer or was he just having a good time?

A human hand has 27 small bones, including eight pebble-shaped bones in the wrist, laced together by a network of ligaments, dozens of tiny muscles to move the joints. Scientists have noted that there are more nerve connections between the hands and the brain than between any other parts of the body, and so the gestures and positions we take with our hands give powerful insights into our emotional state. Because our hands are usually held in front of our body, these signals are easy to see and most of us have several trademark hand positions we continually use. For example, mention the name 'Napoleon' and everyone will describe a man with his hand tucked into his waistcoat with his thumb pointing upwards and will probably volunteer a theory or tell rude jokes about why he did it. These include: he had a stomach ulcer; he was winding his watch; he had a skin disease; that in his era it was impolite to put your hands in your pockets; he had breast cancer; he had a deformed hand; he kept a perfumed sachet in his vest that he'd sniff occasionally; he was playing with himself; and that painters don't like to paint hands. The real story is that in 1738, well before Napoleon's birth, François Nivelon published *A Book Of Genteel Behaviour* describing this posture *'...the hand-held-in was a common stance for men of breeding and manly boldness, tempered with modesty.'* When Napoleon saw the painting he said to the artist, 'You have understood me, my dear David.' So it was a gesture to convey status.

The history books show that Napoleon did not have this gesture in his regular repertoire – in fact, he didn't even sit for the famous painting that featured it – the artist painted him from memory and added the gesture. But the notoriety of this hand gesture highlights how the artist, Jacques-Louis David, understood the authority that the position of the hand and thumb would project.

> *Napoleon was 5'4" (1.64m) tall but those who see the painting perceive him as over 6' (1.85m) tall.*

How the Hands Talk

For thousands of years, the level of status people held in a society would determine the priority order in which they could hold the floor when speaking. The more power or authority you had, the more others would be compelled to stay silent while you spoke. For example, Roman history shows that a low-status person could be executed for interrupting Julius

Caesar. Today, most people live in societies where freedom of speech flourishes and usually anyone who wants to put forward an opinion can do so. In Britain, Australia and the USA it's even permissible to interrupt the President or Prime Minister with your opinion or to give a condescending slow handclap, as happened to Prime Minister Tony Blair in 2003 during a television discussion on the Iraqi crisis. In many countries, the hands have taken on the role of 'punctuation marks' to regulate turn-taking in conversation. The *Hands Raised* gesture has been borrowed from the Italians and French, who are the biggest users of 'hand talking', but it is still rarely seen in England, where waving your hands about when you speak is seen as inappropriate or poor style.

In Italy, the order of talking is simple – the person with his hands raised has the floor and does the talking. The listener will have his hands down or behind his back. So the trick is to try to get your hands in the air if you want to get a word in and this can be done either by looking away and then raising them or by touching the other person's arm to suppress their hand as you raise yours. Many people assume that when Italians talk they are being friendly or intimate because they continually touch each other, but in fact each is attempting to restrict the other's hands and take the floor.

In this chapter we'll evaluate some of the most common hand and thumb gestures in widespread use.

Tie an Italian's hands behind his back and he'll be speechless.

On the One Hand...

Watching how a person summarises a discussion giving both points of view can reveal whether they have a bias one way or another. They usually hold one hand palm up and articulate each point and then give the opposing points on the other hand. Right-handed people reserve their favoured point of view for their right hand and left-handers favour their left.

On the Other Hand, Gestures Improve Recall

Using hand gestures grabs attention, increases the impact of communication and helps individuals retain more of the information they are hearing. At the University of Manchester in England, Geoffrey Beattie and Nina McLoughlin conducted a study where volunteers listened to stories featuring cartoon characters such as Roger Rabbit, Tweetie Pie and Sylvester the Cat. For some listeners, a narrator added hand gestures such as moving the hands up and down quickly to show running, a waving movement to demonstrate a hair dryer and arms wide apart to show a fat opera singer. When the listeners were tested ten minutes later, those who had seen the hand gestures had up to a third higher response when recalling the details of the stories, demonstrating the dramatic effect hand gestures have on our recall ability.

In this chapter, we'll examine 15 of the most common hand gestures you're likely to see every day and we'll discuss what to do about them.

Rubbing the Palms Together

Recently a friend visited us at home to discuss our forthcoming skiing holiday. In the course of the conversation she sat back in her chair, smiled broadly, rubbed her palms together rapidly and exclaimed, 'I can hardly wait!' With her *Raised-Palms-Rub* she had told us non-verbally that she expected the trip to be a big success.

Showing positive
expectancy

Rubbing the palms together is a way in which people communicate positive expectation. The dice thrower rubs the dice between his palms as a sign of his positive expectancy of winning, the master of ceremonies rubs his palms together and says to his audience, 'We have been looking forward to hearing our next speaker,' and the excited salesperson struts into the sales manager's office, rubs his palms together and says excitedly, 'We've just received a big order!' However, the waiter who comes to your table at the end of the evening rubbing his palms together and asking, 'Anything else, sir?' is non-verbally telling you that he has expectancy of a good tip.

The speed at which a person rubs their palms together signals who he thinks will receive the positive benefits. Say, for example, you want to buy a home and you visit an estate agent. After describing the property you want, the agent rubs his palms together quickly and says, 'I've got just the right house for you!' In this way the agent has signalled that he expects the results to be to *your* benefit. But how would you feel if he rubbed his palms together very *slowly* as he told you that he had the ideal property? He'd seem sneaky or devious and you'd get the feeling that he expected the results to benefit him, not you.

The speed of the hand rub signals who the gesturer thinks will get the benefit.

Salespeople are taught to use the palm rub gesture when describing products or services to prospective buyers, and to use a fast hand action to avoid putting buyers on the defensive. When a buyer quickly rubs his palms together and says, 'Let's see what you have to offer!' it signals that he's expecting to see something good and might buy.

'Have I got a deal for you!'

Always remember context: a person who rubs his palms together briskly while standing at a bus terminal on a cold day may not necessarily be doing it because he's expecting a bus. He does it because his hands are cold.

Thumb and Finger Rub

Rubbing the thumb against the index finger or fingertips is commonly used as a money expectancy gesture. Its symbolism is that of rubbing a coin between the thumb and fingertips. It is often used by the street vendor who says, 'I can save you 40%,' or by the person who says to his friend, 'Can you lend me fifty pounds?'

'We can make money out of this!'

This gesture should be avoided at all times by any professional person who deals with clients because it carries negative associations about money.

Hands Clenched Together

At first, this gesture can seem to signal confidence as some people who use it often also smile. On one occasion, we observed a negotiator describing the deal he had just lost. As he went further and further into his story, he had not only taken the *Hands Clenched* position, his fingers were beginning to turn white and looked as if they were welding together. The Hands Clenched gesture shows a restrained, anxious or negative attitude. It's also a favourite of Queen Elizabeth when she is on royal visits and public appearances and it is usually positioned on her lap.

Hands clenched in raised position reveals frustration, even when smiling

Research into the Hands Clenched position by negotiation experts Nierenberg and Calero showed that it was also a frustration gesture when used during a negotiation, signalling that the person was holding back a negative or anxious attitude. It was a position assumed by a person who felt they were either not convincing the other person or thought they were losing the negotiation.

The Hands Clenched gesture has three main positions: hands clenched in front of the face; hands clenched resting on the desk or on the lap; and, when standing, hands clenched in front of the crotch.

Hands clenched in
centre position

Hands clenched in
lower position

We discovered a correlation between the height at which the hands are held and the degree of the person's frustration: that is, a person would be more difficult to deal with when the hands are held high, as in a centre position, than they would be in a lower position (see illustrations). As with all negative gestures, you need to take action to unlock the person's fingers, by offering them a drink or asking them to hold something, or their negative attitude will remain in the same way it does with any arm-crossing position.

The Steeple

So far, we've emphasised that gestures come in clusters, like words in a sentence, and that they must be interpreted in the context in which you observe them. Steepling can be an exception to these rules, as it often occurs in isolation. The fingers of one hand lightly press against those of the other hand to form a church steeple and will sometimes rock back and forth like a spider doing push-ups on a mirror.

We found that the *Steeple* was frequently used in superior-subordinate interaction and that it indicates a confident or self-assured attitude. Superiors often use this gesture position when they give instructions or advice to subordinates and it is particularly common among accountants, lawyers and managers. People who are confident, superior types often use this gesture and, by doing so, signal their confident attitude.

Confident he has
the right answers

Those who use this gesture sometimes convert the Steeple into a praying gesture in an attempt to appear God-like. As a general rule, the Steeple should be avoided when you want to be persuasive or win the other person's confidence, as it can sometimes be read as smugness or arrogance.

President Chirac and Gerry Adams sometimes appear God-like

If you want to look as if you are confident and have all the right answers, the Steeple position will do it for you.

Using Steepling to Win at Chess

Picture this scene – you're playing chess and it's your turn to move. You move your hand over the chessboard and rest your finger on a chess piece, indicating you intend to move that piece. You then notice your opponent sit back and make the Steeple gesture. Your opponent has just told you, non-verbally, that he feels confident about your move so your best strategy is not to make it. You next touch another chess piece and see your opponent assume the Hands Clenched gesture or Arms Crossed position, signalling that he doesn't like your potential move – so you should make it.

The Steeple has two main versions: the *Raised Steeple*, the position often assumed when the Steepler is giving his opinions or ideas or is doing the talking; and the *Lowered Steeple*, which is normally used when the Steepler is listening rather than speaking.

The Lowered Steeple

Women tend to use the Lowered Steeple position more often than the Raised Steeple. When the Raised Steeple is taken with the head tilted back, the person takes on an air of smugness or arrogance.

Although the Steeple gesture is a positive signal, it can be used in either positive or negative circumstances and may be misinterpreted. For example, let's say you are presenting an idea to someone and have seen them using several positive gestures during the presentation, such as open palms, leaning forward, head up, nodding and so on. Let's say that towards the end of your presentation the other person begins to Steeple.

If the Steeple follows a series of other positive gestures and appears when you show the other person the solution to his problem, it's likely you've been given the go-ahead to 'ask for the order'. On the other hand, if the Steeple gesture follows a series of negative gestures such as arm folding, leg crossing, looking away and hand-to-face gestures, he may be confident that he *won't* say 'yes' or that he can get rid of you. In both these cases the Steeple registers confidence, but one has positive results and the other negative consequences. The gestures preceding the Steeple are the key to the outcome.

Summary

Your hands are always in front of you, revealing your emotions and attitudes. Many body language gestures can be difficult to learn but hand gestures can be practised and rehearsed to a point where you can have fairly good control over where your hands are and what they are doing. When you learn to read hand gestures you'll look more confident, feel more successful and win more chess games.

The Face Platter – presenting her face for a man to admire

The Face Platter

This is not a negative gesture – it's a positive one used in courtship. It's used mainly by women and by gay men who want to attract a man's attention. A woman will place one hand on top of the other and present her face to a man as if it was on a platter for him to admire.

If you are going to use flattery – sincere or not – this gesture gives the green light for it.

Holding Hands Behind the Back

The Duke of Edinburgh and several other male members of the British Royal Family are noted for their habit of walking with head up, chin out and one hand holding the other hand behind the back. This gesture is common among leaders and royalty and is used by the policemen patrolling the beat, the headmaster walking around the school playground, senior military personnel and anyone in a position of authority.

Back and front views of the
superiority-confidence gesture

The emotions attached to this gesture are superiority, confidence and power. The person exposes their vulnerable stomach, heart, crotch and throat in a subconscious act of fearlessness. Our experience shows that, if you take this position when you are in a high-stress situation, such as being interviewed by newspaper reporters or waiting outside a dentist's surgery, you'll begin to feel confident and even authoritative, as a result of cause and effect.

Our work with law enforcement officers showed that officers who don't wear firearms use this position regularly and often rock back and forth on the balls of the feet when standing to gain additional height. Police officers who wear firearms seldom use this gesture, preferring to let their arms hang by their side or to have their thumbs tucked into the belt. The firearm gives the officer sufficient power that *Palm-in-Palm* behind the back is not a necessary display of authority.

The *Hand-Gripping-Wrist* gesture communicates a different emotion to Palm-in-Palm behind the back. It's a signal of frustration and an attempt at self-control. One hand grips the other wrist or arm tightly behind the back, as if in an attempt by one arm to prevent the other from striking out.

The Hand-Gripping-Wrist gesture

The higher up one hand grips the opposite arm, the more frustrated or angry the person is likely to be. In the illustration below the person is showing a greater attempt at self-control than in the previous picture, because the hand is gripping the upper arm, not just the wrist. This gesture shows the origin of the expression, 'Get a good grip on yourself.'

The Upper Arm Grip

Wrist-and-arm-gripping behind the back can often be observed outside a courtroom when warring parties are face to face, in salespeople standing in a customer's reception area and in patients waiting for a doctor. It's an attempt to disguise nervousness or self-restraint and, if you catch yourself doing it, change to the Palm-in-Palm behind the back and you will begin to feel more confident and in control.

Thumb Displays

As mentioned earlier, thumbs denote superiority. In palmistry, the thumbs represent strength of character and the ego, and body language signals involving the thumbs also show self-important attitudes. Thumbs are used to display dominance, assertiveness or sometimes aggressive attitudes; thumb gestures are secondary gestures and are usually part of a cluster. Thumb displays are positive signals, often used in the typical pose of the 'cool' individual who uses them to show superiority. A man will use *Protruding Thumbs* around women to whom he is attracted and people who wear high-status or prestige clothing also display their thumbs. You will rarely see a low-status individual, such as a vagrant, doing it.

The Waistcoat Thruster

Thumb displayers also often rock on the balls of their feet to give the impression of extra height.

Thumbs-Protruding-from-Coat-Pocket

Prince Charles using his Thumb-Protruding-from-Coat-Pocket gesture

This gesture is common to men and women who feel they are in a superior position to others. It's one of Prince Charles' regular gestures and reveals the in-control attitude he feels at the time. In a work environment, the boss will walk around the office in the position and, when the boss is away, the person who is next in charge will walk around using it. But none of the subordinates would dare to use it in front of the boss.

Thumb displays can become obvious when a person gives a contradictory verbal message. Take, for example, the lawyer who turns to the jury and in a soft, low voice says, 'In my humble opinion, ladies and gentlemen ...' while displaying his thumbs and tilting back his head to 'look down his nose' at them.

A lawyer pretending to be humble

This can make the jury feel that the lawyer is being insincere or pompous. If a lawyer wanted to appear humble, he should approach the jury with his coat open, with open palms and stoop forward to appear smaller.

'You seem like an intelligent, honest man,' the lawyer said smugly. 'I'd return the compliment, sir,' said the witness. 'But I'm under oath.'

Thumbs sometimes protrude from the back pockets (see below) as if the person is trying to hide their dominant attitude. Women were rarely seen using Thumb Displays until the 1960s when they began to wear trousers and take on more authoritative roles in society.

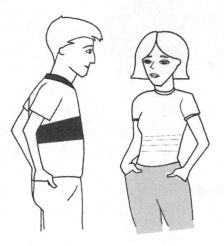

Thumb displays revealing
confident, authoritative attitudes

Arms-Folded-with-Thumbs-Pointing-Upwards is another common thumb cluster. This is a double signal, showing a defensive or negative attitude (folded arms), plus a superior attitude revealed by the thumbs. The person using this cluster usually gestures with his thumbs when he talks, and rocks on the balls of his feet when standing.

Closing himself off
but still feeling superior

The thumb can also be used as a signal of ridicule or disrespect when it is used to point at another person. For example, the husband who leans across to his friend, points towards his wife with his thumb and says 'She always nags', is inviting an argument with her. In this case, the shaking thumb is used as a pointer to ridicule her. Consequently, thumb-pointing is irritating to most women, particularly when a man does it. The Thumb Shaking gesture is not common among women, although they sometimes use the gesture to point at people they don't like.

'She always nags me!'

Summary

The thumbs have been used as a sign of power and authority for thousands of years. In Roman times, the thumb held up or down meant life or death to a gladiator. Even without any training, others intuitively decode thumb signals and seem to understand their meaning. You are now in a position not only to decode thumb signs, but to train yourself to use them.

Chapter 7

EVALUATION AND DECEIT SIGNALS

Decoding Hand-to-Face Gestures

Bill Clinton in front of the Grand Jury –
what do you think he's thinking?

If you told the absolute truth to everyone you interacted with, what would be the result? If you said the *exact words* going through your mind as you thought them, what consequences would it bring? For example:

> To your boss: '*Good morning, boss – you talentless slob.*'
> Man to a female customer: '*Thanks for your business, Susan, and may I say what wonderful firm breasts you have.*'
> Woman to a male neighbour: '*Thanks for helping me with my groceries. You've got a nice tight butt but who the hell cuts your hair?*'
> To your mother-in-law: '*It's nice to see you again – you, interfering, negative old bat.*'

When a woman asks, 'Does this dress make me look fat?' what is your answer? If you are a man, and you know what's good for you, you'd say she looked good. But you might have been thinking, 'The dress doesn't make you look fat – it's all the cake and ice cream you eat that makes you look fat.'

If you told everyone the complete truth all the time, you'd not only end up lonely, you might even finish up in hospital or prison. Lying is the oil that greases our interactions with others and lets us maintain friendly social relationships. These are called *White Lies* because their goal is to make others feel comfortable instead of telling them the cold, hard truth. Research shows that social liars are more popular than those who continually tell the truth, even though we know the social liar is lying to us. *Malicious Lies*, however, are where one person deliberately sets out to deceive another for personal benefit.

Lying Research

The least dependable signs of lying are the ones over which a person has the most control, such as words, because a person can rehearse their lies. The most reliable clues to lying are the gestures a person makes automatically, because they have little or no control over them. These responses are most likely to happen during lies because they are emotionally the most important things to the liar.

Robert Feldman at the University of Massachusetts in Amherst studied 121 couples as they had a conversation with a third person. One third of the participants were told to appear likeable, while another third were instructed to seem competent, and the rest were asked just to be themselves. All participants were then asked to watch the video of themselves and identify any lies they had told during the conversation no matter how big or small. Some lies were white lies, such as saying they liked someone when they really didn't, while other lies were more extreme, such as falsely claiming to be the star of a rock band. Overall, Feldman found that 62% of his participants told an average of two to three lies every ten minutes. James Patterson, author of *The Day America told The Truth*, interviewed over 2000 Americans and found that 91% lied regularly both at home and at work.

So how can you tell when someone is lying, stalling or simply thinking it over? Recognition of deceit, procrastination, boredom and evaluation gestures can be some of the most important observation skills you can learn. In this chapter, you'll learn the body language signals that give people away. The first part of the chapter will deal with lying and deceit.

The Three Wise Monkeys

These monkeys symbolise those who hear no evil, see no evil and speak no evil. Their simple hand-to-face gestures form the basis of the human deceit gestures. In simple terms, when we see, speak and hear lies or deceit, we are likely to attempt to cover our mouth, eyes or ears with our hands.

Hear no evil, see no evil, speak no evil

People who hear bad news or witness a horrific accident will often cover their entire face with their hands to symbolically stop themselves from seeing or hearing the awful news. This was the gesture that was most observed worldwide when people heard about the planes flying into the Twin Towers on 11 September 2001.

As we've already discussed, children often use hand-to-face gestures openly when they lie. If a child tells a lie, he will often cover his mouth with one or both hands in an attempt to stop the deceitful words from coming out. If he doesn't want to listen to a reprimanding parent, he simply covers his ears with his hands to block out the noise. When he sees something he doesn't want to look at, he covers his eyes with his hands or arms. As he becomes older, these hand-to-face gestures become quicker and less obvious, but they still occur when he is lying, covering up or witnessing deceit.

These gestures are also associated with doubt, uncertainty or exaggeration. Desmond Morris conducted research in which nurses were instructed to lie to their patients about their health in a role-play situation. The nurses who lied showed a greater frequency of hand-to-face gestures than those who told the truth to the patients. Men and women also both increase their number of gulps of saliva when lying, but this is usually notice-able only with men, as they have an enlarged Adam's apple.

'I did not have sexual relations with that woman,'
said the politician as he gulped and rubbed his nose.

As mentioned at the beginning of this book, we'll be analysing gestures in isolation and discussing them individually but this is not how they usually occur. They are part of a larger gesture cluster and should be studied in the same way as words in a sentence, that is, how each word is relevant to other words and the overall context in which they are used. When someone uses a hand-to-face gesture, it doesn't always mean that he or she is lying. It does indicate, however, that the person could be holding back information and further observation of other gesture clusters can confirm or deny your suspicions. It's important that you avoid interpreting a single hand-to-face gesture in isolation.

While there is no single guaranteed movement, facial expression or twitch that confirms someone is telling a lie, there are several clusters you can learn to recognise which will dramatically increase your chances of spotting a lie.

How the Face Reveals the Truth

The face is used more than any other part of the body to cover up lies. We use smiles, nods and winks in an attempt to cover up, but unfortunately for us, our body signals will tell the truth and there is a lack of congruence between our body gestures and facial signals. Our attitudes and emotions are continually revealed on our faces and we are completely unaware of it most of the time.

> *Fleeting incongruencies in the face reveal conflicts in the emotions.*

When we're going to try to conceal a lie, or a certain thought flashes into our mind, it can be shown for a split second on our face. We usually interpret someone's quick nose touch as an itch, or that when they rest their hand on their face they are deeply interested in us, without ever suspecting that we're boring them to death. For example, we filmed a man discussing how well he got on with his mother-in-law. Each time he mentioned her name the left side of his face raised in a momentary sneer that lasted only a split second but told us volumes about how he really felt.

Women Lie the Best and That's the Truth

In *Why Men Lie & Women Cry* (Orion) we showed how women are better at reading emotions, and therefore better at manipulating others with an appropriate lie. This trait is seen in baby girls who cry in sympathy with other babies and can then cause other babies to cry by simply bursting into tears at will. Sanjida O'Connell PhD, author of *Mindreading*, conducted a five-month study into how we lie and also concluded that women are far better liars than men. She found that women tell more complicated lies than men, whereas men tell simple lies such as 'I missed the bus' or 'My mobile phone battery was flat – that's why I couldn't call you.' She also found that attractive people are more believed than unattractive ones, explaining why leaders such as John F Kennedy and Bill Clinton were able to get away with as much as they did.

Why It's Hard to Lie

As we said in Chapter 3, most people believe that when someone is lying they smile more than usual, but research shows the opposite is true – they smile less. The difficulty with lying is that the subconscious mind acts automatically and independently of our verbal lie, so our body language gives us away. This is why people who rarely tell lies are easily caught, regardless of how convincing they may sound. The moment they begin to lie, their body sends out contradictory signals, and these give us a feeling that they're not telling the truth. During the lie, the subconscious mind sends out nervous energy which appears as a gesture that can contradict what was said. Professional liars, such as politicians, lawyers, actors and television announcers, have refined their body gestures to the point where it is difficult to 'see' the lie, and people fall for it, hook, line and sinker.

They do it in one of two ways. First, they practise what 'feel' like the right gestures when they tell the lie, but this only works when they have practised telling a lot of lies over long periods of time. Second, they can reduce their gesturing so that they don't use any positive or negative gestures while lying, but that's also hard to do.

> *With practice, liars can become
> convincing, just like actors.*

Try this simple test – tell a deliberate lie to someone face-to-face and make a conscious effort to suppress all body gestures. Even when your major body gestures are consciously suppressed, numerous small micro-gestures will still be transmitted. These include facial muscular twitching, dilation and contraction of pupils, sweating, flushed cheeks, eye-blinking rate increasing from 10 blinks per minute to as many as 50 blinks per minute and many other micro-signals that indicate deceit. Research using slow-motion cameras shows that these micro-gestures can occur within a split second and it's only people such as professional interviewers, salespeople and the very perceptive who can read them.

It's obvious then, that to be able to lie successfully, you need to have your body hidden or out of sight. Interrogation involves placing the person on a chair in the open or placing him under lights with his body in full view of the interrogators; his lies are much easier to see under those circumstances. Lying is easier if you're sitting behind a desk where your body is partially hidden, peering over a fence or from behind a closed door. The best way to lie is over the telephone or in an email.

Eight of the Most Common Lying Gestures

1. The Mouth Cover

The hand covers the mouth as the brain subconsciously instructs it to try to suppress the deceitful words that are being said. Sometimes this

The Mouth Cover

gesture might only be several fingers over the mouth or even a closed fist, but its meaning remains the same.

Some people try to disguise the *Mouth Cover* gesture by giving a fake cough. When actors play gangsters or criminals, they often use this gesture when discussing criminal activities with other gangsters or when being interrogated by the police, so that the audience knows they're being secretive or dishonest.

If the person who is speaking uses this gesture, it indicates that they could be lying. If they cover their mouth while *you* are speaking, it can show they might feel *you* are hiding something. One of the most unsettling sights a conference speaker can see is his audience using this gesture while he's speaking. A speaker should stop and ask, 'Would someone like to ask a question?' or 'I can see some people disagree. Let's take questions.' This allows the audience's objections to be brought into the open, giving the speaker the opportunity to qualify statements and answer questions, just as he would do if they had their arms crossed.

The Mouth Cover may appear as innocuous as the '*Shhh*' gesture where one finger is placed vertically over the lips; this gesture would likely have been used by the person's mother or father when he was a child. As an adult, the person uses it in an attempt to tell themselves not to say something they're feeling. The point is that it alerts you to something that is being withheld.

If your parents or minders used this gesture when you were a child, there's a good chance it's now in your adult repertoire

The Nose Touch

2. The Nose Touch

Sometimes the *Nose Touch* can be several quick rubs below the nose or it may be one quick, almost imperceptible nose touch. Women perform this gesture with smaller strokes than men, perhaps to avoid smudging their make-up.

The important thing to remember is that this type of action should be read in clusters and in context; the person could have hay fever or a cold.

Scientists at the Smell and Taste Treatment and Research Foundation in Chicago found that when you lie, chemicals known as catecholamines are released, causing tissue inside the nose to swell. They used special imaging cameras that show blood flow in the body to reveal that intentional lying also causes an increase in blood pressure. This technology indicates that the human nose actually expands with blood during lying, and is known as the 'Pinocchio Effect'. Increased blood pressure inflates the nose and causes the nerve endings in the nose to tingle, resulting in a brisk rubbing action to the nose with the hand to satisfy the 'itch'.

You can't see the swelling with the naked eye but this is what appears to cause the Nose Touch gesture. The same phenomenon occurs when a person is upset, anxious or angry.

American neurologist Alan Hirsch and psychiatrist Charles Wolf did an extensive analysis of Bill Clinton's testimony to the Grand Jury on his affair with Monica Lewinsky and found that, when he told the truth, he rarely touched his

'I did not have sexual relations with that woman!'

nose. When he lied, however, he gave a split-second frown before he answered and touched his nose once every four minutes for a grand total of 26 nose touches. Conversely, Bill Clinton did not touch his nose at all when he answered truthfully, they said.

Studies with Body Imaging cameras have revealed that a man's penis also swells with blood when he tells a lie. Maybe the Grand Jury should have pulled Bill's trousers down instead.

Grand Jury prosecutor: *'Mr Clinton - why did the chicken cross the road?'*

Bill Clinton: *'What do you mean by chicken? Could you define chicken please? And I did not cross the road with that chicken.'*

3. What About an Itchy Nose?

The itch of a person's nose is normally satisfied by a deliberate rubbing or scratching action, as opposed to the light strokes of the Nose Touch gesture. As with the Mouth Cover, the Nose Touch can be used both by the speaker to disguise his own deceit and by the listener who doubts the speaker's words. An itch is usually an isolated repetitive gesture and is incongruent or out of context with the person's overall conversation.

'I just can't see it'

4. The Eye Rub

'See no evil,' said one of the wise monkeys. When a child doesn't want to look at something he'll cover his eyes with one or both hands. When an adult doesn't want to look at something distasteful, the *Eye Rub* is likely to occur. The Eye Rub is the brain's attempt to block out the deceit, doubt or distasteful thing it sees, or to avoid having to look at the face of the person who is being lied to. Men usually rub their eyes vigorously and if the lie is a real whopper they will often look away. Women are less likely to use the Eye Rub – instead, they will use small, gentle touching motions just below the eye, because they either have been conditioned as girls to avoid making robust gestures, or to avoid smudging make-up. They also avoid a listener's gaze by looking away.

'Lying through your teeth' is a commonly used phrase. It refers to a gesture cluster of clenched teeth and a false smile, combined with the Eye Rub. This gesture is used by movie actors to portray insincerity and by 'polite' cultures such as the English, who prefer not to tell you exactly what they're thinking.

5. The Ear Grab

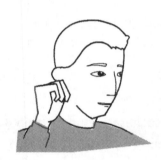

'I don't want to hear it.'

Imagine you tell someone, 'It only costs £300' and the person grabs their ear, looks away to the side and says, 'It sounds like a good deal to me.' This is a symbolic attempt by the listener to 'hear no evil': trying to block the words he is hearing by putting the hand around or over the ear or tugging at the earlobe. This is the adult version of the *Hands-Over-Both-Ears* gesture used by the child who wants to block out his parent's reprimands. Other variations of the *Ear Grab* include rubbing the back of the ear, the *Finger Drill* – where the fingertip is screwed back and forth inside the ear, pulling at the earlobe or bending the entire ear forward to cover the ear hole.

The Ear Grab can also be a signal that the person has heard enough or may want to speak. As with the Nose Touch, the Ear Grab is used by a person who is experiencing anxiety. Prince Charles often uses both the Ear Grab and the Nose Touch when he enters a room full of people or walks past a large crowd. His anxiety is revealed here and we have never seen a photo or film footage of him using these gestures when he is in the relative safety of his car.

In Italy, however, the Ear Grab is used to indicate that someone is effeminate or gay.

6. The Neck Scratch

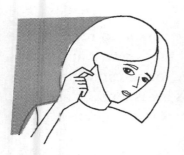

Showing uncertainty

The index finger – usually of the writing hand – scratches the side of the neck below the earlobe. Our observations of this gesture reveal the person scratches an average of five times. Rarely is the number of scratches less than five and hardly ever more than five. This gesture is a signal of doubt or uncertainty and is characteristic of the person who says, 'I'm not sure I agree.' It is very noticeable when the verbal language contradicts it, for example, when the person says something like, 'I can understand how you feel' but the *Neck Scratch* indicates they don't.

7. The Collar Pull

Getting hot under the collar

Desmond Morris was one of the first to discover that lies cause a tingling sensation in the delicate facial and neck tissues, and a rub or scratch was required to satisfy it. This not only accounts for why people who are uncertain will scratch their neck, it presents a good explanation as to why some people use the *Collar Pull* when they lie and suspect they have been caught out. Increased blood pressure from the deceit causes sweat to form on the neck when the deceiver feels that you suspect he's not telling the truth.

It also occurs when a person is feeling angry or frustrated and needs to pull the collar away from his neck in an attempt to let the cool air circulate. When you see someone use this gesture, ask, 'Could you repeat that, please?' or, 'Could you clarify that point, please?' This can cause the would-be deceiver to give the game away.

8. Fingers-in-the-Mouth

This is an unconscious attempt by the person to revert to the security of the child sucking on his mother's breast and occurs when a person feels under pressure. A young child substitutes his thumb or a blanket for his mother's breast and, as an adult, he puts his fingers to his mouth and sucks on cigarettes, pipes, pens and glasses, and chews gum.

Reassurance is needed here

Most Hand-to-Mouth gestures can be connected to lying or deception but the *Fingers-in-Mouth* gesture is an outward indication of an inner need for reassurance so giving the person guarantees and assurances is a positive move.

Evaluation and Procrastination Gestures

A good speaker is said to be one who 'instinctively' knows when his audience is interested in what he's saying and can also tell when his listeners have had enough. A good salesperson senses when he is hitting his client's 'hot buttons' and finding out where the buyer's interest lies. Every presenter knows the empty feeling that results when he or she is giving a presentation to someone who says very little and just sits there watching. Fortunately, there are a number of *Hand-to-Cheek* and *Hand-to-Chin* gestures that can be used as a thermometer to test how hot or cold the other person's attitude is, and to tell the speaker how well he is doing.

Boredom

When the listener begins to use his hand to support his head, it is a signal that boredom has set in and his supporting hand is an attempt to hold his head up to stop himself from falling asleep. The degree of the listener's boredom is related to the extent to which his arm and hand are supporting his head. It usually begins with the chin being supported by the thumb and then by the fist as interest wanes. Extreme lack of interest is shown when the head is fully supported by the hand (see illustration), and the ultimate boredom signal occurs when the head is fully supported by the hands and snoring sounds are evident.

The hand supporting the head to stop from falling asleep

Drumming the fingers on the table and continual tapping of the feet on the floor are often misinterpreted by professional speakers as boredom signals, but in fact signal impatience. If you are addressing a group of people and see these signals, a strategic move must be made to get the finger drummer or foot tapper involved in the conversation to avoid his negative effect on the other listeners. Any audience that displays boredom and impatience signals together is telling the speaker that it is time for him to end.

> '*Do you talk in your sleep?' he asked the speaker.*
> '*No,' came the reply. 'Then please don't talk in mine.'*

The speed of the finger or foot tap is related to the extent of the person's impatience – the faster the taps, the more impatient the listener is becoming.

Evaluation Gestures

Evaluation is shown by a closed hand resting on the chin or cheek, often with the index finger pointing upwards. When the person begins to lose interest but still wants to appear interested for courtesy's sake, the position will alter so that the heel of the palm supports the head as boredom sets in.

Interested evaluation – the head supports itself and the hand rests on the cheek

Middle managers often use this gesture to feign interest to the company president who is giving a dull, boring speech. Unfortunately for them, however, as soon as the hand begins to support the head in any way, it gives the game away and the president is likely to feel that some of the managers are being insincere or using false flattery.

Having negative thoughts

He's heard enough or
is not impressed

Genuine interest is shown when the hand lightly rests on the cheek and is not used as a head support. When the index finger points vertically up the cheek and the thumb supports the chin, the listener is having negative or critical thoughts about the speaker or his subject. Sometimes the index finger may rub or pull at the eye as the negative thoughts continue.

This gesture is often mistaken as a signal of interest, but the supporting thumb under the chin tells the truth about the critical attitude. Holding a gesture cluster affects a person's attitude so the longer a person holds it, the longer their critical attitude will remain. This gesture cluster is a signal that immediate action is required by the speaker, either by involving the listener in what he is saying or by ending the encounter. A simple move, such as handing something to the listener to alter his pose, can cause a change in attitude.

Rodin's The Thinker showed a thoughtful, evaluative attitude, but the body posture and hand supporting the head also reveal a dejected person

The Lying Interviewee

We interviewed a man who had arrived from abroad to apply for a position with our company. Throughout the interview he kept his arms and legs crossed, used critical evaluation clusters, had very little palm use and he looked away frequently. Something was obviously worrying him, but in the early stages of the interview we didn't have sufficient information for an accurate assessment of his negative gestures. We asked questions about his previous employers in his native country. His answers included a series of eye-rubbing and nose-touching gestures and he continued to look away. We eventually decided not to hire him, based on what we had seen as opposed to what he had said. We were curious about his deceit gestures and when we checked with his overseas referees, we discovered that he had given false information about his past. He assumed that a potential employer in another country probably wouldn't bother to check overseas references and, had we not been aware of the body language cues and signals, we could have made the mistake of hiring him.

Chin Stroking

The next time you have the opportunity to present an idea to a group of people, watch them carefully as you give your idea and you may notice that most will bring one hand up to their face and use an evaluation gesture. When you come to the end of your presentation and ask the group to give opinions or suggestions about your ideas, the evaluation gestures will usually stop and a *Chin Stroking* gesture begins. This Chin Stroke is the signal that the listener is going through the decision-making process.

Making a decision   Female version of Chin Stroking

When you've asked the listeners for their decision and they start Chin Stroking, their next gestures will signal whether their decision is negative or positive. Your best strategy is to stay quiet and watch their next gestures, which will indicate the decision reached. For example, if the Chin Stroke is followed by crossed arms and legs and the person sits back in their chair, it's a fair bet the answer will be 'no'. This gives you an early opportunity to resell the benefits before the other person verbalises 'no' and makes it harder to reach agreement.

If the Chin Stroke is followed by leaning forward with arms open or picking up your proposal or sample, chances are you have a 'yes' and can proceed as if you have agreement.

Stalling Clusters

Someone who wears glasses sometimes follows an evaluation cluster by taking off their glasses and putting one arm of the frame in the mouth instead of using the Chin Stroke when making their decision. A cigarette smoker will take a puff of smoke. When a person puts a pen or a finger in their mouth after you've asked for a decision, it's a signal that he is unsure and reassurance is needed. The object in the mouth allows him to stall and not feel any urgency in giving an immediate response.

Sometimes boredom, evaluation and decision-making gestures come in combinations, each showing different elements of the person's attitude.

The next illustration shows the evaluation gesture moved to the chin, and the hand may also be stroking the chin. This person is evaluating the proposition and drawing conclusions simultaneously.

Evaluation/decision-making cluster

When the listener begins to lose interest in the speaker, the head begins to rest on the hand. The next picture shows evaluation with the head supported by the thumb as the listener becomes uninterested.

Evaluation, decision, boredom cluster

Arnold Schwarzenegger drives home his
point while the TV host thinks it over

Head Rubbing and Slapping Gestures

When you say someone 'gives you a pain in the neck', you are
referring to the ancient reaction of the tiny erector pillae

muscles on the neck – often called
goosebumps – attempting to make
your non-existent fur pelt stand on
end to make yourself appear more
intimidating because you are feeling
threatened or angry. It's the same hair-
raising reaction an angry dog has
when it's confronted by another
potentially hostile dog. This reaction
causes the tingling feeling you experience on the back of your neck when
you feel frustrated or fearful. You'll
usually rub your hand over the area to

'Pain in the neck' gesture   satisfy the sensation.

Let us assume, for example, that you asked someone to do a small favour for you and that they had forgotten to do it. When you ask them for the result, they slap either their forehead or back of the neck, as if they were symbolically beating themselves. Although slapping of the head is used to communicate forgetfulness, it's important to watch whether they slap the forehead or neck. If they slap their forehead, they signal that they are not intimidated by you mentioning their forgetfulness. When they slap the back of the neck to satisfy the raised erector pillae muscles, however, it tells you that you are literally a 'pain-in-the-neck' for mentioning it. If the person slaps their rear end however...

Gerard Nierenberg, of the Negotiation Institute in New York, found that those who habitually rub the back of the neck have a tendency to be negative or critical, whereas those who habitually rub their foreheads to non-verbalise an error tend to be more open and easy-going.

Punishing oneself by slapping oneself

Acquiring the ability to interpret hand-to-face gestures accurately in a given set of circumstances takes time and observation. When a person uses any of the hand-to-face gestures discussed in this chapter, it's reasonable to assume a negative thought has entered his mind. The question is, however, what is the negative thought? It could be doubt, deceit, uncertainty, exaggeration, apprehension or outright lying. The real skill is the ability to interpret which negative is the correct one. This can best be done by an analysis of the gestures preceding the hand-to-face gesture and interpreting it in context.

Why Bob Always Lost at Chess

We have a colleague, Bob, who enjoys playing chess. We challenged him to a competition, which we secretly videotaped for later analysis of his body language. The video revealed that Bob often rubbed his ear or touched his nose during the game, but only when he was unsure of his next move. We discovered that when we signalled an intention to move a chess piece by touching it, Bob's body language would signal what he thought about the proposed move. When he felt he could beat a move, and had probably already thought of a counter move, he'd signal his confidence by Steepling; when he was uncertain or unhappy he'd use the Mouth Cover, Ear Pull or Neck Scratch. This happened with such predictability that when we secretly explained Bob's cues to the other members of our chess group, soon most could beat poor old Bob by anticipating his thoughts from his body language. Bob has not been offered a copy of this book.

The Double Meaning

During a videotaped role-play interview, our interviewee suddenly covered his mouth and rubbed his nose after he had been asked a question by the interviewer. He used the Mouth Cover for several seconds before answering, then returned to his open pose. Up to that point in the role-play, the interviewee had kept an open posture with his coat unbuttoned, palms visible, nodding his head and leaning forward when he answered questions, so we thought the gestures might have been isolated or out of context. On reviewing the videotape, we asked him about the hand-to-mouth gesture and he said that when he was asked the question, he thought he could have responded in two ways: one negative, one positive. As he thought about the negative answer and of how the interviewer might react to it, he covered his mouth. When he thought of the positive answer, however, his hand dropped away from his mouth and he resumed an open posture. His uncertainty about the interviewer's possible reaction to the negative reply had resulted in the sudden Mouth Cover.

This illustrates how easy it can be to misinterpret a hand-to-face gesture and to jump to wrong conclusions.

Chapter 8
EYE SIGNALS

Some men have the ability to see
through solid surfaces

Throughout history, we've been preoccupied with the eyes and their effect on human behaviour. Eye contact regulates conversation, gives cues of dominance, 'He looked down his nose at me' or forms the basis for suspecting a liar, 'Look me in the eye when you say that!' We spend much of our face-to-face time looking at the other person's face, so eye signals are a vital part of being able to read a person's attitude and thoughts. When people meet for the first time they make a series of quick judgements about each other, based largely on what they see.

We use phrases such as 'She looked daggers at him', 'He had that gleam in his eye', 'She has big baby eyes', 'He has shifty eyes', 'She has inviting eyes', 'She gave him a look to kill', 'She gave an icy stare' or 'He gave me the evil eye'. We also say a person has Bette Davis eyes, Spanish eyes, bedroom eyes, hard, angry, blank, private, sad, happy, defiant, cold, jealous, unforgiving and piercing eyes. When we use these phrases we are unwittingly referring to the size of the person's pupils and to his gaze behaviour. The eyes can be the most revealing and accurate of all human communication signals because they are a focal point on the body and the pupils work independently of conscious control.

The Dilating Pupils

In given light conditions, your pupils will dilate or contract as your attitude and mood change from positive to negative and vice versa. When someone becomes excited, their pupils can dilate to up to four times their original size. Conversely, an angry, negative mood causes the pupils to contract to what are commonly known as 'beady little eyes' or 'snake eyes'. Lighter eyes can look more attractive because it's easier to see the dilation taking place.

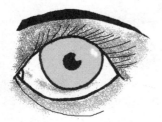

'Beady' eyes

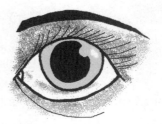

Bedroom eyes

Eckhard Hess, the former head of the Department of Psychology at the University of Chicago and pioneer of the studies of pupillometry, found that pupil size is affected by one's general state of arousal. In general, pupil size increases when people view something that stimulates them. Hess found that the pupils of both heterosexual men and women dilate when viewing pin-ups of the opposite sex and constrict when viewing same-sex pin-ups. Similar findings have also been obtained when people were asked to look at pleasant or unpleasant pictures including foods, political figures, a disabled child or war scenes, or when listening to music. Hess also found that increases in pupil size are positively correlated with mental activity associated with problem solving, reaching maximum dilation as a person arrives at the solution.

We applied this research to the business world and demonstrated how people rate models in photographs as more attractive if the photo has been altered to make the pupil area larger. This was an effective way to increase the sales of any product that used a close-up of the face, such as women's cosmetics, hair products and clothing. Using brochures in a direct mail campaign, we were able to help increase the direct catalogue sales of Revlon lipsticks by 45% by enlarging the pupil size of the models in the photographs.

Which picture do you find more attractive?

The eyes are a key signal in courtship and the purpose of eye make-up is to emphasise eye display. If a woman is attracted to a man, she will dilate her pupils at him and he is likely to decode this signal correctly without knowing it. This is why romantic encounters are most successful in dimly lit places because everyone's pupils dilate and create the impression that couples are interested in each other.

....

*When a man is excited by a woman, which part of
his body can grow to almost three times its size?*

....

When lovers gaze deep into each other's eyes, they are
unknowingly looking for pupil-dilation signals and each
becomes excited by the dilation of the other's pupils. Research
has shown that when pornographic films are shown to men,
their pupils can dilate to almost three times their size. Most
women's pupils gave the greatest dilation when looking at pictures of mothers and babies. Young babies and children have
larger pupils than adults, and babies' pupils constantly dilate
when adults are present in an attempt to look as appealing as
possible and therefore receive constant attention. This is why
the bestselling children's toys almost always have oversized
pupils.

Research also shows that pupil dilation has a reciprocal
effect on the person who sees the dilated pupils. Men looking
at pictures of women with dilated pupils showed greater pupil
dilation than when they looked at pictures of women with
constricted pupils.

Take the Pupil Test

The ability to decode pupil dilation is hardwired into the brain
and happens completely automatically. To test this, cover diagram B with your hand and ask someone to stare at the
'pupils' in illustration A. Then switch them to staring at illustration B and you'll see how their pupils dilate to match the
illustration, because their brain thinks it's looking at eyes that
find it attractive. Women's pupils dilate faster than men's to
create rapport with what their brain sees as another person's
eyes.

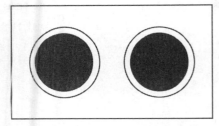
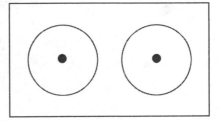

Diagram A   Diagram B

Hess conducted a pupil response experiment by showing five pictures to respondents: a naked male, a naked female, a baby, a mother and baby, and a landscape. Predictably, men's pupils dilated most at the naked female, gay men dilated most at the naked male but women's pupils dilated most at the picture of the mother and baby with the naked male picture coming in second.

Tests conducted with expert card players show that fewer games were won by the experts when their opponents wore dark glasses. For example, if an opponent was dealt four aces in a game of poker, his rapid pupil dilation could be unconsciously detected by the expert, who would 'sense' he should not bet on the next hand. Dark glasses worn by the opponents eliminated pupil signals and, as a result, the experts won fewer hands than usual.

Pupil decoding was used by the ancient Chinese gem traders who watched for the pupil dilation of their buyers when negotiating prices. Centuries ago, prostitutes put drops of belladonna, a tincture containing atropine, into their eyes to dilate their pupils and to make themselves appear more desirable.

David Bowie has different-coloured eyes – one blue and one hazel – and one is permanently dilated; this condition is called Heterochromia and it affects 1% of the population. Bowie's eye variations are the result of a punch-up over a girl-friend at the age of 12

An old cliché says, 'Look a person in the eye when you talk to them' when you are communicating or negotiating, but it's better to practise 'looking them in the pupil' as the pupils will tell you their real feelings.

Women Are Better at It, as Usual

Dr Simon Baron-Cohen at Cambridge University conducted some tests where subjects were shown photographs in which only a narrow strip of the face across both eyes was visible. The subjects were asked to choose between mental states expressed in the photographs such as 'friendly', 'relaxed', 'hostile' and 'worried' and attitudes such as 'desire for you' and 'desire for someone else'.

Statistically, pure guesswork would result in half the answers being correct but men's average score was 19 out of 25 while women scored 22 out of 25. This test shows that both sexes have a greater ability to decode eye signals than body signals and that women are better at it than men. Scientists don't yet know how this eye information is sent or decoded, they simply know that we can do it. Autistic people – who are nearly all males – scored the lowest. Autistic brains lack the ability to read people's body language and this is one reason why autistic people have difficulty in forming social relationships, even though many have very high IQs.

Giving Them the Eye

Humans are the only primates that have whites of the eye, known as the sclera – apes' eyes are completely dark. The white of the eye evolved as a communication aid to allow humans to see where other people were looking, because direction is linked to emotional states. Women's brains have more hardwiring than men's to read emotions, and one consequence of this is that women have more white of the eye than men. Apes lack eye-whites, which means that their prey don't know where the ape is looking or whether they have been spotted, giving the ape a greater chance of hunting success.

Humans are the only primates with pronounced whites of the eye.

The Eyebrow Flash

This gesture is a long-distance 'hello' greeting signal which has been used everywhere since ancient times. The *Eyebrow Flash* is universal and is also used by monkeys and apes as a social greeting signal, confirming that it's an inborn gesture. The eyebrows rise rapidly for a split second and then drop again and its purpose is to draw attention to the face so that clear signals can be exchanged. The only culture that doesn't use it is the Japanese, where it's considered improper or impolite and has definite sexual connotations.

The Eyebrow Flash

This is an unconscious signal that acknowledges the other person's presence and is probably linked to the fear reaction of being surprised, or saying, 'I'm surprised and afraid of you', which translates to 'I acknowledge you and am not threatening'. We don't Eyebrow Flash strangers we pass in the street or people we don't like, and people who don't give the Eyebrow Flash on initial greeting are perceived as potentially aggressive. Try this simple test and you'll discover first hand the power of the Eyebrow Flash – sit in the lobby of a hotel and Eyebrow Flash everyone who goes past. You'll see that not only do others return the Flash and smile, many will come over and begin to talk to you. The golden rule is always Eyebrow Flash people you like or those who you want to like you.

Eye Widening

Lowering the eyebrows is how humans show dominance or aggression towards others, whereas raising the eyebrows shows submission. Keating & Keating found that several species of apes and monkeys use exactly the same gestures for the same purpose. They also found that people who intentionally raise their eyebrows are perceived as submissive by both humans and apes, and that those who lower them are perceived as aggressive.

In *Why Men Lie & Women Cry* (Orion) we showed how women widen their eyes by raising their eyebrows and eyelids to create the 'baby face' appearance of a small infant. This has a powerful effect on men by releasing hormones into the brain, which stimulate the desire to protect and defend females. Women pluck and redraw their eyebrows higher up the forehead to appear more submissive because, on a subconscious level at least, they know it appeals to men. If men trim their eyebrows they do it from the top of the eyebrow down to make their eyes appear narrower and more authoritative.

High-placed eyebrows gave Marilyn Monroe a submissive appearance while low-set eyebrows gave James Cagney his aggressive look and JFK's turned-in eyebrows made him appear both authoritative and concerned

John F Kennedy had what are known as 'medially down-turned' eyebrows, which gave his face a permanently concerned look that appealed to voters. If he'd had big bushy eyebrows like actor James Cagney's he would have had a less powerful impact on the electorate.

The 'Looking Up' Cluster

Princess Diana at the age of eight – like most young girls, she silently understood the impact of putting the head down and looking up

Lowering the head and looking up is another sub-missive gesture that appeals to men because it makes the eyes appear larger and makes a woman appear more child-like. This is because children are so much smaller than adults and spend their looking time gazing up and this creates a parenting reaction in both men and women.

Princess Diana used the 'Looking Up' cluster to evoke world empathy during her marital problems

Princess Diana made an art form out of keeping her chin down while looking up and exposing her vulnerable neck. This child-like gesture cluster triggered maternal and paternal reactions towards her in millions of people, especially when she seemed to be under attack by the British Royal Family. People who use these submissive clusters usually don't practise them consciously but know that when they use them, they get a result.

How Men's Fires Get Lit

Marilyn Monroe was the master of using female pre-orgasmic expressions and body language, and she understood, at least on a subconscious level, how it could make most men go weak at the knees

Lowering the eyelids while simultaneously raising the eyebrows, looking up and slightly parting the lips is a cluster that has been used by women for centuries to show sexual submissiveness. This is one of the trademarks of the sex sirens such as Marilyn Monroe, Deborah Harry and Sharon Stone.

Not only does this gesture maximise the distance between the eyelid and eyebrows, it also gives the person a mysterious, secretive look and new research shows that this is the expression many women have on their faces immediately before having an orgasm.

Gaze Behaviour – Where Do You Look?

It is only when you see 'eye to eye' with another person that a real basis for communication can be established. While some people can make us feel comfortable when they talk with us, others make us feel ill at ease and some seem untrustworthy. Initially, this has to do with the length of time that they look at us or with how long they hold our gaze as they speak.

Michael Argyle, a pioneer of social psychology and non-verbal communication skills in Britain, found that when Westerners and Europeans talk, their average gaze time is 61%, consisting of 41% gaze time when talking, 75% when listening and 31% mutual gazing. He recorded the average gaze length to be 2.95 seconds and the length of a mutual gaze was 1.18 seconds. We found that the amount of eye contact in a typical conversation ranges from 25% to 100%, depending on who's talking and what culture they're from. When we talk we maintain 40 to 60% eye contact with an average of 80% eye contact when listening. The notable exception to this rule is Japan and some Asian and South American cultures, where extended eye contact is seen as aggressive or disrespectful. The Japanese tend to look away or at your throat, which can be disconcerting for culturally inexperienced Westerners and Europeans.

Argyle found that when person A likes person B, he will look at him a lot. This causes B to think that A likes him, so B will like A in return. In other words, in most cultures, to build a good rapport with another person, your gaze should meet theirs about 60 to 70% of the time. This will also cause them to begin to like you. It is not surprising, therefore, that the nervous, timid person who meets our gaze less than one-third of the time is rarely trusted. This is also why, in negotiations, dark tinted glasses should be avoided as they make others feel you are either staring at them or trying to avoid them.

....

He married her for her looks, but not the ones she's been giving him lately.

....

As with most body language and gestures, the length of time that one person gazes at another can be culturally determined. Always be sure to consider cultural circumstances before jumping to conclusions. The safest rule when travelling to places such as Japan is to mirror the gaze time of your hosts.

When two people meet and make eye contact for the first time, it's usually the person who is subordinate who looks away first. This means that *not* looking away becomes a subtle way to deliver a challenge or show disagreement when someone gives their opinion or point of view. Where the status of the other person is higher, however, for example, the person is your boss, you can send a clear message of disagreement by holding his gaze for only several seconds longer than would be usually acceptable. But it's not a good idea to do this regularly with your boss if you want to keep your job.

How to Keep Eye Contact in a Nudist Colony

We sent a group of non-nudists to a nudist colony and filmed where they were looking when they were introduced to new people. All the non-nudist men reported that they had trouble resisting the urge to look down and the video replay showed how obvious it was when they *did* look down. The women said they did not experience these problems and rarely was a woman filmed intentionally gazing towards the nether regions. This is because men are equipped with a form of tunnel vision that makes them far better than women at seeing directly in front of them and over long distances for spotting targets. Most men's close range and peripheral vision is far poorer than women's, however, which is why men have difficulty seeing things in refrigerators, cupboards and drawers. Women's peripheral vision extends to at least 45 degrees to each side, above and below, which means she can appear to be looking at someone's face while, at the same time, she is inspecting their goods and chattels.

Women's wider peripheral vision lets them appear to be looking in
one direction when they are, in fact, looking in another.

How to Grab a Man's Attention

When a woman wants to get a man's attention across a room
she will meet his gaze, hold it for two to three seconds, then
look away and down. This gaze is long enough for her to send
him a message of interest and potential submission. An experiment by Monika Moore PhD, of Websters University, showed
that most men are not hardwired to read a woman's first gaze
signal so she usually needs to repeat it three times before the
average man picks up on it, four times for really slow men and
five or more times for the especially thick. When she finally
gets his attention she will often use a small version of the
Eyebrow Flash that is a small, subtle eye-widening gesture that
tells him the signal was intended for him.

Sometimes a simple face-to-face verbal approach of 'Hey, I
like you!' is more effective on men who are slow on the uptake.

Most Liars Look You in the Eye

As we said earlier, many people associate lying with looking
away. We conducted a series of experiments where participants

were told to tell a series of lies to others in recorded interviews. The recordings were used in our communication seminars where viewers were asked to judge who was lying and who wasn't. What we discovered was contrary to a popular belief about liars. Approximately 30% of the liars constantly looked away when they lied and the viewers spotted these lies around 80% of the time, with women having a better catch rate than men. The other 70% of the liars maintained strong eye contact with their victim, assuming they were less likely to get caught if they did the *opposite* of what people expected. They were right. Lie-catching dropped to an average of 25%, with men scoring a dismal 15% success and women 35%. Women's more intuitive brains were better than men's in detecting voice changes, pupil dilation and other cues that gave the liar away. This shows that gaze alone is not a reliable signal of lying and you need to observe other gestures as well.

When a person's gaze meets yours for more than two-thirds of the time, it can mean one of two things: first, he finds you interesting or appealing, in which case he'll also have dilated pupils; or second, he's hostile towards you and could be issuing a challenge, in which case the pupils will be constricted. As mentioned, women are good at deciphering pupil signals and can differentiate interest from aggression, but men are significantly worse at doing it. This is why the average man can't tell if a woman is about to give him a kiss or a slap in the face.

How to Avoid being Attacked or Abused

Most primates avert their gaze to show submission. If an ape is going to display aggression or is likely to attack, it will lock eyes onto its victim. To avoid being attacked, the victim will look away and try to make itself appear smaller. Scientific evidence shows that submission behaviour appears to be hardwired into primate brains for survival reasons. Under attack, we make ourselves appear smaller by hunching our shoulders, pulling our arms in close to the body, pressing our knees together and locking our ankles under a chair, dropping our chin to the chest to protect the throat and averting our gaze by looking away. These gestures activate an 'off switch' in the brain of the aggressor and the attack can be avoided.

Making yourself appear smaller turns off the aggression switch in an aggressor's brain.

This is an ideal position to take if you are being reprimanded by a superior when you actually deserve the reprimand, but it would be detrimental against a random street attack. From a person who is walking past a group of possible assailants in the street it would signal fear and this can contribute to inciting an attack. If you walk upright with larger movements, swinging your arms and legs and having your front open, you will project that you could defend yourself if necessary and so are less likely to be attacked.

The Sideways Glance

The *Sideways Glance* is used to communicate interest, uncertainty or hostility. When it is combined with slightly raised eyebrows or a smile, it communicates interest and is frequently used as a courtship signal, mostly by women. If it is clustered with down-turned eyebrows, furrowed brow or the corners of the mouth down-turned, it signals a suspicious, hostile or critical attitude.

Extended Blinking

A normal, relaxed blinking rate is six to eight blinks per minute and the eyes are closed for only about one tenth of a second. People under pressure, for instance when they are lying, are likely to dramatically increase their blinking rate.

Extended Blinking is an unconscious attempt by the person's brain to block you from their sight because they've become bored or disinterested or feel they're superior to you. It's as if their brain can no longer tolerate dealing with you so their eyes shut for two to three seconds or longer to wipe you from sight and remain closed as the person momentarily removes you from his mind.

Shutting you out

Superior types may also tilt their head back to give you a 'long look', commonly known as 'looking down one's nose'; this is also done by a person who feels that their importance is not being noticed. This is mainly a Western cultural gesture and a speciality of English people who feel they are upper-class. If you see this happening during a conversation, it's a signal that you're not doing well and that a new tack is needed. If you believe the person is simply arrogant, try this: when they've closed their eyes for the third or fourth time, quickly step a pace to your left or right. When their eyelids lift again, it gives the illusion that you've disappeared and materialised in another place and this can really rattle them. If the person also starts snoring, you can safely assume that your communication has failed.

Darting Eyes

When the eyes dart from side to side it can look as if the person is checking out the activity in the room but the reality is that the brain is searching for escape routes (just as happens in monkeys and apes), revealing a person's insecurity about what is happening.

When you're with a particularly boring individual, your natural urge is to look away for escape routes. But because most of us are aware that looking away shows a lack of interest in the other person and signals our desire to escape, we look *more* at the boring individual and use a Tight-Lipped Smile to feign interest. This behaviour parallels what liars are doing when they increase their eye contact to appear convincing.

The Geography of the Face

The geographical area of a person's face and body that you gaze upon can also dramatically affect the outcome of a face-to-face encounter.

When you've finished reading this next section, try out the techniques we discuss as soon as possible – without warning anyone – and you'll experience the powerful effect these skills can have. It takes about a week of practice for these eye techniques to become a normal part of your communication skills.

There are three basic types of gazing: *Social Gazing, Intimate Gazing* and *Power Gazing*.

1. The Social Gaze
Experiments into gazing reveal that during social encounters the gazer's eyes look in a triangular area on the other person's face between the eyes and the mouth for about 90% of the gaze time.

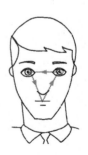

This is the area of the face we look at in a non-threatening environment. The other person will perceive you as non-aggressive.

The Social
Gazing area

2. The Intimate Gaze
When people approach each other from a distance, they look quickly between the other person's face and lower body to first

establish what the sex of the person is and then a second time to determine a level of interest in them. This gaze is across the eyes and below the chin to lower parts of the person's body. In close encounters, it's the triangular area between the eyes and the chest and for distant gazing it's from the eyes to the groin or below.

Men and women use this gaze to show interest in each other, and those who are interested will return the gaze. We usually give two quick glances and then look at their face and, despite most people's strong denials about it, hidden camera studies reveal that everyone does it, including nuns.

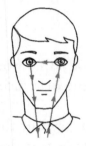

The Intimate Gaze zone

As we said earlier, a woman's wider-ranging peripheral vision, however, allows her to check out a man's body from head to toe without getting caught. Male tunnel vision is why a man will move his gaze up and down a woman's body in a very obvious way. This is also the reason why men are constantly accused of ogling women's bodies at close range but women are rarely accused of the same, even though research shows that women do more of it than men. It's not that men are bigger oglers than women – men's tunnel vision means they keep getting caught.

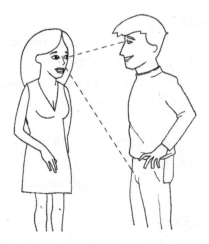

Women's wider peripheral vision means never getting caught;
Men's Tunnel Vision means always getting caught

Looking down towards the ground during conversation serves different purposes for men and women. For a man, it lets him give a woman the once over. For a woman, it has the dual purpose of letting her check him out and at the same time send a submissive signal of looking away and down.

Why do men have trouble making eye contact?
Breasts don't have eyes.

3. The Power Gaze

Imagine the person has a third eye in the centre of their forehead and look in a triangular area between the person's 'three' eyes. The impact this gaze has on the other person has to be experienced to be believed.

Not only does it change the atmosphere to very serious, it can stop a bore dead in their tracks. By keeping your gaze directed at this area, you keep the screws firmly on them.

The Power Gaze

Provided your gaze doesn't drop below the level of their eyes, the pressure will stay on them. Never use this in friendly or romantic encounters. But it works a treat on the person who you want to intimidate or on the person who simply won't shut up.

The Power Stare

If you have soft, weak or wimpy eyes practise using the *Power Stare* to give yourself more authority. When you are under attack from someone, try not to blink while maintaining eye contact. When you look at the attacker, narrow your eyelids and focus closely on the person. This is what predatory animals do just before they strike their prey. When you pan your eyes from one person to another without blinking it has an unnerving effect on anyone who watches you do it.

Don't mess with the
Terminator

To do this, move your eyeballs first and then let your head
follow, but your shoulders should remain still. The Power Stare
was used by Arnold Schwarzenegger as The Terminator and
can strike fear into the hearts of would-be intimidators. Better
still, have a policy of dealing only with pleasant people so
you'll never need to whip out your Power Stare.

The Politician's Story

When someone looks around from side to side or won't look us
in the eye when they talk, our trust in their credibility diminishes dramatically, even though they may be doing it because of
shyness. We had a politician client who was a novice at being
interviewed on television and he constantly flicked his eyes
between the reporters and the cameras when he was being interviewed. This had the effect of making him look shifty-eyed on
the screen and each time he appeared on television his popular-
ity decreased. By training him simply to look at only the
reporter and ignore the cameras, his credibility increased. We
trained another politician to address his answers mainly to the
lens of the television camera when he participated in a televised
political debate. While this alienated the 150 studio audience
guests it impressed millions of television viewers, who felt as if
the politician was talking directly to them.

Look Deep Into My Eyes, Baby

For a television show, we conducted an experiment using a dating agency. A selected number of men were told that their next date was well matched to them and that they should expect to have a successful, fun time. We explained to each man that his date had suffered an injury to one eye as a child and that she was very sensitive about it because the eye didn't track properly. We said we weren't sure which eye it was, but if he looked closely he'd be able to pick it. Each woman was also told the same story about her date and that if she too looked closely she'd be able to spot the slow eye. On their dates, the couples spent the evening gazing into each other's eyes searching in vain for the 'problem eye'. The outcome was that each couple reported high levels of intimacy and romance on their dates and the likelihood of the couple meeting again for a second date was 200% higher than the agency average.

Extended gazing can create intimate feelings.

You can also drive couples apart by telling them that their date has a hearing problem and that they'd need to talk about 10% louder than their date to be heard. This results in a couple talking louder and louder as the evening progresses to the point where they are yelling at each other.

The First 20 Seconds of an Interview

Many people are taught that, in a sales or job interview, you should maintain strong eye contact with the other person and keep it up until you are seated. This creates problems for both the interviewer and interviewee because it's contrary to the process we like to go through when we meet someone new. A man wants to check out a woman's hair, legs, body shape and overall presentation. If she maintains eye contact it restricts this process so he's left trying to steal glances at her during the interview without getting caught and so he becomes distracted from the actual job of interviewing. Some women are disappointed that, in a supposedly equal business world, men still do this, but hidden cameras show this to be a fact of business life whether we like it or not.

Like it or not, everyone steals a look at a woman's rear when she leaves a room, even if they don't like her front view.

Video cameras also reveal that women interviewers go through the same evaluation process with both male and female interviewees but women's wider peripheral vision means they rarely get caught. Women are also more critical than men of female interviewees whose appearance doesn't stack up. Women look at a male candidate's hair length, clothes design and co-ordination, the creases in his trousers and shine on his shoes. Most men are completely unaware that women look at the condition of the *back* of his shoes as he walks out.

Solution

When you go for an interview, shake hands and then give the interviewer a two- to three-second frame of uninterrupted time for them to complete the process of looking you over. Look down to open your briefcase or folder, or to arrange any papers you might need, turn to hang up your coat, or move your chair in closer, and then look up. In filming sales interviews, we found that not only did the interviews feel better for the salespeople who used this strategy, it added up to a better outcome in sales results.

What Channel Are You Tuned to?

A person's eye movements can reveal what their mind is focusing on by telling you whether they are remembering something they have seen, heard, smelled, tasted or touched. This technique is a development of American psychologists Grinder and Bandler and is known as *Neurolinguistic Programming*, or *NLP*.

In simple terms, if a person is remembering something that they saw, their eyes will move upward. If they are recalling something they heard, they look to the side and tilt their head as if listening. If they are recalling a feeling or emotion, they'll look down and to the right. When a person is mentally talking to themselves, they look down and to the left.

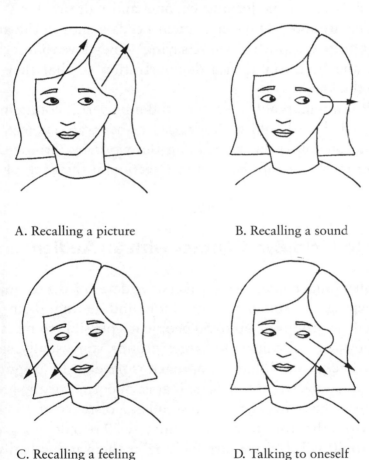

A. Recalling a picture	B. Recalling a sound
C. Recalling a feeling	D. Talking to oneself

The difficulty is that these eye movements can occur in a fraction of a second and come in clusters making it harder to read 'live'. A videotape replay, however, can let you see discrepancies between what a person says and what they really think.

Thirty-five per cent of people prefer the visual information channel and will use phrases such as 'I see what you mean', 'Can you look into that?', 'That's perfectly clear' or 'Can you show me that?' and you will get their attention by showing them photos, charts and graphs and asking if they 'Get the picture'.

Twenty-five per cent prefer the auditory channel and use words such as 'That rings a bell', 'I hear you', 'That doesn't sound right' and that they want to be 'in tune' with you. The other 40% prefer the feelings channel and will say 'Let's kick that idea around', 'Our department needs a shot in the arm', 'I can't quite grasp what you're saying'. They love to test drive things and be involved in a demonstration so that they can 'grasp the idea'.

NLP is a remarkable discovery and a powerful communications tool that should be addressed as separate subject. We suggest you follow up by reading the work by Grinder and Bandler mentioned in the reference section at the back of this book.

How to Hold Eye Contact with an Audience

As professional conference speakers, we developed a technique for keeping an audience's attention and letting them feel involved. In groups of up to 50 people it's possible to meet the gaze of each individual. In larger groups you usually stand further back, so a different approach is needed. By pegging a real or imaginary point or person at each corner of the group and one in the centre, when you stand at a distance of 10 yards (10m) from the front row, approximately 20 people in a group of up to 50 will feel you are looking at them individually as you speak and so you can create an intimate bond with most of your audience.

How to Present Visual Information

When you are giving a visual presentation using books, charts, graphs or a laptop it's important to know how to control where the other person is looking. Research shows that of the information relayed to the brain in visual presentations, 83% comes via the eyes, 11% via the ears, and 6% through the other senses.

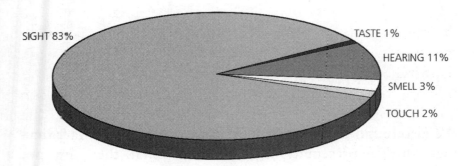

Impact on the brain of information from the senses during a visual presentation

The Wharton study in the United States found that the retention of verbal presentations was only 10%. This means that a verbal presentation requires frequent repetition of key points to be effective. By comparison, the retention rate of combined verbal and visual presentations is 50%. This means you will achieve a 400% increase in efficiency through the use of visual aids. The study also found that using visual aids cuts the average business meeting time from 25.7 minutes to 18.6 minutes – a 28% time saving.

The Power Lift

To keep control of where a person is looking, use a pen to point to the presentation and, at the same time, verbalise what he sees. Next, lift the pen from the presentation and hold it between his eyes and your eyes. This has the magnetic effect of lifting his head so that now he is looking at you and he sees and hears what you are saying, achieving maximum absorption of your message. Keep the palm of your other hand open when you are speaking.

The Power Lift – using the pen to control where a
person looks during a presentation

We also found that women hold more direct eye contact than men during presentations, especially when they are not talking. When women are talking, however, they avert their eyes more than men do.

Men stare more at women than vice versa and men give less direct eye contact when listening to other men than when listening to women.

Summary

Where you direct your gaze has a powerful impact on the outcome of a face-to-face encounter. If you were a manager who was going to reprimand an errant subordinate or a parent reprimanding a child, which gaze would you use? If you use Social Gazing, the sting would be taken out of your words, regardless of how loud or threatening you might try to sound. Social Gazing would weaken your words but Intimate Gazing could either intimidate or embarrass them. Power Gazing, however, has a powerful effect on the receiver and tells them you mean business.

Using the right gaze gives credibility.

What men describe as the 'come-on' look that women use relates to a sideways glance, dilated pupils and Intimate Gazing. If a woman wants to play hard to get, she needs to avoid using an Intimate Gaze and use Social Gazing instead. But most men miss a lot of it anyway. To use a Power Gaze during courting would leave a man or woman labelled as cold or unfriendly. When you use an Intimate Gaze on a potential partner, however, you give the game away. Women are expert at sending and receiving this gaze but, unfortunately, most men are not. When men use the Intimate Gaze it's usually blatantly obvious to women and men are generally unaware of having been given an Intimate Gaze by a woman, much to the frustration of the woman who gave it.

Chapter 9

SPACE INVADERS – TERRITORIES AND PERSONAL SPACE

'Excuse me…but you're sitting in my seat!'

Thousands of books and articles have been written about the staking out and guarding of territories by animals, birds, fish and primates, but only in recent years has it been discovered that man also has territories. When you understand the implications of this, you can gain enormous insights into your own behaviour, and the face-to-face reactions of others can be predicted. American anthropologist Edward Hall was one of the pioneers in the study of man's spatial needs and in the early 1960s he coined the word 'proxemics', from 'proximity' or nearness. His research into this field led to new understanding about our relationships with each other.

Every country is a territory staked out by clearly defined boundaries and sometimes protected by armed guards. Within each country there are usually smaller territories in the form of states and counties. Within these are even smaller territories called cities and towns, within which are suburbs, containing many streets that, in themselves, represent a closed territory to those who live there. In the cinema it's an armrest where we do silent battle with strangers who try to claim it. The inhabitants of each territory share an intangible allegiance to it and have been known to turn to savagery and killing in order to protect it.

A territory is also an area or space around a person that he claims as his own, as if it were an extension of his body. Each person has his own personal territory, which includes the area that exists around his possessions, such as his home, which is bounded by fences, the inside of his motor vehicle, his own bedroom or personal chair and, as Dr Hall discovered, a defined air space around his body.

This chapter will deal mainly with the implications of this air space, how people react when it is invaded and the importance of sometimes keeping an 'arms-length' relationship.

Personal Space

Most animals have a certain air space around their bodies that they claim as their personal space. How far the space extends depends mainly on how crowded the conditions were in which the animal was raised and the local population density. So personal territory can expand or contract depending on the local circumstances. A lion raised in the remote regions of Africa may have a territorial space with a radius of 30 miles (50 kilometres) or more, depending on the density of the lion population in that area, and it marks its territory by urinating or defecating around the boundaries. On the other hand, a lion raised in captivity with other lions may have a personal space of only several yards (metres), the direct result of crowded conditions.

Like most animals, each human has his own personal portable 'air bubble', which he carries around with him; its size is dependent on the density of the population in the place where he grew up. *Personal Space* is therefore culturally determined. Where some cultures, such as the Japanese, are accustomed to crowding, others prefer the 'wide open spaces' and like you to keep your distance.

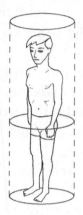

Personal space – the portable bubble
we all carry around with us

Research shows that people in prisons appear to have larger personal space needs than most of the community, which results in the prisoners being constantly aggressive when approached by others. Solitary confinement, where no others are in the prisoner's space, always has a calming effect. Violence from passengers on aircraft increased during the 1990s when the airlines started packing people close together in the seats to compensate for revenue lost as a result of price discounting.

Zone Distances

We'll now discuss the radius of the 'air bubble' around suburban middle-class people living in places such as Australia, New Zealand, Great Britain, North America, Northern Europe, Scandinavia, Canada or anywhere a culture is 'Westernised' such as Singapore, Guam and Iceland. The country in which you personally live may have larger or smaller territories than those we discuss here, but they will be proportionately the same as the ones we discuss here. Children have learned this spacing by age 12 and it can be broken down into four distinct zone distances:

1. The Intimate Zone between 6 and 18 inches (15–45 centimetres). Of all the zone distances, this is by far the most important, as it is this zone that a person guards as if it were his own property. Only those who are emotionally close to us are permitted to enter. These include lovers, parents, spouse, children, close friends, relatives and pets. There is a sub-zone that extends up to 6 inches (15cm) from the body that can be entered only during intimate physical contact. This is the close *Intimate Zone*.

2. The Personal Zone between 18 inches and 48 inches (46cm–1.22m). This is the distance that we stand from others at cocktail parties, office parties, social functions and friendly gatherings.

3. The Social Zone between 4 and 12 feet (1.22–3.6m). We stand at this distance from strangers, the plumber or carpenter doing repairs around our home, the postman, the local shopkeeper, the new employee at work and people whom we don't know very well.

4. The Public Zone is over 12 feet (3.6m). Whenever we address a large group of people, this is the comfortable distance at which we choose to stand.

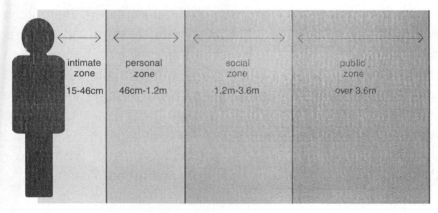

Personal Zone distances

All these distances tend to reduce between two women and increase between two men.

Practical Applications of Zone Distances

Our Intimate Zone (between 6 and 18 inches, 15–45cm) is normally entered by another person for one of two reasons: first, the intruder is a close relative or friend, or he or she may be making sexual advances; second, the intruder is hostile and may be about to attack. While we will tolerate strangers moving within our *Personal* and *Social Zones*, the intrusion of a stranger into our Intimate Zone causes physiological changes to take place within our bodies. The heart pumps faster, adrenalin pours into the bloodstream, and blood is pumped to the brain and the muscles as physical preparations for a possible fight or flight situation are made.

This means that putting your arm, in a friendly way, around someone you've just met may result in that person feeling negative towards you, even though they may smile and appear to enjoy it in order not to offend you.

Women stand slightly closer to one another, face each other more and touch more than men do with other men.

If you want people to feel comfortable around you, the golden rule is 'keep your distance'. The more intimate our relationship is with other people, the closer they will permit us to move within their zones. For example, a new work employee may initially feel that the other staff members are cold towards him, but they are only keeping him in the Social Zone until they know him better. As he becomes better known to them, the distance between them decreases until eventually he is permitted to move within their Personal Zones and, in some cases, their Intimate Zones.

Who Is Moving In on Whom?

The distance that two people keep their hips apart when they embrace reveals clues about the relationship between them.

Lovers press their torsos against each other and move within each other's close Intimate Zones. This differs from the kiss received from a stranger on New Year's Eve, from your best friend's spouse or dear old Aunt Sally, all of whom keep their pelvic area at least 6 inches (15cm) away from yours.

One of the exceptions to the distance/intimacy rule occurs where the spatial distance is based on the person's social standing. For example, the CEO of a company may be the weekend fishing buddy of one of his subordinates and when they go fishing each may move within the other's personal or Intimate Zone. At the office, however, the CEO keeps his fishing buddy at the social distance to maintain the unwritten code of social strata rules.

Why We Hate Riding in Lifts

Crowding at concerts, cinemas, in trains or buses results in unavoidable intrusion into other people's Intimate Zones, and people's reactions are fascinating to watch. There is a list of unwritten rules that most cultures follow rigidly when faced with a crowded situation such as a packed lift, in a line at the sandwich shop or on public transport.

Here are the common lift-riding rules:

1. There will be no talking to anyone, including a person you know.
2. Avoid eye contact with others at all times.
3. Maintain a 'poker face' – no emotion is permitted to be shown.
4. If you have a book or newspaper, pretend to be deeply engrossed in it.
5. In bigger crowds, no body movement is allowed.
6. At all times, you must watch the floor numbers change at all times.

This behaviour is called 'masking' and is common everywhere.

It's simply each person's attempt to hide their emotions from others by wearing a neutral mask.

We often hear words such as 'miserable', 'unhappy' and 'despondent' used to describe people who travel to work in the rush hour on public transport. These labels are used to describe the blank, expressionless look on the faces of the travellers, but are misjudgements on the part of the observer. What the observer sees, in fact, is a group of people masking – adhering to the rules that apply to the unavoidable invasion of their Intimate Zones in a crowded public place.

> *The people travelling on the Underground aren't unhappy; they're just masking their emotions.*

Notice how you behave next time you go alone to a crowded cinema. As you choose a seat that is surrounded by a sea of unknown faces, notice how, like a pre-programmed robot, you will begin to obey the unwritten rules of masking in a crowded public place. As you compete for territorial rights to the armrest with the stranger beside you, you will begin to realise why those who often go to a crowded cinema alone do not take their seats until the lights are out and the film begins. Whether we are in a crowded lift, cinema or bus, people around us become non-persons – that is, they don't exist as far as we're concerned and so we don't respond as if we were being attacked if someone inadvertently encroaches on our territory.

Why Mobs Become Angry

An angry mob or group of protesters fighting for a mutual purpose does not react in the same way as an individual does when his territory is invaded; in fact, something very different occurs. As the density of the crowd increases, each individual has less personal space and starts to feel hostile, which is why, as the size of the mob increases, it becomes angrier and uglier and fights may break out. The police try to break up the crowd so that each person can regain his own personal space and become calmer.

Only in recent years have governments and town planners begun to understand the effect that high-density housing projects have in depriving individuals of their personal territory. The consequences of high-density living and overcrowding were seen in a study of the deer population on James Island, an island about a mile (2 kilometres) off the coast of Maryland in Chesapeake Bay in the United States. Many of the deer were dying in large numbers, despite the fact that at the time there was plenty of food, predators were not evident and infection was not present. Similar studies in earlier years with rats and rabbits revealed the same trend and further investigation showed that the deer had died as a result of overactive adrenal glands, resulting from the stress caused by the degradation of each deer's personal territory as the population increased. The adrenal glands play an important part in the regulation of growth, reproduction and the level of the body's defences. A physiological reaction to the stress of overpopulation had caused the deaths, not starvation, infection or aggression from others. This is why areas that have the highest human population density also have the highest crime and violence rates.

> *One of our deepest urges is the desire to own land. This compulsion comes from the fact that it gives us the space freedom we need.*

Interrogators use territorial invasion techniques to break down the resistance of criminals being questioned. They seat the criminal on an armless, fixed chair in an open area of the room and encroach into his intimate and close Intimate Zones when asking questions, remaining there until he answers. It often takes only a short while for this territorial harassment to break down the criminal's resistance.

Spacing Rituals

When a person claims a space or an area among strangers, such as a seat at the cinema, a place at the conference table or a towel hook at the health club, he does it in a predictable way. He usually looks for the widest space available between two others and claims the area in the centre. At the cinema he will choose a seat that is halfway between the end of a row and where the nearest person is sitting. At the health club, he chooses the towel hook that is in the largest available space, midway between two other towels or midway between the nearest towel and the end of the towel rack. The purpose of this ritual is to avoid offending the other people by being either too close or too far away from them.

....

Doctors and hairdressers are given permission to enter our Intimate Zones. We allow pets in at any time because they're not threatening.

....

At the cinema, if you choose a seat more than halfway between the end of the row and the nearest other person, that other person may feel offended if you are too far away from him or he may feel intimidated if you sit too close. The main purpose of this spacing ritual is to maintain harmony and it appears to be a learned behaviour.

An exception to this rule is the spacing that occurs in public toilet blocks. We found that people choose the end toilets about 90% of the time and, if they are occupied, the midway principle is used. Men always try to avoid standing beside strangers at a public urinal and always obey the unwritten law of 'Death before eye contact'.

Try the Luncheon Test

Try this simple test next time you eat with someone. Unspoken territorial rules state that a restaurant table is divided equally down the middle and the staff carefully place the salt, pepper, sugar, flowers and other accessories equally on the centre line. As the meal progresses, subtly move the salt cellar across to the other person's side, then the pepper, flowers and so on. Before long this subtle territorial invasion will cause a reaction in your lunch-mate. They either sit back to regain their space or start pushing everything back to the centre.

Cultural Factors Affecting Zone Distances

A young Italian couple migrated from Italy to live in Sydney, Australia and were invited to join a local social club. Several weeks after joining, three female members complained that the Italian man was making sexual advances towards them and that they felt uncomfortable around him. The male members of the club felt that the Italian woman had also been behaving as if she could be sexually available.

This situation illustrates the complications that can happen when cultures with different space needs come together. Many Southern Europeans have an intimate distance of only 8 to 11 inches (20–30cm) and in some places it's even less. The Italian couple felt at ease and relaxed when standing at a distance of 10 inches (25cm) from the Australians but were totally unaware of their intrusion into the Australians' 46-centimetre Intimate Zone. Italian people also use more eye contact and touch than Australians, which gave rise to further misjudgements about their motives. The Italians were shocked when this was pointed out to them but they resolved to practise standing back at a more culturally accepted distance.

Moving into the Intimate Zone of the opposite sex is a way of showing interest in that person and is commonly called an 'advance'. If the advance into the Intimate Zone is rejected, the other person will step backwards to reclaim their space. If the advance is accepted, the other person holds his ground and allows the intruder to remain. To measure a man's level of interest in her, a woman will step into his Intimate Zone and then step back out again. If he's interested, this cues him to step into her space whenever he makes a point.

The closer people feel emotionally to each other the closer they will stand to each other.

What seemed to the Italian couple to be a perfectly normal social encounter was being interpreted by the Australians as a sexual advance. The Italians thought the Australians were being cold and unfriendly because they kept moving away from the Italians to keep a comfortable distance.

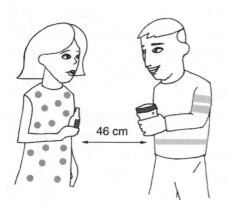

The acceptable conversational distance for most Western, Northern European and Scandinavian city dwellers

A man with a smaller spatial need forcing a woman to lean back to defend her space

The above illustration shows the negative reaction of a woman on whose territory a man is encroaching. She leans backward, attempting to keep a comfortable distance. However, the man may be from a culture with a smaller Personal Zone and he is moving forward to a distance that is comfortable for him. The woman may interpret this as a sexual move.

Why Japanese Always Lead When They Waltz

At our international conferences, city-born Americans usually stand 18 to 48 inches (46–122cm) from each other and stand in the same place while talking. If you watch a Japanese and an American talking, the two will slowly begin to move around the room, the American moving backwards away from the Japanese and the Japanese moving forward. This is an attempt by both the American and Japanese to adjust to a culturally comfortable distance from the other. The Japanese, with his smaller 10-inch (25cm) Intimate Zone, continually steps forward to adjust to his spatial need, but this invades the American's Intimate Zone, forcing him to step backwards to make his own spatial adjustment. Video recordings of this phenomenon replayed at high speed give the illusion that the two men are waltzing around the room with the Japanese leading. This is one of the reasons why, when negotiating business, Asians, Europeans or Americans often look at each other with suspicion. The Europeans or Americans refer to the Asians as 'pushy' and 'familiar' and the Asians refer to the Europeans or Americans as 'cold', 'stand-offish' and 'cool'. This lack of awareness of Intimate Zone variations between cultures can easily lead to misconceptions and inaccurate assumptions about one culture by another.

Country vs. City Spatial Zones

As mentioned, the amount of Personal Space someone needs is

relative to the population density where they live. People raised in sparsely populated rural areas for example, need more Personal Space than those raised in densely populated cities. Watching how far a person extends his arm to shake hands gives a clue to whether he is from a large city or a country area. City dwellers typically have their private 18-inch (46cm) 'bubble'; this is also the measured distance between wrist and torso when they reach to shake hands.

Two men from the city greet each other; their hands reaching to 18 inches (46cm)

This allows the hands to meet on neutral territory. People raised in a country town with a small population may have a space 'bubble' of up to 36 inches (1m) or more and this is the average measured distance from the wrist to the body when the country person shakes hands.

Two people from a country town reaching out to 36 inches (1m)

Rural people tend to stand with their feet firmly planted on the ground and lean forward to meet your handshake, whereas a city dweller will step forward to greet you. People raised in remote areas can have an even larger Personal Space need, which could be as wide as 18 feet (6 metres). They often prefer not to shake hands but would rather stand at a distance and wave.

People from a sparsely populated area keeping their distance

Farming equipment salespeople who live in cities find this information useful for calling on farmers in sparse rural areas. Considering, for example, that a farmer could have a 'bubble' of 3 to 6 feet (1–2m) or more, a handshake could be seen as a territorial intrusion, causing the farmer to react negatively or defensively. Successful country salespeople state almost unanimously that the best negotiating conditions exist when they greet the rural customer with an extended handshake and the farmer from a remote area with a distant wave.

Territory and Ownership

Property a person owns or a space he regularly uses constitutes a private territory and, just as with his personal bubble, he'll fight to defend it. A person's home, office and car represent a territory, each having clearly marked boundaries in the form of walls, gates, fences and doors. Each territory may have several sub-territories. For example, in a home a person's private territory may be their kitchen and they'll object to anyone invading it when they're using it; a businessman has his favourite place at the conference table; diners have their favourite seat in the café; and Mum or Dad have their favourite chair at home. These areas are usually marked either by leaving personal possessions on or around the area, or by frequent use of it. The café diner may even go so far as to carve his initials into 'his' place at the table and the businessman marks his territory at the conference table with things such as a personal folder, pens, books and clothing spread around his 18-inch (46cm) Intimate Zone border.

Studies carried out by Desmond Morris into seating positions in libraries showed that leaving a book or personal object on a library desk reserved that place for an average of 77 minutes; leaving a jacket over a chair reserved it for two hours. At home a family member might mark his or her favourite chair by leaving a personal object, such as a handbag or magazine, on or near it to show their claim and ownership of the space.

If the boss of the house asks a visitor to be seated and the person innocently sits in the wrong chair, the boss can become agitated about this invasion of his territory and be put on the defensive. A simple question such as, 'Which chair is yours?' can avoid the negative results of making such a territorial error.

Car Territory

People driving a car can react in a way that's often completely unlike their normal social, territorial behaviour.

A motor vehicle seems to have a magnifying effect on the size of a person's Personal Space. In some cases, this territory is magnified up to 10 times the normal size, so the driver feels that he has a claim to an area of 25 to 30 feet (8-10 metres) in front of and behind his car. When another driver cuts in front of him, even if it wasn't dangerous, the driver may go through a physiological change, becoming angry and even attacking the other driver in what is now known as 'Road Rage'. Compare this to the situation that occurs when the same person is stepping into a lift and another person steps in front of him, invading his personal territory. His reaction in those circumstances is normally apologetic and he allows the other person to go first: dramatically different from what happens when the same person cuts in front of him on the open road.

In a car, many people think they're invisible. That's why they make intimate adjustments in full view of everyone.

For some people, the car becomes a protective cocoon in which they can hide from the outside world. As they drive slowly beside the kerb, almost in the gutter, they can be as big a hazard on the road as the driver with the expanded Personal Space. Italians, with their smaller spatial needs, are often accused of being tail-gaters and pushy on the motor-ways because they are closer than is culturally accepted elsewhere.

Take the Test

Look at the next illustration and decide what the possible scenarios could be between the two people, based entirely on their spatial distances. A few simple questions and further observation of these people can reveal the correct answer and can help you avoid making incorrect assumptions.

Who is who and from where?

We could make any one of the following assumptions about these people:

1. Both people are city dwellers and the man is making an intimate approach to the woman.
2. The man has a smaller Intimate Zone than the woman and is innocently invading hers.
3. The woman is from a culture with smaller Intimate Zone needs.
4. The couple feel emotionally close to each other.

Summary

Others will invite or reject you, depending on the respect that you have for their Personal Space. This is why the happy-go-lucky person, who slaps everyone he meets on the back or continually touches people during a conversation, is secretly disliked by everyone. Many factors can affect the spatial distance a person takes in relation to others, so it's wise to consider every criterion before making a judgement about why a person is keeping a certain distance.

Chapter 10

HOW THE LEGS REVEAL WHAT THE MIND WANTS TO DO

Mark sat there with his legs wide apart, stroking his tie and massaging the salt shaker. He hadn't noticed that, for the past 20 minutes, her legs had been crossed away from him and pointing towards the nearest exit.

The farther away from the brain a body part is positioned, the less awareness we have of what it is doing. For example, most people are aware of their face and what expressions and gestures they are displaying and we can even practise some expressions to 'put on a brave face' or 'give a disapproving look', 'grin and bear it' or 'look happy' when Grandma gives you ugly underwear again for your birthday. After our face, we are less aware of our arms and hands, then our chest and stomach and we are least aware of our legs and almost oblivious to our feet.

This means that the legs and feet are an important source of information about someone's attitude because most people are unaware of what they are doing with them and never consider faking gestures with them in the way that they would with their face. A person can look composed and in control while their foot is repetitively tapping or making short jabs in the air, revealing their frustration at not being able to escape.

> *Jiggling the feet is like the brain's attempt to run away from what is being experienced.*

Everybody's Talking About a New Way of Walking

The way people swing their arms when they walk gives insight into their personality – or what they want you to believe they're like. When young, healthy, vibrant people walk, they walk faster than older people, which results in their arms swinging higher in front and behind, and can even make it look as if they're marching. This is partly due to their additional speed and greater muscle flexibility. As a consequence of this, the army march evolved as an exaggerated walk to portray the effect that the marchers are youthful and vigorous. This same walk has been adopted by many politicians and public figures who want to send out a message of their vitality. That is why striding is a popular gait with many politicians. Women's arms tend to swing even further back because their arms bend further out from the elbow to enable them to carry babies more effectively.

How Feet Tell the Truth

We conducted a series of tests with managers, who were instructed to lie convincingly in a series of staged interviews. We found that the managers, regardless of gender, dramatically increased the unconscious number of foot movements they made when they were lying. Most managers used fake facial expressions and tried to control their hands while lying but almost all were unaware of what their feet and legs were doing. These results were verified by psychologist Paul Ekman, who discovered that not only do people increase their lower body movements when they lie but observers have greater success exposing a person's lies when they can see the liar's entire body. This explains why many business executives feel comfortable only when sitting behind a desk with a solid front, where their lower body is hidden.

> *If you're not sure whether you're being lied to or not, look under their desk.*

Glass-topped tables cause us more stress than solid tables, as our legs are in full view and so we don't feel as if we are in full control.

The Purpose of the Legs

The legs evolved in humans to serve two purposes: to move forward to get food and to run away from danger. Because the human brain is hardwired for these two objectives – to go towards what we want and move away from what we don't want – the way a person uses their legs and feet reveals where they want to go. In other words, they show a person's commitment to leaving or staying in a conversation. Open or uncrossed leg positions show an open or dominant attitude, while crossed positions reveal closed attitudes or uncertainty.

A woman who is not interested in a man will fold her arms on her chest and cross her legs away from him giving him the 'no-go' body language while an interested woman would open herself to him.

The Four Main Standing Positions

1. At Attention

This is a formal position that shows a neutral attitude with no commitment to stay or go. In male–female encounters, it is used more by women than men as it effectively keeps the legs together like a 'No Comment' signal. Schoolchildren use it when talking to a teacher, junior officers use it when talking to senior officers, people meeting royalty do it and employees use it when talking to the boss.

The Attention Stance

2. Legs Apart

As mentioned earlier, this is predominantly a male gesture and is like a standing *Crotch Display*. The Crotch Displayer plants both feet firmly on the ground, making a clear statement that he has no intention of leaving. It is used as a dominance signal by men because it highlights the genitals, giving the Crotch Displayer a macho-looking attitude.

The Crotch Display – putting his masculinity on show

Male participants at sports matches can be seen standing around with each other in this position at half time and giving their crotch a continual adjustment. These adjustments have nothing to do with itching – they allow males to highlight their masculinity and show solidarity as a team by all performing the same actions.

The Crotch Display is used by
macho men and tough guys

3. The Foot-Forward

The body weight is shifted to one hip, which leaves the front foot pointing forward. Paintings done during the Middle Ages often show high status men standing in the *Foot-Forward Position* as it allowed them to display their fine hosiery, shoes and breeches.

The Foot-Forward Position –
pointing at where the mind wants
to go

This a valuable clue to a person's immediate intentions, because we point our lead foot in the direction our mind would like to go and this stance looks as if the person is beginning to walk. In a group situation, we point our lead foot at the most interesting or attractive person but when we want to leave, we point our feet at the nearest exit.

4. Leg Cross

The next time you attend a meeting with men and women you will notice some groups of people standing with their arms and legs crossed. Look more closely and you'll also see that they are standing at a greater distance from each other than the customary social distance.

The Standing-Leg-Cross

If they are wearing coats or jackets, they are likely to be buttoned. This is how most people stand when they are among people whom they don't know well. If you interact with them you would find that one or all of them are unfamiliar with others in the group.

While open legs can show openness or dominance, crossed legs shows a closed, submissive or defensive attitude as they symbolically deny any access to the genitals.

The Scissors – 'No comment' but he's not leaving

For a woman, positions like the *Scissors* and the *Single-Leg-Cross* send two messages: one, that she intends to stay, not leave; and two, that access is denied. When a man does it, it also shows he'll stay but wants to be sure you don't 'kick him where it hurts'. Open legs display masculinity; closed legs protect masculinity. If he's with men he feels are inferior to him, the Crotch Display feels right; if he's with superior males, however, this gesture makes him look competitive and he feels vulnerable. Studies show that people who lack confidence also take Leg Cross positions.

Open legs show male confidence;
closed legs show male reticence.

Imagine now that you notice another group of people standing with arms unfolded, palms visible, coats unbuttoned, relaxed appearance and leaning back on one leg with the other pointing towards others in the group. All are gesturing with their hands and moving in and out of each other's Personal Space. Closer investigation would reveal that these people are friends or are known personally to each other. The first group of people with the closed arms and legs may have relaxed facial expressions and conversation that sounds free and easy, but the folded arms and legs tell us that they are not as relaxed or confident with each other as they are trying to appear.

Try this: join a group where you know no one and stand with your arms and legs tightly crossed and wear a serious expression. One by one the other group members will cross their arms and legs and remain in that position until you, the stranger, leave. Walk away and watch how, one by one, the members of the group assume their original open poses once again.

Crossing the legs not only reveals negative or defensive emotions, it makes a person appear insecure and causes others to react accordingly.

Defensive, Cold or 'Just Comfortable'?

Some people will claim that they are not defensive or feeling insecure when they cross their arms or legs, but do it because they're cold. When someone wants to warm his hands he'll thrust them under his armpits rather than tucking them under the elbows, as is the case with a defensive arm-cross. Second, when a person feels cold he may use a type of body hug and when the legs are crossed they are usually straight, stiff and pressed hard against each other as opposed to the more relaxed leg posture of the defensive stance or position.

She's more likely to be cold or just looking for the rest room

People who habitually cross their arms or legs prefer to say that they are cold rather than admit that they could be nervous, anxious or defensive. Others simply say they're 'comfortable'. That's probably true – when someone feels defensive or insecure, crossed arms and legs feel comfortable because it matches their emotional state.

How We Move from Closed to Open

As people begin to feel more comfortable in a group and get to know others, they move through a series of movements taking them from the defensive crossed arms and legs position to the relaxed open position. This standing 'opening-up' procedure follows the same sequence everywhere.

1. Uncertain about each other   2. Openness and acceptance

It begins with the closed position, arms and legs crossed (illustration 1). As they begin to feel comfortable with each other and rapport builds, their legs uncross first and their feet are placed together in the Attention Position. Next, the arm folded on top in the arm-cross comes out and the palm is occasionally flashed when speaking but is eventually not used as a barrier. Instead, it may hold the outside of the other arm in a

217

Single-Arm-Barrier. Both arms unfold next, and one arm gestures or may be placed on the hip or in the pocket. Finally, one person takes the Foot-Forward Position, showing acceptance of the other person (illustration 2).

The European Leg Cross

One leg is crossed neatly over the other, with 70% of people crossing left over right. This is the normal crossed-leg position used by European, Asian and British cultures.

The European/British
Leg Cross

When a person crosses both legs and arms they have emotionally withdrawn from the conversation and it can be futile to try to be convincing when they sit like this.

Not open to communicating
on any level

In business contexts, we have found that people sitting like this talk in shorter sentences, reject more proposals and can recall less detail of what was discussed than those who sit with their arms and legs in an open position.

The American Figure Four

This position is a seated version of a Crotch Display as it highlights the genitals and is used by American males or any cultures that are becoming 'Americanised', such as the youth of Singapore, Japan and the Philippines. It shows that an argumentative or competitive attitude exists. Monkeys and chimps also use genital displays when they are being aggressive, because a good display can avoid the damage that could be inflicted from a physical fight. With all primates, the male with the most impressive display is seen by the others as the winner. Places like Australia and New Zealand use both European leg crossing and the *Figure Four*. During the Second World War, the Nazis kept a lookout for the Figure Four as anyone using it was clearly not German or had spent time in the USA.

Ready to argue the point – the American Figure Four

The Figure Four is still uncommon in Britain and Europe among older people but is now seen in diverse cultures such as Russia, Japan, Sardinia and Malta among the younger generations who are addicted to American films and television and are mirroring what they see. Men who sit like this are not only perceived as being more dominant, they are also seen as relaxed and youthful. In parts of the Middle East and Asia however, the Figure Four is seen as an insult because it shows the sole of the shoe and that's the part that walks in dirt.

Women who wear trousers or jeans can sometimes be seen sitting in the Figure Four position, but they usually do it only around other women, not men, as they don't want to appear too masculine or to signal sexual availability.

Studies also show that most people make most of their final decision to do something when both feet are on the ground, so the Figure Four is not conducive to asking someone to make a decision.

When the Body Closes, so Does the Mind

We attended a conference where the audience was split 50/50 male and female and was comprised of about 100 managers and 500 salespeople. A controversial issue was being discussed – the treatment of salespeople by corporations. A well-known speaker who was head of the salespersons' association was asked to address the group. As he took the stage almost all the male managers and around 25% of the female managers took the defensive Arms-and-Legs-Crossed position, revealing how threatened they felt by what they thought he would say. Their fears were well founded. He raged about the poor quality of management and how this was a major contributing factor to the industry's staffing problems. Throughout his speech, most salespeople in the audience were either leaning forward showing interest or using evaluation gestures, but the managers held their defensive position.

When the mind closes,
the body follows.

The salesperson then discussed what he believed the manager's role should be, relative to salespeople. Almost as if they were players in an orchestra who had been given a command by the orchestra leader, most of the male managers shifted to the Figure Four position. They were now mentally debating the salesperson's point of view and many later confirmed that this had been the case. We noticed that some managers had not changed their posture. Even though most had also disagreed with the speaker's views, some were unable to take the Figure Four because of physical or medical conditions such as being overweight, having leg problems or arthritis.

If you're trying to persuade someone who sits in any of these positions you should attempt to get them to uncross before continuing. If you have something to show, invite them to sit beside you or give them things to do or to hold so that they lean forward to write notes or hold brochures and samples. Offering tea or coffee also works well as it makes it hard for a person to cross their arms and legs without burning themselves.

Figure Four Leg Clamp

Not only does this person have a competitive attitude, they lock the Figure Four into a permanent position using one or both hands as a clamp. This is a sign of the tough-minded, stubborn individual who rejects any opinion other than their own.

The Leg Clamp – locking a
competitive attitude into place

The Ankle Lock

The male version of the *Ankle Lock* is often combined with clenched fists resting on the knees or with the hands tightly gripping the arms of the chair and a seated Crotch Display (see below). The female version varies slightly: the knees are held together, the feet may be to one side and the hands rest side by side or one on top of the other resting on the upper legs.

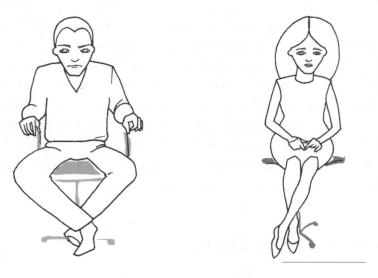

The Ankle Lock: A woman minimising her leg space
and a man taking up more space

Over three decades of interviewing and selling to people, we have noted that when an interviewee locks his ankles, he is mentally 'biting his lip'. The gesture shows that he is holding back a negative emotion, uncertainty or fear. The feet are usually withdrawn under the chair, showing that the person also has a withdrawn attitude. When people are *involved* in a conversation, they also put their feet *into* the conversation.

Our work with lawyers showed that defendants who sat outside the courtroom just prior to a hearing were three times more likely than the plaintiffs to have their ankles tightly locked under their chairs as they tried to control their emotional state. Our study of 319 dental patients showed that 88%

locked their ankles as soon as they sat in the dental chair to have work done. Patients who were only having a check-up locked their ankles 68% of the time compared to 98% who locked ankles when the dentist administered an injection.

> *More people lock their ankles with*
> *the taxman than with the dentist.*

Our work with law enforcement and government bodies, such as the police, customs and the tax office, showed that most people who were being interviewed locked their ankles at the beginning of the interviews, but this was just as likely to be from fear as out of guilt.

We also analysed the human resources profession and found that most interviewees lock their ankles at some point during an interview, indicating that they were holding back an emotion or attitude. Nierenberg and Calero found that when one party locked his ankles during a negotiation it often meant that he was holding back a valuable concession. They found that by using questioning techniques they could often encourage him to unlock his ankles and reveal the concession.

> *Asking positive questions about their feelings*
> *can often get others to unlock their ankles.*

In the initial stages of studying the Ankle Lock, we found that asking questions was reasonably successful (42%) in getting interviewees to relax and unlock their ankles. We discovered, however, that if an interviewer walks around to the interviewee's side of the desk and sits beside him, removing the desk as a barrier, the interviewee would often relax and unlock his ankles and the conversation would take on an open, more personal tone.

We were advising a company on effective customer telephone contact when we met a man who had the unenviable job of customer debt collection. We watched him make a number of calls and although he sounded relaxed, we noticed that, when he talked with customers, his ankles were continually locked together beneath his chair, but he didn't do this when he was talking with us. When asked 'How do you enjoy this work?', he replied, 'Fine! It's a lot of fun.' The verbal statement was inconsistent, however, with his non-verbal signals, although he did look and sound convincing. 'Are you sure?' we asked. He paused for a moment, unlocked his ankles and, with open palms, said, 'Well, actually, it drives me crazy!' He said that he receives several calls each day from customers who are rude or aggressive and he practised holding back his feelings in order not to communicate them to customers. We also recorded that salespeople who don't enjoy using the telephone commonly sit in the Ankle Lock position.

The Short Skirt Syndrome

Women who wear mini-skirts cross their legs and ankles for obvious, necessary reasons. Through years of habit, however, many older women still sit in this position, which can not only make them feel restrained, but others are likely to unconsciously read it as negative and react towards these women with caution.

> *Mini-skirts can give a woman the*
> *appearance that she's not approachable.*

Some people will still claim they sit in the Ankle Lock position, or for that matter any negative arm and leg position, because they feel 'comfortable'. If you are in this category, remember that any arm or leg position will feel comfortable when you hold a defensive, negative or reserved attitude.

A negative gesture can increase or prolong a negative attitude, and other people will read you as being apprehensive, defensive or non-participant. Practise using positive and open gestures; this will improve your self-confidence and others will perceive you in a more positive way.

The Leg Twine

This gesture is almost exclusively used by women and is a trademark of shy and timid women and part-time contortionists. The top of one foot locks around the other leg to reinforce an insecure attitude and shows she has retreated into her shell like a tortoise, despite how relaxed her upper body may appear. A warm, friendly, low-key approach is needed if you eventually hope to open this clam.

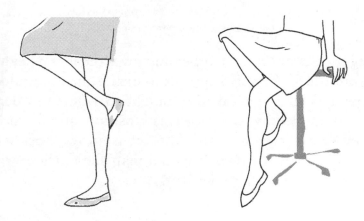

Shy, timid people use the Leg Twine

Parallel-Legs

Because of the bone configuration of female legs and hips, most men can't sit like this so it becomes a powerful signal of femininity. Not surprisingly, over 86% of male participants in our leg rating surveys voted this the most attractive female sitting position.

225

Men voted Parallel-Legs as their number one favourite
position in women who are seated

One leg presses against the other and gives the legs a healthier, more youthful look, which appeals to men from a reproductive standpoint. This is the position taught to women in deportment and modelling classes. This position should not be confused with the woman who constantly crosses and uncrosses her legs when she's with a man she fancies – this is done to draw attention to her legs.

Put Your Right Foot In, Put Your Right Foot Out

When we're interested in either a conversation or a person, we put one foot forward to shorten the distance between us and that person. If we're reticent or not interested, we put our feet back, usually under a chair if seated.

He's coming on strong with
One-Foot-Forward and Crotch
Display; she's either undecided
or not keen

In the above scene, the man is trying to show interest in the
woman by using typical male courtship body language: foot
forward, legs apart, Crotch Display and Arms-Splayed to try
to enlarge his overall perceived size and take up more space.

She's also using typical female no-go body language: legs
together, body facing away, arms folded and minimising the
amount of space she occupies. He's probably wasting his time.

Summary

Our feet tell others where we want to go and who we do or
don't like. If you are a woman, avoid crossing your legs when
you're sitting with businessmen unless you are wearing an A-
line dress or at least one that is below the knee-line. The sight
of a woman's thighs is distracting to almost all men and
detracts from her message. They'll remember who she was but
won't remember much of what she had to say. Many women
wear shorter dresses in business because this appearance is
continually thrust at them by the media; over 90% of all
female television hosts are presented with short dresses and
exposed legs. This is because studies prove that male viewers
will watch the programme for longer, but the same studies also

show that the more leg a woman shows, the less men can remember the content of what she said. The rule here is simple – for social contexts, exposed crossed legs are fine but don't do it in business. If you're a man dealing with women in business the same rule applies – keep your knees together.

Chapter 11

THE 13 MOST COMMON GESTURES YOU'LL SEE DAILY

The number one gesture cluster women
can't tolerate men doing at work

People rarely think consciously about the effect of many of the seemingly simple non-verbal things they do. For example, when one person hugs another, most observers silently assume that the back patting that occurs towards the end of the hug is a gesture of affection and that the air kisses made – the sound made on the side of someone's cheek – is also affection. The reality is that the pat is used in the same way professional wrestlers use it – to tell the other person to end the hug and break the clinch. If you are really not too keen about hugging someone but are forced into it because the people ahead of you did it, you're likely to begin the back patting in the air even before the hug begins. The air kiss – with its accompanying sound – is given as a displacement of a real kiss that we don't want to give either.

Most people use the Shoulder Tap to break a clinch – sincere huggers hold on tight. While she was holding firmly, he was tapping rapidly

This chapter covers some of the most common head gestures and body language clusters you are likely to see in your day-to-day dealings with others.

The Head Nod

In most cultures the *Head Nod* is used to signify 'Yes' or agreement. It's a stunted form of bowing – the person symbolically goes to bow but stops short, resulting in a nod. Bowing is a submissive gesture so the Head Nod shows we are going along with the other person's point of view. Research conducted with people who were born deaf, dumb and blind shows that they also use this gesture to signify 'Yes', so it appears to be an inborn gesture of submission.

In India, the head is rocked from side to side, called the *Head Wobble*, to signal 'Yes'. This is confusing for Westerners and Europeans, who use this gesture to communicate 'Maybe yes – maybe no'. As we've already said, in Japan, head nodding doesn't necessarily mean 'Yes, I agree' – it usually means 'Yes I hear you.'

Head nodding has its origins in bowing to appear subordinate.

In Arab countries they use a single, upward head movement, which means 'no' while Bulgarians use the common 'no' gesture to mean 'yes'.

Why You Should Learn to Nod

Most people have never considered the power of head nodding as a persuasion tool. Research shows that people will talk three to four times more than usual when the listener nods their head using groups of three nods at regular intervals. The speed of the nod signals the patience – or lack of patience – of the listener. Slow nodding communicates that the listener is interested in what the speaker is saying so give slow, deliberate clusters of three head nods when the other person is making a point. Fast nodding tells the speaker you've heard enough or that you want them to finish or give you a turn to speak.

How to Encourage Agreement

There are two powerful uses of the Head Nod. Body language is an unconscious outward reflection of inner feelings so, if you feel positive or affirmative, your head will begin to nod as you speak. Conversely, if you simply start nodding your head intentionally, you will begin to experience positive feelings. In other words, positive feelings cause the head to nod – and the reverse is also true: nodding the head causes positive feelings. It's cause and effect again.

Head nodding is also very contagious. If someone nods their head at you, you will usually nod too – even if you don't necessarily agree with what they are saying. Head nodding is an excellent tool for creating rapport, getting agreement and co-operation. By finishing each sentence with a verbal affirmation such as, 'Isn't it?', 'Wouldn't you?', 'Isn't that true?' or 'Fair enough?', and with the speaker and listener both nodding their heads, the listener experiences positive feelings which create a greater likelihood of getting them to agree with you.

Head nodding encourages
co-operation and agreement.

After you've asked a question and the listener gives his answer, nod your head during his answer. When he finishes speaking *continue* to nod your head *another five times* at the rate of about one nod per second. Usually, by the time you have counted to four, the listener will begin speaking again and give you more information. And as long as you nod and stay silent with your hand on your chin in an Evaluation position, there's no pressure on you to speak and you won't come across like an interrogator. When you listen, put your hand on your chin and give it light strokes because, as previously stated, research shows that this encourages others to keep talking.

The Head Shake

Research also indicates that the *Head Shake*, usually meaning 'No', may also be an inborn action and evolutionary biologists believe that it's the first gesture humans learn. This theory says that when the newborn baby has had enough milk, it shakes its head from side to side to reject its mother's breast. Similarly, a child who has had enough to eat uses the Head Shake to reject attempts to spoon feed him.

Shaking the head owes its origin to breastfeeding.

When someone is trying to convince you, watch if they use the Head Shake gesture while saying they agree. The person who says, 'I can see your point of view', or, 'It sounds good', or, 'We'll definitely do business', while shaking his head from side to side might sound convincing, but the Head Shake gesture signals a negative attitude and you would be well advised to be sceptical about it.

No woman believes a man who says 'I love you' while shaking his head. When Bill Clinton uttered his famous phrase, 'I did not have sex with that woman' during the Monica Lewinsky inquest, he did not use a Head Shake.

The Basic Head Positions

1. Head Up

The neutral head position

There are three basic head positions. The first is with *Head Up* and is the position taken by the person who has a neutral attitude about what is being said. The head remains still and the conversation may be punctuated by occasional small nods. Hand-to-cheek evaluation gestures are often used with this position.

When the head is lifted high with the chin jutting forward it signals superiority, fearlessness or arrogance. The person intentionally exposes their throat and they gain additional height which allows them to 'look down their nose' at you. Large chins are the result of high testosterone levels which is why chin-jutting is associated with power and aggression.

Margaret Thatcher using her defiant Chin Thrust

2. The Head Tilt

Tilting the head to the side is a submission signal because it exposes the throat and neck and makes the person look smaller and less threatening. Its probable origin is in the baby resting its head on its parent's shoulder or chest, and the submissive, non-threatening meaning it conveys seems to be unconsciously understood by most people, especially women.

The Head Tilt displays the vulnerable neck and makes a person appear smaller and more submissive

Charles Darwin was one of the first to note that humans, as well as animals – especially dogs – tilt their heads to one side when they become interested in something. Women will use this gesture to show interest in men they fancy because a woman who is non-threatening and shows submission is attractive to most men.

Tilting the head to reveal the vulnerable neck appears to be intuitively understood by most people

Studies of paintings from the last two thousand years show that women are depicted three times as often as men using the *Head-Tilt* and women are shown in advertisements tilting their heads three times as often as men. This shows how most people understand, on an intuitive level, that displaying the neck shows submission. In a business negotiations with men, however, a woman should keep her head up at all times.

If you are giving a presentation or delivering a speech, make a point of looking for this gesture among your audience. When you see an audience tilting their heads and leaning forward using hand-to-chin evaluation gestures, you're getting the point across. When you listen to others, use the Head-Tilt and Head Nods and the listener will begin to feel trusting towards you because you appear non-threatening.

3. Head Down

When the chin is down, it signals that a negative, judgemental or aggressive attitude exists. Critical evaluation clusters are normally made with the head down and until the person's head lifts or tilts, you can have a problem. Professional presenters and trainers are often confronted by audiences who are seated with their heads down and arms folded on their chests.

Experienced conference speakers and presenters will take action to involve their audience and get participation before they begin their presentation. This is intended to

Head Down
shows disapproval
or dejection

get the audience's heads up and to get involvement. If the speaker's tactic is successful, the audience's next head position will be the Head Tilt.

The English have a peculiar greeting gesture called the *Head Twist*, which involves putting the head down while simultaneously twisting the head to one side. This comes from medieval times when men would doff their hat as a form of greeting; this evolved into just dipping the head and touching the hat, which, in modern times, is now the Head Twist, the salute or simply tapping the forehead when meeting someone.

The Head Shrug

Raising the shoulders and pulling the head down between them lets a person protect the vulnerable neck and throat from injury. It's the cluster used when a person hears a loud bang behind them or if they think something will fall on them. When it's used in a personal or business context it implies a submissive apology, which detracts from any encounter where you are trying to appear confident.

When someone walks past others who are talking, admiring a view or listening to a speaker, they pull their head down, turn their shoulders in and try to appear smaller and less significant. This is known as the *Head Duck*. It is also used by subordinates approaching superiors, and reveals the status and power play between individuals.

The Head Duck – trying to
appear smaller in order
not to cause offence to others

Picking Imaginary Lint

When a person disapproves of the opinions or attitudes of
others but doesn't want to say anything, displacement gestures
are likely to occur, that is, apparently innocent body language
gestures that reveal a withheld opinion. Picking imaginary
pieces of lint from one's own clothing is one such gesture. The
Lint-Picker usually looks down and away from others while
performing this seemingly minor, irrelevant action. This is a
common signal of disapproval and is a good sign that he
doesn't like what's being said, even when he sounds as if he's
agreeing with everything.

The Lint-Picker has a
secret opinion and
prefers not to state it

Open your palms and say, 'What do you think?' or, 'I can see
you have some thoughts on this. Would you mind telling me
what they are?' Sit back, arms apart, palms visible, and wait for
the answer. If the person says he is in agreement with you but

continues to pick the imaginary lint, you may need to take an even more direct approach to discover his hidden objections.

How We Show We're Ready for Action

To appear bigger for fighting or courting rituals, birds will fluff their feathers, fish can expand their body size by sucking in water and cats or dogs make their fur stand on end. The hairless human, however, no longer has a thick pelt to expand to make himself look more imposing when he is fearful or angry. When we describe a scary movie we often say, 'It made my hair stand on end'; if we become angry with someone, 'He made the hackles on my neck rise'; and when we are smitten with someone, they can give us 'goose bumps'. All these are the body's mechanical reactions to circumstances in which we attempt to make ourselves appear larger and are caused by the erector pillae muscles on the skin, which attempt to make our non-existent pelt stand up. Modern humans, however, have invented a gesture to help them achieve a bigger physical presence – the *Hands-on-Hips* gesture.

Elbows up and pointed shows readiness
to dominate; elbows in and head tilted show submission

Hands-on-Hips is used by the child arguing with its parent, the athlete waiting for his event to begin, the boxer waiting for the bout to start and males who want to issue a non-verbal challenge to other males who enter their territory. In each instance, the person takes the Hands-on-Hips pose and this is a universal gesture used to communicate that a person is ready for assertive action. It lets the person take up more space and has the threat value of the pointed elbows that act as weapons, preventing others from approaching or passing. The arms being half raised show readiness for attack and this is the position taken by cowboys in a gunfight. Even one hand on the hip will send the intended message, particularly when it's pointed at the intended victim. It's used everywhere and in the Philippines and Malaysia it carries the even stronger message of anger or outrage.

Also known as the 'readiness' gesture, that is, the person is ready for assertive action, its basic meaning carries a subtly aggressive attitude everywhere. It has also been called the achiever stance, related to the goal-directed person who is ready to tackle their objectives or is ready to take action on something. Men often use this gesture around women to display an assertive male attitude.

Hands-on-Hips makes you look bigger and more noticeable because you take up more space.

It's important to consider the context and other body language immediately preceding the Hands-on-Hips pose in order to make an accurate assessment of the person's attitude. For example, is the coat open and pushed back on to the hips, or is it buttoned when the aggressive pose is taken? *Closed-Coat-Readiness* shows frustration, whereas coat open and pushed back is directly aggressive because the person is openly exposing their front in a display of fearlessness. This position is further reinforced by placing the feet evenly apart on the ground or by adding clenched fists to the gesture cluster.

Hands-on-Hips used by
models to make clothing
more appealing

These aggressive–readiness clusters are used by professional models to give the impression that their clothing is for the modern, assertive, forward-thinking woman. Occasionally the gesture may be done with only one hand on the hip and the other displaying another gesture and this is commonly used by women who want to draw attention to themselves by using this cluster with a pelvic tilt to emphasise their hips-to-waist ratio, which indicates fertility. Hands-on-Hips is regularly used by both men and women in courtship to draw attention to themselves.

The Cowboy Stance

Thumbs tucked into the belt or into the tops of the pockets, frames the genital area and is a display used mainly by men to show a sexually aggressive attitude. It is the most common gesture used in television Westerns to show viewers the virility of their favourite gunslinger.

Also jokingly called the *Man-of-the-Long-Thumbs* gesture, the arms take the readiness

The cowboy stance – his fingers point
at what he wants you to notice

position and the hands serve as central indicators, highlighting the crotch. Men use this gesture to stake their territory or to show other men that they are unafraid. Apes use the same gesture, but without a belt or trousers.

This gesture tells others, 'I am virile – I can dominate' which is why it's a regular for men on the prowl. Any man talking to a woman while he's standing like this – with dilated pupils and one foot pointing towards her – is easily read by most women. It's one of the gestures that gives the game away for most men, as they unwittingly declare to her what's on their mind.

The sexually assertive female

This gesture is principally used by men, but women wearing jeans and trousers can occasionally be seen doing it too. When wearing dresses or skirts, the sexually assertive female displays one or both thumbs tucked into a belt or pocket.

Sizing Up the Competition

The next illustration shows two men sizing each other up, using the characteristic Hands-on-Hips and *Thumbs-in-Belt* gestures. Considering that they are both turned at an angle away from each other and the lower halves of their bodies appear relaxed, it's reasonable to assume that they are unconsciously evaluating each other and that confrontation is unlikely.

Sizing up the competition

Their conversation may sound casual or friendly but a relaxed atmosphere won't exist until their Hands-on-Hips gestures are dropped and open gestures or head tilting are used.

If these two men were directly facing each other with their feet planted firmly on the ground and legs apart, a fight could be likely.

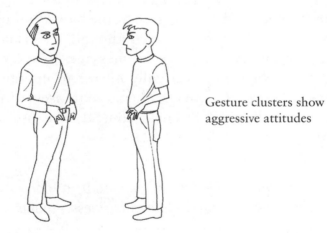

Gesture clusters show aggressive attitudes

Even though Adolf Hitler used the Hands-on-Hips gesture to try to appear authoritative for publicity photographs he still could not stop his left hand from crossing his body and attempting to cover his solitary testicle.

Ein Volk, ein Reich, ein Führer

Contradictory signals: his right arm shows pointed aggression while his left hand attempts to protect his front

The Legs-Spread

This is almost entirely a male gesture and is also seen among apes who are trying to establish authority over other apes. Rather than risk injury fighting, they spread their legs and the one with the biggest display is seen as the most dominant. And so it is with male humans; even though it's usually done unconsciously, it sends a powerful message. If one man does the *Legs-Spread* the others usually mirror to maintain status but it has very negative effects when a man uses it in front of women, especially in a business context, because she can't mirror it.

A woman will feel intimidated by a man who uses the Legs-Spread in business situations.

Our videotaped meetings reveal that many women respond by crossing their legs and arms, which immediately puts them on the defensive. The advice for men here is clear – keep your legs together in business meetings. If you're a woman who is constantly confronted by a crotch-displaying male, don't react when he does it. It can work against you only if you respond defensively. Instead, try talking to his crotch – responses such as 'You've got a good point there, Bob' and 'I can see where you're coming from' can teach a valuable lesson as well as causing riotous laughter when used at the right time.

Leg-Over-the-Arm-of-Chair

This is mainly done by men because it also uses the Legs-Spread. It not only signifies the man's ownership of the chair, it also signals that he has an informal, aggressive attitude.

Informality, indifference and lack of concern

It is common to see two male friends laughing and joking with each other while sitting this way, but let's consider its impact in different circumstances. Let's say an employee has a personal problem and goes to ask his boss for advice. As the employee explains, he leans forward in the chair, his hands on his knees, his head down, with a dejected expression and voice lowered. The boss listens, sitting motionless, then leans back in his chair and puts one leg over the arm. The boss's attitude has now changed to lack of concern or indifference. In other words, he has little concern for the employee or his problem and he may even feel that his time is being wasted with the 'same old story'.

So what was the boss indifferent about? He may have considered the employee's problem, decided that it's not much of a problem anyway and become disinterested. He may even tell his employee not to worry and that the problem will simply go away.

As long as the boss's leg stays over the arm of the chair, his indifferent attitude will persist. When the employee leaves the office, the boss breathes a sigh of relief and says to himself, 'Thank heavens he's gone!' and takes his leg off the arm of the chair.

The *Leg-Over-the-Arm-of-Chair* can be annoying when it occurs during negotiation, and it is vital to make that person change position because the longer he stays in it, the longer he will have an indifferent or aggressive attitude. An easy way to do this is to ask him to lean across and look at something, or, if you have a wicked sense of humour, tell him there's a split in his trousers.

Straddling a Chair

Centuries ago, men used shields to protect themselves from the spears and clubs of the enemy, and today, civilised man uses whatever he has at his disposal to symbolise this same protective behaviour when he is under physical or verbal attack. This includes standing behind a gate, doorway, fence, desk or the open door of his motor vehicle and straddling a chair.

The Straddler wants to dominate or control while, at the same time, protecting his front

The back of the chair acts as a shield to protect the body and can transform a person into an aggressive, dominant personality. Men also have their legs spread in a wide Crotch Display, adding male assertion to the position. Most Straddlers are dominant types who will try to take control of others when they become bored with the conversation, and the back of the chair serves as good protection from any 'attack' by other members of the group. The Straddler is often discreet and can slip into the straddle position almost unnoticed.

The easiest way to disarm the Straddler is to stand up or sit behind him, making him feel vulnerable to attack and forcing him to change his position. This can work well in a group situation because the Straddler will have his back exposed and this compels him to change to another position.

So what would you do with a Straddler on a swivel chair? It is pointless to try to reason with a crotch-displaying man on a merry-go-round, so the best defence is non-verbal. Conduct your conversation standing up and looking down on the Straddler, and move into his Personal Space. This is unnerving for him and he can even fall backwards off his chair in an attempt to move away.

Next time you have a Straddler coming to visit you, be sure to seat him on a fixed chair that has arms to stop him from taking his favourite position. When he can't straddle, his usual next move is to use the *Catapult*.

The Catapult

This is a seated version of the Hands-on-Hips pose except the hands are behind the head with the elbows menacingly pointed out. Again, it's almost entirely a male gesture used to intimidate others or it infers a relaxed attitude to lull you into a false sense of security just before he ambushes you.

The Catapult: cool, confident, knows it all and thinks he has more bananas than anyone

This gesture is typical of professionals such as accountants, lawyers, sales managers or people who are feeling superior, dominant or confident about something. If we could read this person's mind, he would be saying things such as, 'I have all the answers', or 'Everything's under control', or even 'Maybe one day you'll be as smart as me'. Management personnel regularly use it and newly appointed male managers suddenly begin to use it, despite the fact that they seldom used it prior to their promotion. It is also used by 'Know-It-All' individuals and it intimidates most people. It's the trademark gesture of men who like you to realise just how knowledgeable they are. It can also be used as a territorial sign to show that the person has staked a claim to that particular area.

It is usually clustered with a Figure-Four leg position or Crotch Display, which shows that he not only feels superior, he's also likely to argue or try to dominate. There are several ways you can deal with this gesture, depending on the circumstances. You can lean forward with palms up and say, 'I can see that you know about this. Would you care to comment?' then sit back and wait for an answer.

Women quickly develop a dislike for men who use the Catapult in business meetings.

You could place something just out of his reach and ask, 'Have you seen this?', forcing him to lean forward. If you are a man, copying the gesture can be a simple way to handle the Catapulter because mirroring creates equality. This doesn't work for a woman however, because it puts her breasts on display, leaving her at a disadvantage. Even flat-chested women who attempt the *Catapult* are described as aggressive by both men and women.

The Catapult doesn't work for women, even flat-chested ones.

If you are a woman and a man does this, continue the conversation standing up. This forces the Catapulter to change position so he can continue the conversation. When he stops the Catapult, sit down again. If he catapults again, stand up. This is a non-aggressive way of training others not to try to intimidate you. On the other hand, if the person using the Catapult is your superior and is reprimanding you, you will intimidate him by copying this gesture. For example, two equals will use the Catapult in each other's presence to show equality and agreement, but if a mischievous schoolboy did it, it would infuriate the school principal.

In one insurance company, we found that 27 out of 30 male sales managers used the Catapult regularly around their salespeople or subordinates but rarely in the presence of their superiors. When they were with their superiors, however, the same managers were more likely to use submissive and subordinate gesture clusters.

Gestures That Show When a Person is Ready

One of the most valuable gestures a negotiator can learn to recognise is seated readiness. When you are presenting a proposal, for example, if the other person were to take this gesture at the end of the presentation, and the interview had gone well up to that point, you could ask for agreement and would be likely to get it.

The classic position showing readiness for action

Our video replays of salespeople interviewing potential buyers revealed that, whenever the *Seated Readiness* gesture followed a Chin-Stroke (decision-making), the client said 'yes' to the proposal more than half the time. In contrast, if during the close of the sale the client took the Arms-Crossed position immediately after the Chin-Stroke, the sale was usually not made. The Seated Readiness gesture can also be taken by the angry person who is ready for something else – to throw you out. The preceding gesture clusters indicate the person's real intentions.

The Starter's Position

Readiness gestures that signal a desire to conclude a meeting include leaning forward with both hands on both knees, or leaning forward with both hands gripping the chair as if they were at the start of a race. If either of these occur during a conversation it would be wise for you to take the lead and resell, change direction or terminate the conversation.

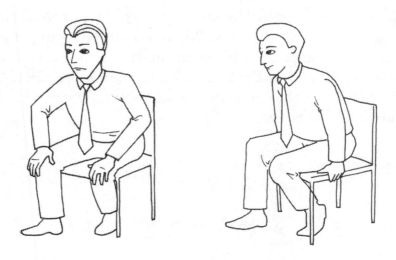

On your marks, get set: in the starting blocks –
readiness to end an encounter or a conversation

Summary

The body language signals covered in this chapter are fairly easy to observe because most involve big gestures. Not only is it important to understand the significance of these signals, it's vital to good communication that you eliminate any negative gestures from your own repertoire and practise using the things that will give you positive results.

Chapter 12

MIRRORING – HOW WE BUILD RAPPORT

They all look the same, dress the same way, use the same facial expressions
and body language but each will tell you he's 'doing his own thing'

When we meet others for the first time, we need to assess
quickly whether they are positive or negative towards us, just
as most other animals do for survival reasons. We do this by
scanning the other person's body to see if they will move or
gesture the same way we do in what is known as 'mirroring'.
We mirror each other's body language as a way of bonding,
being accepted and creating rapport, but we are usually oblivious to the fact that we are doing it. In ancient times, mirroring
was also a social device which helped our ancestors fit in successfully with larger groups; it is also a left-over from a
primitive method of learning which involved imitation.

One of the most noticeable forms of mirroring is yawning –
one person starts and it sets everyone off. Robert Provine
found that yawning is so contagious you don't even need to see
another person yawn – the sight of a wide-open mouth is
enough to do it. It was once thought that the purpose of

yawning was to oxygenate the body but we now know that it's a form of mirroring that serves to create rapport with others and to avoid aggression – just as it also does for monkeys and chimps.

Wearing the same outfit as another woman is a mirroring no-no. But if two men show up at a party wearing the same outfit, they could become lifelong friends.

Non-verbally, mirroring says 'Look at me; I'm the same as you. I feel the same way and share the same attitudes.' This is why people at a rock concert will all jump to their feet and applaud simultaneously or give a 'Mexican Wave' together. The synchronicity of the crowd promotes a secure feeling in the participants. Similarly, people in an angry mob will mirror aggressive attitudes and this explains why many usually calm people can lose their cool in this situation.

The urge to mirror is also the basis on which a queue works. In a queue, people willingly co-operate with people they have never met and will never see again, obeying an unwritten set of behavioural rules while waiting for a bus, at an art gallery, in a bank or side by side in war. Professor Joseph Heinrich from the University of Michigan found that the urges to mirror others are hardwired into the brain because co-operation leads to more food, better health and

Learning to mirror our parents begins early: Prince Philip and a young Prince Charles in perfect step

economic growth for communities. It also offers an explanation as to why societies that are highly disciplined in mirroring, such as the British, Germans and ancient Romans, successfully dominated the world for many years.

Mirroring makes others feel 'at ease'. It's such a powerful rapport-building tool that slow-motion video research reveals that it even extends to simultaneous blinking, nostril-flaring, eyebrow-raising and even pupil dilation, which is remarkable as these micro-gestures cannot be consciously imitated.

Creating the Right Vibes

Studies into synchronous body language behaviour show that people who feel similar emotions, or are on the same wavelength and are likely to be experiencing a rapport, will also begin to match each other's body language and expressions. Being 'in sync' to bond with another person begins early in the womb when our body functions and heartbeat match the rhythm of our mother, so mirroring is a state to which we are naturally inclined.

When a couple are in the early stages of courtship it's common to see them behave with synchronous movements, almost as if they are dancing. For example, when a woman takes a mouthful of food the man wipes the corner of his mouth; or he begins a sentence and she finishes it for him. When she gets PMT, he develops a strong desire for chocolate; and when she feels bloated, he farts.

When a person says 'the vibes are right' or that they 'feel right' around another person, they are unknowingly referring to mirroring and synchronous behaviour. For example, at a restaurant, one person can be reluctant to eat or drink alone for fear of being out of sync with the others. When it comes to ordering the meal, each may check with the others before ordering. 'What are you having?' they ask as they try to mirror their meals. This is one of the reasons why playing background music during a date is so effective – the music gets a couple to beat and tap in time together.

Mirroring the other person's body language and appearance
shows a united front and doesn't let either get one-up on the other

Mirroring on a Cellular Level

American heart surgeon, Dr Memhet Oz, reported some remarkable findings from heart recipients. He found that, as with most other body organs, the heart appears to retain cellular memories, and this allows some patients to experience some of the emotions experienced by the heart donor. Even more remarkably, he found some recipients also assume the same gestures and posture of the donor even though they have never seen the donor. His conclusion was that it appears that the heart cells instruct the recipient's brains to take on the donor's body language. Conversely, people suffering from disorders such as autism have no ability to mirror or match the behaviour of others, which makes it difficult for two-way communication with others. The same goes for drunk people whose gestures are out of sync with their words, making it impossible for any mirroring to occur.

Because of the phenomenon of cause and effect, if you *intentionally* assume certain body language positions you will begin to experience the emotions associated with those gestures. For example, if you feel confident, you may unconsciously assume the Steeple gesture to reflect your confidence, but if you intentionally Steeple you will not only begin to feel more confident, others will perceive that you're confident. This, then, becomes a powerful way to create a rapport with others by intentionally matching their body language and posture.

Mirroring Differences Between Men and Women

Geoffrey Beattie, at the University of Manchester, found that a woman is instinctively four times more likely to mirror another woman than a man is to mirror another man. He also found that women mirror men's body language too, but men are reluctant to mirror a woman's gestures or posture – unless he is in courtship mode.

When a woman says she can 'see' that someone doesn't agree with the group opinion she is actually 'seeing' the disagreement. She's picked up that someone's body language is out of sync with group opinion and they are showing their disagreement by not mirroring the group's body language. How women can 'see' disagreement, anger, lying or feeling hurt has always been a source of amazement to most men. It's because most men's brains are simply not well equipped to read the fine detail of others' body language and don't consciously notice mirroring discrepancies.

As we said in our book *Why Men Don't Listen & Women Can't Read Maps* (Orion), men and women's brains are programmed differently to express emotions through facial expressions and body language. Typically, a woman can use an average of six main facial expressions in a ten-second listening period to reflect and then feed back the speaker's emotions. Her face will mirror the emotions being expressed by the speaker. To someone watching, it can look as if the events being discussed are happening to both women.

A woman reads the meaning of what is being said through

the speaker's voice tone and his emotional condition through his body language. This is exactly what a man needs to do to capture a woman's attention and to keep her interested and listening. Most men are daunted by the prospect of using facial feedback while listening, but it pays big dividends for the man who becomes good at it.

Some men say 'She'll think I'm effeminate!', but research with these techniques shows that when a man mirrors a woman's facial expressions as she talks she will describe him as caring, intelligent, interesting and attractive.

Men, on the other hand, can make fewer than a third of the facial expressions a woman can make. Men usually hold expressionless faces, especially in public, because of the evolutionary need to withhold emotion to stave off possible attack from strangers and to appear to be in control of their emotions. This is why most men look as if they are statues when they listen.

The emotionless mask that men wear while listening allows them to feel in control of the situation, but does not mean men don't experience emotions. Brain scans reveal that men can feel emotion as strongly as women, but avoid showing it publicly.

What to Do About It if You're Female

The key to mirroring a man's behaviour is in understanding that he doesn't use his face to signal his attitudes – he uses his body. Most women find it difficult to mirror an expressionless man but with males this is not required. If you're a woman, it means that you need to reduce your facial expressions so that you don't come across as overwhelming or intimidating. Most importantly, don't mirror what you think he *might* be feeling. That can be disastrous if you've got it wrong and you may be described as 'dizzy' or 'scatterbrained'. Women in business who listen with a more serious face are described by men as more intelligent, astute and sensible.

When Men and Women Start to Look Alike

When two people live together for a long time and have a good working relationship, they often begin to look alike. This is because they are constantly mirroring each other's facial expressions, which, over time, builds muscle definition in the same areas of the face. Even couples who don't look facially similar can appear similar in a photograph because they use the same smile.

The Beckhams don't look at all alike until they smile

Forty years of mirroring – the Beckhams at retirement with their dog, Spot

In 2000, psychologist Dr John Gottman of the University of Washington, Seattle, and his colleagues, discovered that marriages are more likely to fail when one partner not only does not mirror the other's expressions of happiness, but instead shows expressions of contempt. Instead, this opposite behaviour affects the smiling partner, even when they are not consciously aware of what is happening.

Do We Resemble Our Pets?

You can also see mirroring occur in the pets some people choose. Without realising it, we unconsciously tend to favour pets that

physically resemble us, or that appear to reflect our attitudes.
To demonstrate the point, here are a few examples:

Do we choose pets that resemble us?

Monkey See, Monkey Do

The next time you attend a social function or go to a place
where people meet and interact, notice the number of people
who have taken the identical gestures and posture of the
person with whom they're talking. Mirroring is the way one

person tells another that he is in agreement with his ideas and attitudes. One is non-verbally saying to the other, 'As you can see, I think the same as you.' The person with the highest status often makes the first moves and the others copy, usually in pecking order.

Thinking alike

Take, for example, the two men standing at the bar in the above illustration. They are mirroring so it's reasonable to assume that they are discussing a topic on which they have similar thoughts and feelings. If one man uses an evaluation gesture or stands on the other foot, the other will copy. One puts a hand in his pocket, the other copies again. Mirroring will continue for as long as the two are in agreement.

Even when Presidents Bush and Chirac disagree verbally, they still usually mirror each other – this shows they have mutual respect

Mirroring happens among friends or between people of the same status and it is common to see married couples walk, stand, sit and move in identical ways. Albert Scheflen found that people who are strangers studiously *avoid* holding mirror positions.

Matching Voices

Intonation, voice inflection, speed of speaking and even accents also synchronise during the mirroring process to further establish mutual attitudes and build rapport. This is known as 'pacing' and it can almost seem as if the two people are singing in tune. You will often see a speaker beating time with his hands while the listener matches the rhythm with head nods. As a relationship grows over time, the mirroring of the main body language positions becomes less as each person begins to anticipate the other's attitudes, and vocal pacing with the other person becomes a main medium for maintaining rapport.

Never speak at a faster rate than the other person. Studies reveal that others describe feeling 'pressured' when someone speaks more quickly than they do. A person's speed of speech shows the rate at which their brain can consciously analyse information. Speak at the same rate or slightly slower than the other person and mirror their inflection and intonation. Pacing is critical when attempting to make appointments by telephone because voice is your only communication medium.

Intentionally Creating Rapport

The significance of mirroring is one of the most important body language lessons you can learn because it's a clear way in which others tell us that they agree with us or like us. It is also a way for us to tell others that we like them, by simply mirroring their body language.

If a boss wants to develop a rapport and create a relaxed atmosphere with a nervous employee, he could copy the employee's posture to achieve this end. Similarly, an up-and-coming employee may be seen copying his boss's gestures in an attempt to show agreement when the boss is giving his opinion. Using this knowledge, it is possible to influence others by mirroring their positive gestures and posture. This has the effect of putting the other person in a receptive and relaxed frame of mind, because he can 'see' that you understand his point of view.

Mirroring the other person's body language to gain acceptance

Before you mirror someone's body language, however, you must take into consideration your relationship with that person. Let's say, for example, the junior employee of a corporation has asked for a pay rise and is called into the manager's office. The employee enters the manager's office, the manager asks him to sit down and assumes the Catapult with a Figure-Four showing the employee a superior, dominant attitude. But what would happen if the junior then copied the manager's dominant body language while discussing the potential salary rise?

A boss would perceive a subordinate's mirroring behaviour as arrogance

Even if the employee's talk was on a subordinate level, the manager could feel affronted by the employee's body language and his job could be in jeopardy. Mirroring is also effective for intimidating or disarming 'superior' types who try to take control. Accountants, lawyers and managers are notorious for using superiority body language clusters around people they consider inferior. By mirroring, you can disconcert them and force a change of position. But never do it to the boss.

They have the same posture and body language and
the close distance between them shows thay are friends
going about business in the same way with similar goals.

Who Mirrors Whom?

Research shows that when the leader of a group assumes certain gestures and positions, subordinates will copy, usually in pecking order. Leaders also tend to be the first of a group to walk through a doorway and they like to sit on the end of a sofa, table or bench seat rather than in the centre. When a group of executives walks into a room, the person with the highest status usually goes first. When executives are seated in the boardroom, the boss usually sits at the head of the table, often furthest from the door. If the boss sits in the Catapult, his subordinates are likely to copy in order of their importance within the group. You can see this in a meeting where people 'take sides' with others by mirroring their body language. This lets you see who will vote with you and who will vote against you.

Mirroring is a good strategy to use if you are part of a presentation team. Decide, in advance, that when the team spokesperson makes a gesture or takes a posture when speaking, the entire team will mirror. This not only gives your team the powerful appearance of being cohesive, it can frighten the hell out of competitors who suspect something is up, even though they can't quite figure out what it is.

Bill Clinton may have been the world's most powerful
man but when Hillary gestured, he copied – and when
they walk hand-in-hand, she often has the front-hold position

When presenting ideas, products and services to couples, watching who mirrors whom reveals where the ultimate power or final decision-making ability lies. If the woman makes the initial movements, however small, such as crossing her feet, lacing her fingers or using a Critical Evaluation cluster and the man copies, there is little point in asking him for a decision – he doesn't have the authority to make it.

Walking in step – Charles leads, Camilla follows slightly behind;
after the beginning of the Iraqi conflict in 2003, Tony Blair began
to mirror George Bush's Thumbs-in-Belt gesture

Summary

Mirroring someone's body language makes them feel accepted and creates a bond and is a phenomenon that occurs naturally between friends and people of equal status. Conversely, we make a point of not mirroring those we don't like or strangers, such as those riding with us in a lift or standing in the queue at the cinema.

Mirroring the other person's body language and speech patterns is one of the most powerful ways to build rapport quickly. In a new meeting with someone, mirror his seating position, posture, body angle, gestures, expressions and tone of voice. Before long, they'll start to feel that there's something about you they like – they'll describe you as 'easy to be with'. This is because they see themselves reflected in you. A word of warning, however: don't do it too early in a new encounter as many people have become aware of mirroring strategies since our original book *Body Language* was published and over 100 million people watched the television series that followed. When someone takes a position you have one of three choices – ignore it, do something else or mirror it. Mirroring pays big dividends. But never mirror a person's negative signals.

Chapter 13

THE SECRET SIGNALS
OF CIGARETTES,
GLASSES AND MAKE-UP

Smoking is an outward signal of inner turmoil or conflict and most smoking has less to do with nicotine addiction and more to do with the need for reassurance. It is one of the displacement activities that people use in today's high-pressure society to release the tensions that build up from social and business encounters. For example, most people experience inner tension while waiting outside the dentist's surgery to have a tooth removed. While a smoker might cover up his anxiety by sneaking out for a smoke, non-smokers perform other rituals such as grooming, gum-chewing, nail-biting, finger-and-foot-tapping, cufflink-adjusting, head-scratching, playing with something, or other gestures that tell us they need reassurance. Jewellery is also popular for exactly the same reason – it has high fondle value and allows its owner to displace their insecurity, fear, impatience or lack of confidence onto the item.

Studies now show a clear relationship between whether an infant was breast-fed and its likelihood of becoming a smoker as an adult. It was found that babies who were largely bottle-fed represent the majority of adult smokers and the heaviest smokers, while the longer a baby was breast-fed, the less chance there was that it would become a smoker. It seems that breast-fed babies receive comfort and bonding from the breast that is unattainable from a bottle, the consequence being that the bottle-fed babies, as adults, continue the search for comfort by sucking things. Smokers use their cigarettes for the same reason as the child who sucks his blanket or thumb.

> *Bottle-fed babies are three times more likely to become smokers than breast-fed babies.*

Not only were smokers three times more likely to have been thumb-suckers as children, they have also been shown to be more neurotic than non-smokers and to experience oral fixations such as sucking the arm of their glasses, nail-biting, pen-munching, lip-biting and enough pencil-chewing to embarrass an average beaver. Clearly, many desires, including the urge to suck and feel secure, were satisfied in breast-fed babies but not in bottle-fed babies.

The Two Types of Smokers

There are two basic types of smokers – addicted smokers and social smokers.

Studies show that smaller, quicker puffs on a cigarette stimulate the brain, giving a heightened level of awareness whereas longer, slower puffs act as a sedative. Addicted smokers are dependent on the sedative effects of nicotine to help them deal with stress and they take longer, deeper puffs and will also smoke alone. Social smokers usually smoke only in the presence of others or 'when I have a few drinks'. This means that this smoking is a social display to create certain impressions on others. In social smoking, from the time the cigarette is lit until it's extinguished it's being smoked for only 20% of the time in shorter, quicker puffs while the other 80% is devoted to a series of special body language gestures and rituals.

Most social smoking is part of a social ritual.

A study conducted by Andy Parrot of the University of East London reports that 80% of smokers say they feel less stressed when they smoke. However, the stress levels of adult smokers are only slightly higher than those of non-smokers anyway, and stress levels increase as the smokers develop a regular smoking habit. Parrot also found that stopping smoking actually leads to a reduction of stress. Science now shows that smoking is not an aid for mood control because nicotine dependency *heightens* stress levels. The supposed relaxing effect of smoking only reflects the reversal of the tension and irritability that develops during a smoker's nicotine depletion. In other words, the smoker's mood is normal during smoking, and stressed when *not* smoking. That means that for a smoker to feel normal, the smoker must always have a lit cigarette in his mouth! Furthermore, when smokers quit smoking, they gradually become less stressed over time. Smoking reflects the reversal effect of the tension and stress caused by the lack of nicotine in the blood.

Studies show poor moods occur during the first few weeks after quitting, but there is dramatic improvement once the nicotine is completely gone from the body, reducing craving for the drug and the stress that results from it.

Smoking is similar to hitting yourself over the head with a hammer because, when you stop, you feel better.

Even though smoking is now banned in many places and contexts, it's an advantage to understand the connection between smoking body language signals and a person's attitude. Smoking gestures play an important part in assessing emotional states as they are usually performed in a predictable, ritualistic manner that can give important clues to the smoker's state of mind or to what they are trying to achieve. The cigarette ritual involves tapping, twisting, flicking, waving and other mini-gestures indicating that the person is experiencing more tension than may be normal.

Differences Between Men and Women

When women smoke they will often hold the cigarette high with their wrist bent back in a wrist display gesture, leaving the front of the body open. When men smoke they keep their wrist straight to avoid looking effeminate and drop their smoking hand down below chest level after they puff, keeping the front of the body protected at all times.

Twice as many women smoke as men and both sexes take the same number of puffs per cigarette, but men hold the smoke in their lungs longer, making them more susceptible to lung cancer than women.

Women use the cigarette as a social display
to open the body and display the wrist; men close their
bodies when they smoke and prefer secretive holds

Men will often use the *Pinch Hold* when smoking, especially if they are trying to be secretive, keeping the cigarette hidden inside the palm. This gesture is commonly used in the movies by actors who play tough guys or who are acting sneaky or suspicious.

Smoking as a Sexual Display

Films and media advertising have always portrayed smoking as sexy. Smoking is another opportunity to emphasise our sex differences: it allows a woman to use wrist displays (we'll discuss this in Chapter 15) and open her body to a man and it allows the cigarette to be used like a small phallus being seductively sucked between her lips. A man can highlight his masculinity by holding the cigarette secretively and seductively. Previous generations used a seductive smoking ritual as an acceptable form of courtship with a man offering to light a woman's cigarette while she touched his hand and held his gaze longer than usual as she thanked him. In many places today, however, smoking is as popular as a fart in a spacesuit so the smoking courtship ritual is virtually dead. The key to the perceived female sexual attraction behind smoking is the submissive attitude it implies; in other words, it carries the subtle message that a woman who smokes can be persuaded to do things that are not in her best interests. While blowing smoke in a person's face is unacceptable everywhere, in Syria it's seen as a sexual invitation when a man does it to a woman!

How to Spot a Positive or Negative Decision

Whether a person has a positive or negative attitude towards his circumstances is revealed by the direction in which his smoke is exhaled, whether it's up or down. We are assuming here that the smoker is not blowing the smoke upwards to avoid offending others and that he could have blown the smoke in either direction. A person who is feeling positive, superior or confident about what he sees or hears will blow the smoke in an upward direction most of the time. Conversely, a person in a negative, secretive or suspicious frame of mind will blow the smoke down most of the time. Blowing down and from the corner of the mouth indicates an even more negative or secretive attitude.

Smoke blown up: confident, superior, positive;
smoke blown down: negative, secretive, suspicious

In films, the leader of a motorcycle gang or criminal syndicate is usually portrayed as a tough, aggressive man who, as he smokes, tilts his head back sharply and with controlled precision blows the smoke towards the ceiling to demonstrate his superiority to the rest of the gang. In contrast, Humphrey Bogart was often cast as a gangster or tough guy who held his cigarette inverted in his hand and blew the smoke down from the corner of his mouth as he planned a jailbreak or other devious activity. There also appears to be a relationship between how positive or negative the person feels and the speed at which he exhales the smoke. The faster the smoke is blown upwards the more superior or confident; the faster it is blown down, the more negative he feels.

If a smoker is playing cards and is dealt a good hand, he is likely to blow the smoke upwards, whereas a poor hand may cause him to blow it downwards. While some card players use a 'poker face' when playing cards as a way of not showing any body signals that may give them away, other players like to be actors and use misleading body language to lull the other players into a false sense of security. If, for example, a poker player was dealt four of a kind and he wanted to bluff the other players, he could throw the cards face down on the table in disgust, curse, cross his arms and put on a non-verbal display indicating he'd been dealt a poor hand. But then he quietly sits back and draws on his cigarette and blows the smoke upwards. And then he Steeples. It would be unwise for the other players to now bet on the next hand, as they would probably be beaten. Observation of smoking gestures in selling situations shows that when smokers are asked to buy, those who have already reached a positive decision blow the smoke upwards, whereas those who have decided not to buy, blow downwards.

The original study of smokers we carried out in 1978 showed that smokers took significantly longer to reach a decision in a negotiation than non-smokers and that the smoking ritual is performed most often during the tense moments of the negotiations. Smokers, it seems, are able to stall decision-making by diverting their attention to the smoking process. So if you want quicker decisions from smokers, negotiate in a room that displays a large 'No Smoking' sign.

Cigar Smokers

Cigars have always been used as a means of displaying superiority because of their cost and size. The big-time business executive, the gang leader and those in high-status positions are often portrayed as smoking cigars. Cigars are used to celebrate a victory or achievement such as the birth of a baby, a wedding, clinching a business deal or winning the lottery. It is not surprising that most of the smoke exhaled by cigar smokers is blown upwards. At a celebration dinner where cigars were distributed freely we noted that of 400 recorded cigar smoke exhalations, 320 were in an upward direction.

How Smokers End a Session

Most smokers smoke their cigarette down to a certain length before extinguishing it in an ashtray. Women tend to slowly stub the cigarette out while men are likely to crush it with the thumb. If the smoker lights a cigarette and suddenly extinguishes it earlier than he normally would, he has signalled his decision to terminate the conversation. Watching for this termination signal can allow you to take control or to close the conversation, making it appear that it was your idea to end things.

How to Read Glasses

Almost every artificial aid a person uses gives them an opportunity to perform a number of revealing gestures and this is certainly the case with those who wear glasses. One of the most common gestures is placing one arm of the frame in the mouth.

Using the glasses to stall for time

As Desmond Morris pointed out, the act of putting objects against the lips or in the mouth is a momentary attempt by the person to relive the security he experienced as a baby at his mother's breast. This means that the *Glasses-Arm-in-Mouth* gesture is essentially a reassurance gesture.

If you wear glasses you may sometimes feel as if you are looking at life through two toilet paper rolls, but you are perceived by others as being more studious and intelligent, particularly in the early stages of a meeting. In one study, people pictured wearing glasses were judged by respondents as being 14 IQ points more intelligent compared to when they were not wearing them. This effect lasted less than five minutes, however, so you would be wise to consider wearing them only for short interviews.

The 'intelligent' look is reduced, however, if you wear glasses with oversized lenses, Elton John-style coloured frames or designer glasses with distracting initials on the frame. Wearing glasses that are one size larger than the face can make younger people look older, more studious and more authoritative.

Solid frame glasses can make you look more sincere
and intelligent; over-the-top frames don't

In our study using pictures of people's faces, we found that when you add glasses to a face in a business context, respondents describe that person as studious, intelligent, conservative, educated and sincere. The heavier the frame on the glasses the more frequently these descriptions were likely to be used and it made little difference whether the face was male or female. This could be because the leaders of business who wear glasses use heavier frames. So in a business environment, glasses are a statement of power. Frameless, small or spindly frames convey a powerless image and say that you are more interested in fashion than business. The reverse holds true in social contexts but in these situations you are selling yourself as a friend or mate. We advise people in positions of power to wear stronger frames to make serious points, such as reading a financial budget, and frameless styles when conveying a 'nice guy' image or being 'one of the boys'.

Stalling Tactics

As with cigarette smoking, the Glasses-Arm-in-Mouth action can be used to stall or delay a decision. In negotiating, it has been found that this gesture appears most frequently at the close when the person has been asked for a decision. Continually taking the glasses off and cleaning the lenses is another method used by glasses wearers to gain time for a decision. When this gesture is seen immediately after a decision has been asked for, silence is the best tactic.

The gestures that follow Glasses-Arm-in-Mouth signal the person's intention and allow an alert negotiator to respond accordingly. For example, if the person puts the glasses back on, this often means that he wants to 'see' the facts again. Folding the glasses and putting them away signals an intention to terminate the conversation and throwing the glasses onto the desk is symbolically rejecting the proposal.

Peering-Over-the-Glasses

Actors in films made during the 1920s and 1930s used *Peering-Over-the-Glasses* to portray, for example, a critical or judgemental person such as a teacher in an English public school. Often the person would be wearing reading glasses and find it more convenient to look over the tops, rather than removing them to look at the other person. But whoever is on the receiving end of this look may feel as though he is being judged or scrutinised. The habit of looking over the glasses can be a very costly mistake because the listener may respond to this look with negatives such as folded arms, crossed legs or an argumentative attitude. If you wear glasses, remove them when speaking and put them back on to listen. This not only relaxes the other person, but allows you to have control of the conversation. The listener quickly becomes conditioned that when you take your glasses off, you're taking the floor, and when you put them back on, it's his turn to talk.

Peering-Over-the-Glasses intimidates everyone

Contact lenses can make your pupils appear dilated and moist and can also reflect lights. This can give you a softer, more sensual appearance, which is fine for social contexts but can be disastrous in business, especially for women. A woman can find herself trying her best to persuade a businessman to buy her ideas while he is mesmerised by the sensual effect of her contact lenses and doesn't hear a word she says.

Tinted glasses and sunglasses are never acceptable in business contexts and arouse suspicions in social environments. When you want to convey that you see things clearly and precisely you must have clear glass in the frames – keep sunglasses and tinted lenses for outdoors.

Wearing Glasses on the Head

People who wear dark sunglasses during meetings are seen as suspicious, secretive and insecure while those who wear them on their head are perceived to be relaxed, youthful and 'cool' – just back from Club Med, in fact. This is because they give the wearer the appearance that they have two huge eyes with dilated pupils on the top of their head; this mimics the non-threatening effect that babies and cuddly toys with painted large pupils have on us.

Creating the 'Four Eyes' effect of dilated pupils

The Power of Glasses and Make-up

Wearing make-up definitely adds to perceived credibility, especially for women in business. To demonstrate this we conducted a simple experiment. We hired four similar looking female assistants to help sell our training products at a seminar. Each woman was given her own separate merchandise table and all were dressed in similar clothing. One assistant wore glasses and make-up, the second wore glasses and no make-up, the third had make-up and no glasses and the fourth had neither make-up nor glasses. Customers would approach the table and talk with the assistants about the programmes, spending an average discussion time of between four and six minutes. When the customers left the tables they were asked to recall information about each woman's personality and appearance and to choose adjectives from a list that best described each woman. The woman wearing both make-up and glasses was described as confident, intelligent, sophisticated and the most outgoing. Some female customers saw her as confident but also cold, arrogant and/or conceited – indicating they may have seen her as a possible competitor, because the men never saw her this way. The assistant who wore make-up and no glasses received good ratings on appearance and personal presentation but lower on personal skills such as listening and building rapport.

> *Wearing make-up definitely adds to*
> *a woman's perceived self-confidence.*

The assistants who wore no make-up were rated worst on personal skills and personal presentation and wearing glasses without make-up made little difference to the customers' attitudes and recall. Most female customers had noted when make-up was not being worn by the assistant while most men could not recall whether she wore it or not. Interestingly, both women who wore make-up were thought to be wearing shorter skirts than those without make-up, demonstrating that make-up also presents a sexier image than wearing none. The bottom line here is clear – make-up gives a woman a more intelligent, confident and sexier image and the combination of glasses and make-up in business has the most positive and memorable impact on observers, so having a pair of non-correctable glasses could be an excellent strategy for business meetings.

A Little Lippy, Lady?

For one of our television shows, we asked nine women to turn up for a series of interviews with both male and female interviewers. For half the interviews, each woman wore lipstick but they did not wear it to the other half. The interviewer's attitudes after the experiment quickly became clear – the women wearing red lipstick and using larger lip displays were seen as more interested in themselves and in men's attention, while women with reduced lip displays and muted or pastel colours were seen as more career oriented and businesslike. The women with no lipstick were seen as more serious about work than men but lacking in personal skills. Almost all female interviewers had noticed whether the candidates wore lipstick or not, while only half of the men noticed when women were not wearing it. This means that a woman should wear larger displays of bright red lipsticks for going on dates but smaller, more understated displays for business meetings. If she works in businesses that promote female image, such as clothing, cosmetics and hairdressing, bright displays are seen as positive because they sell female attractiveness.

Briefcase Signals

The size of a briefcase is linked to perceptions of the status of its owner. Those who carry large, bulging briefcases are thought to do all the work and probably take work home because they are poor time managers. Slim briefcases say that the owner is only concerned with the bottom line and therefore has more status. Always carry a briefcase to one side, preferably in your left hand, which allows you to shake hands smoothly with your right hand without fumbling. If you're a woman, never carry a briefcase and handbag at the same time – you will be perceived as less businesslike and more disorganised. And never use a briefcase as a barrier between you and another person.

Summary

Regardless of what type of object or thing we choose to handle, wear or smoke, there are special signals and rituals we display without awareness. The more of these objects we use, the more we signal our intentions or emotions. Learning how to read these signals gives you a second set of body language cues to observe.

Chapter 14

HOW THE BODY POINTS TO WHERE THE MIND WANTS TO GO

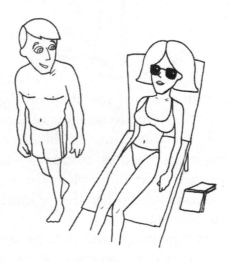

Often, the body goes one way while
the mind goes another

Have you ever been talking with someone and had the feeling he would rather be elsewhere than with you, even though he seems to be enjoying your company? A still photograph of that scene would probably reveal two things: first, the person's head is turned towards you and facial signals such as smiling and nodding are evident; and second, the person's body and feet are pointing *away* from you, either towards another person or towards an exit. The direction in which a person points his body or feet is a signal of where he would prefer to be going.

The man on the right
indicating he wants
to leave

The above illustration shows two men talking in a doorway. The man on the left is trying to hold the other man's attention, but his listener wants to continue in the direction his body is pointing, although his head is turned to acknowledge the other man's presence. It is only when the man on the right turns his body towards the other that a mutually interesting conversation can take place.

In any face-to-face meeting, when one person has decided to end the conversation or wants to leave, he will turn his body or feet to point towards the nearest exit. If this was a conversation involving you, it's a signal that you should do something to get the person involved and interested or else terminate the conversation on your terms, allowing you to maintain control.

What Body Angles Say

1. Open Positions
We stated earlier that the distance between people is related to their degree of interest or intimacy. The angle at which people orient their bodies also gives non-verbal clues to their attitudes and relationships.

Most animals, if they want to fight with another animal, will signal this by approaching head on. If the other animal accepts the challenge, it will reciprocate by also standing head on. The same applies to humans. If, however, the animal wants to check out the other animal at close range but doesn't intend to attack it will approach side on, just as friendly dogs do. And so it is with humans. A speaker who takes a strong attitude to his listener while standing straight and facing them directly is perceived as aggressive. The speaker who delivers exactly the same message but points his body away from the listener is seen as confident and goal oriented but not as aggressive.

To avoid being seen as aggressive, we stand with our bodies angled at 45 degrees to each other during friendly encounters to form an angle of 90 degrees.

Each standing at 45-degree angles to avoid coming across as aggressive

The picture above shows two men with their bodies angled towards an imaginary third point to form a triangle shape. The angle formed indicates that a non-aggressive conversation is probably taking place and they are also displaying similar status by mirroring. The formation of the triangle invites a third person to join in the conversation. If a fourth person is accepted into the group, a square is formed and, for a fifth and sixth person, either a circle or two new triangles are formed.

In confined spaces like lifts, crowded buses and underground trains, where it's not possible to turn your body away from strangers to a 45-degree angle, we turn our heads to the angle instead.

2. Closed Positions

When two people want intimacy, their body angle changes from 45 degrees to 0 degrees, that is, they face each other. A man or woman who wants to monopolise a person's attention uses this position, as well as other courtship gestures, when they make their play. A man will not only point his body towards a woman, he also closes the distance between them as he moves into her Intimate Zone. To accept his approach, she need only orient her body angle to 0 degrees and allow him to enter her space. The distance between two people standing in a *Closed Position* is usually less than in the open formation.

Direct body pointing in the Closed Position to attempt to get a captive audience

In addition to courtship displays, both may mirror each other's gestures and increase eye contact if they are both interested. The Closed Position can also be used between people who are hostile towards each other in order to issue a challenge.

Research has shown that men fear attack from the front and are more wary of a frontal approach, while women fear attack from behind and are wary of approaches from the rear. So never stand front-on with a male you have just met. He perceives it as aggression from a man and sexual interest from a woman. If you are male, it's acceptable to approach a woman from the front and eventually you can angle yourself to 45 degrees.

How We Exclude Others

The next illustration shows the 45-degree *Open Position* taken by the first two people, which invites a third person to join in the conversation.

Open triangular position encouraging the entry of a third person

If a third person wants to join two others who are standing in a Closed Position, he'll be invited only when the other two angle their bodies to form the triangle. If the third person is not accepted, the others will hold the Closed Position and turn only their heads towards him as a sign of recognition; and they will probably give tight-lipped smiles.

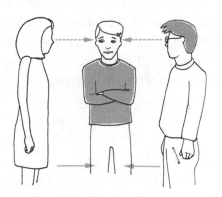

Time to leave – the new person is not accepted by the others

A conversation between three people may begin in the open triangle position but eventually two people may take the Closed Position to exclude the third person. This group formation is a clear signal to the third person that he should leave the group to avoid embarrassment.

Seated Body Pointing

Crossing the knees towards another person shows a sign of interest in or acceptance of that person. If the other person also becomes interested, he will cross knees towards the first person. As the two people become more involved with each other they begin to mirror each other's movements and gestures.

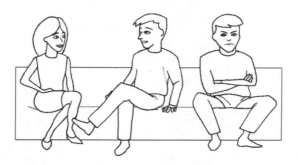

Body Pointing is used to close off a couple
and exclude the man on the right

In the picture above, the man and woman to the left have formed a closed position that excludes all others, such as the man on the right. The only way in which the man on the right could participate in the conversation would be to move a chair to a position in front of the couple and attempt to form a triangle, or take some other action to break their closed formation. But, for now, they'd like him to take a long walk off a short pier.

Foot Pointing

Not only do the feet serve as pointers indicating the direction in which a person's mind is going, they also point at people who we find the most interesting or attractive. Imagine you are at a social function and you notice a group of three men and one woman. The conversation seems to be dominated by the men, and the woman is just listening. Then you notice that the men all have their front foot pointing towards the woman.

Feet signalling what's
on the owner's mind

With this simple non-verbal cue, the men are each telling the woman they're interested in her. On a subconscious level, she sees the foot gestures and is likely to stay with the group for as long as she is receiving this attention. She's standing with both feet together (neutral) and could eventually point one foot towards the man she finds the most interesting.

Summary

Few people ever consider the effect that body and foot pointing play in influencing the attitudes and the responses of others. If you want to make others feel comfortable use the 45-degree Open Position and, when you need to exert pressure, use the direct body point. The 45-degree position allows the other person to think and act independently, without feeling pressured. Never approach men directly from the front or women from behind.

These body pointing skills take a little practice to master but they can become natural before long. In your day-to-day encounters with others, foot pointing, body pointing and positive gesture clusters such as open arms, visible palms, leaning forward, head tilting and smiling can make it easy for others not only to enjoy your company, but to be influenced by your point of view.

Chapter 15

COURTSHIP DISPLAYS AND ATTRACTION SIGNALS

1. A man and woman approaching on a beach

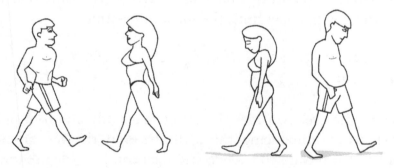

2. They see each other   3. They pass

Dr Albert Scheflen, author of *Body Language and the Social Order*, found that, when a person enters the company of the opposite sex, certain physiological changes take place. He found that high muscle tone became evident in preparation for a possible sexual encounter, 'bagging' around the face and eyes decreased, body sagging disappeared, the chest protruded, the stomach was automatically pulled in, pot-bellied slumping disappeared, the body assumed an erect posture and the person appeared to become more youthful in appearance. He noted that both men and women walked with a livelier, springier gait as a display of health and vitality and to convey their suitability as a partner. A man will stand taller, protrude his jaw and expand his chest to make himself appear dominant. A woman who is interested will respond by emphasising her breasts, tilting her head, touching her hair, exposing her wrists and thereby making herself appear submissive.

The ideal place to observe these changes is on a beach when a man and a woman approach each other from a distance. The changes take place when they are close enough to meet each other's gaze and will continue until after they have passed each other, at which time their original posture returns.

Body language is a fundamental part of courtship because it reveals how available, attractive, ready, enthusiastic, sexy or desperate we are. While some courtship signals are studied and deliberate, others, such as those just mentioned, are completely unconscious. It is still unclear how we learn these signals but research now shows that many may be inborn.

The Emergence of the Colourful Male

In the majority of mammals, it's the male that 'dresses up' to impress the less than colourful females. Humans, however, do it the other way around. For centuries, women have done most of the sexual advertising by decorating themselves in colourful clothing and jewellery and painting their faces. The exception to this was during the sixteenth and seventeenth centuries in Europe when men adorned themselves with beautiful wigs and colourful clothing and out-dressed the average woman. Keep in mind also that, historically, while women have dressed to attract men, men have dressed in clothing to either show status or to frighten away enemies. Today we see the re-emergence of the self-obsessed male who is again beginning to decorate himself like a peacock. We see footballers having facials and manicures, and wrestlers tinting their hair. In the USA we have seen the emergence of the 'metro-sexual' male – a heterosexual male who copies women's behaviour patterns – he has manicures, pedicures and hair colouring, wears fancy clothes, goes to the jacuzzi, eats organic vegetarian food has botox, a face-lift and is in touch with his 'feminine side'. While the 'metro-sexual' male seems an oddity to many straight men, our observation shows 'metro-sexuals' fall into three categories: gay men; effeminate men; and men who realise that assuming traditional female behaviours is a great way to meet lots of women.

Graham's Story

Graham was a man who developed a skill that most men would kill to have.

He would attend a social function and somehow quickly 'scope out' the available women, make his choice and, in almost record-breaking time, would be seen heading towards the exit with her, escorting her to his car and driving back to his apartment. He would return to the function and repeat this process, sometimes several times in the same evening. He seemed to have a built-in radar for finding the available women at the right time and getting them to go with him. No one knew how he did it.

Research by animal courtship behaviour zoologists and behavioural scientists reveals that male and female animals use a series of intricate courtship gestures, some obvious and others subtle, and that most of this is done subconsciously. In the animal world, courtship behaviour in each species follows specific and pre-determined patterns. For example, in several species of bird, the male struts around the female giving a vocal display, puffing up his feathers and performing many intricate body movements to gain her attention, while the female appears to display little or no interest. This ritual is similar to that performed by humans when courtship begins.

Human flirtation involves sequences of gestures and expressions not unlike the courtship dances of birds and other animals, as seen on wildlife programmes.

The bottom line is that when a person wants to attract the opposite sex they do so by emphasising sexual differences. To discourage the opposite sex we play down or hide these differences.

....

Highlighting gender differences is
what makes a person look 'sexy'.

....

Graham's technique was first to spot women whose body language indicated they were available and then to respond with his own male courtship gestures. Those who were interested would return the appropriate female signals, giving him the non-verbal green light to proceed to the next stage.

The success women have in intimate encounters is directly related to their ability to send courtship signals to men and to decode those being sent back. For a man, success in the mating game relies mainly on his ability to read the signals being sent to him, as opposed to being able to initiate his own moves. Most women are aware of courtship signals but men are far less perceptive, often being completely blind to them, which is why so many men have difficulty finding potential mates. Women's difficulty in finding partners is not about reading signals, it's more about finding a man who'll match their criteria.

Graham somehow knew exactly what to look for and women would describe him as sexy, masculine, humorous and 'someone who makes me feel feminine'. This was their reaction to the constant attention he'd give them and the courtship signals he used. Men, on the other hand, described him as 'aggressive', 'insincere', 'arrogant' and 'not particularly funny' – their reaction to the competition Graham represented. Consequently, Graham had few male friends for obvious reasons – no man likes a potential rival for the attentions of his woman. This chapter is devoted to the female signals Graham could see and to the body language he used in return.

Why Women Always Call the Shots

Ask any man who usually makes the first move in courtship and he will invariably say that men do. All studies into courtship, however, show that women are the initiators 90% of the time. A woman does this by sending a series of subtle eye, body and facial signals to the targeted man, who, assuming he is perceptive enough to pick them up, responds to them. There are men who will approach women in a club or bar without being sent the green light but, while some of these men are regularly successful with finding partners, their overall statistical success rate is low because they weren't invited first – they're simply playing the numbers game.

In courtship, women call the tunes most of the time – men do most of the dancing.

In these cases, if a man detects that his approach will be unsuccessful he's likely to pretend he's come to talk to her about other unrelated things and he will use corny lines like, 'You work at the National Bank don't you?' or 'Aren't you John Smith's sister?' To be successful in courtship by playing the numbers game a man has to approach a lot of women to make a sale – unless, of course, he looks like Brad Pitt. Any man who crosses the floor to chat up a woman has usually done so at her request after picking up her body language signals. It just *looks* as if he made the first move because he made the walk across the floor. Women do initiate up to 90% of flirtatious encounters but it is done so subtly that most men think they are the ones taking the lead.

Differences Between Men and Women

Men find it difficult to interpret the more subtle cues in women's body language and research shows that men tend to mistake friendliness and smiling for sexual interest. This is because men see the world in more sexual terms than women; men have 10 to 20 times more testosterone than women, which makes them see the world in terms of sex.

....

To some men, when a lady says 'no' she means maybe; when she says 'maybe' she means 'yes'; but if she says 'yes' she's no lady.

....

When they meet a possible partner, women send out subtle, but often deceptive, courting signals to see whether he's worth pursuing. Women tend to bombard men with courting rituals in the first minutes of meeting them. Men may misinterpret these signals and make a clumsy pass. By sending erratic and ambiguous signals in the early stages, women manipulate men into showing their hand. This is one reason why many women have trouble attracting men – men become confused and won't make an approach.

The Attraction Process

As with other animals, human courtship follows a predictable five-step sequence that we all go through when we meet an attractive person.

Stage 1. Eye contact: She looks across the room and spots a man she fancies. She waits till he notices her then holds his gaze for about five seconds and then turns away. He now keeps watching her to see if she does it again. A woman needs to deliver this gaze, on average, three times before the average man realises what's happening. This gaze process can be repeated several times and is the start of the flirting process.

Stage 2. Smiling: She delivers one or more fleeting smiles. This is a quick half smile that is intended to give a prospective man the green light to make an approach. Unfortunately, many men are not responsive to these signals, leaving the woman feeling that he's not interested in her.

Stage 3. Preening: She sits up straight to emphasise her breasts and crosses her legs or ankles to show them to best advantage or, if she's standing, she tilts her hips and tilts her head sideways towards one shoulder, exposing her bare neck. She plays with her hair for up to six seconds – suggesting she is grooming herself for her man. She may lick her lips, flick her hair and straighten her clothing and jewellery. He'll respond with gestures such as standing up straight, pulling his stomach in, expanding his chest, adjusting his clothing, touching his hair and tucking his thumbs into his belt. They both point their feet or entire bodies towards each other.

Stage 4. Talk: He approaches and attempts to make small talk, using clichés such as, 'Haven't I seen you somewhere before?' and other well-worn lines that are purely intended to break the ice.

Stage 5. Touch: She looks for an opportunity to initiate a light touch on the arm, either 'accidental' or otherwise. A hand touch indicates a higher level of intimacy than a touch on the arm. Each level of touch is then repeated to check that the person is happy with this level of intimacy and to let them know that the first touch was not accidental. Lightly brushing or touching the shoulder of a man is done to give the impression that the woman cares about his health and appearance. Shaking hands is a quick way to move to the touch stage.

These first five stages of courtship may seem minor or even incidental but they are critical to starting any new relationship and are the stages that most people, especially men, find difficult. This chapter will examine the signals that are most likely to be sent by men and women – and Graham - during these stages.

The 13 Most Common Female Courtship Gestures and Signals

Women use most of the same basic preening gestures as men, including touching the hair, smoothing the clothing, one or both hands on hips, foot and body pointing towards the man, extended intimate gaze and increasing eye contact. Some women will also adopt the thumbs-in-belt gesture, which, although it's a male assertion gesture, is used more subtly: usually only one thumb is tucked into a belt or protrudes from a handbag or pocket.

Women become more sexually active in the middle of their menstrual cycle, when they are most likely to conceive. It's during this time that they are more likely to wear shorter dresses and higher heels, to walk, talk, dance and act more provocatively and to use the signals we are about to discuss. What follows is a list of the 13 most common courtship gestures and signals used by women everywhere to show a man that she could be available.

1. The Head Toss and Hair Flick

This is usually the first display a woman will use when she's around a man she fancies. The head is flicked back to toss the hair over the shoulders or away from the face. Even women with short hair will use this gesture. It's a way for a woman subtly to show that she cares about how she looks to a man. This also lets her expose her armpit, which allows the 'sex perfume' known as pheromone to waft across to the target man.

Preening the hair and letting pheromones
in the armpit work their magic

2. Wet Lips and Pouting, Mouth Slightly Open

At puberty, a boy's facial bone structure alters dramatically as testosterone gives him a stronger, protruding jaw-line, larger nose and more pronounced forehead – all the essentials for protection to the face during encounters with animals or enemies. Girls' bone structure remains largely unchanged and child-like with more subcutaneous fat, which makes the female adolescent face appear thicker and fuller, particularly the lips. Larger, thicker lips therefore become a signal of femaleness because of their contrast in size to male lips. Some women have collagen injected into their lips to overstate this sexual difference and thereby make themselves more appealing to men. Pouting simply increases the lip display.

A woman's outer genital lips are proportionately the same thickness to her facial lips. Desmond Morris describes this as 'self-mimi-cry', as it is intended to symbolise the female genital region. The lips can be made to appear wet either by the use of saliva or cosmetics, giving a woman the appearance of sexual invitation.

When a woman becomes sexually aroused her lips, breasts and genitals become larger and redder as they fill with blood. The use of lipstick is an Egyptian invention that is four thousand years old and is intended to

Sex sirens instinctively know how to use mouth and lip displays to get attention

mimic facially the reddened genitals of the sexually aroused female. This explains why, in experiments using photos of women wearing various lipstick colours, men consistently find the bright reds the most attractive and sensual.

3. Self-Touching

As stated earlier, our minds get our bodies to act out our secret desires – and so it is with *Self-Touching*. Women have dramatically more nerve sensors for experiencing touch than men, making them more sensitive to touch sensations. When a woman slowly and sensually strokes her thigh, neck or throat it infers that, if a man plays his cards right, he may be able to touch her in these same ways. At the same time, her self-touch lets her imagine what it might feel like if the man was initiating the touch.

Most pictures of women in sensual poses include plenty of Self-Touching

4. The Limp Wrist

Walking or sitting while holding a *Limp Wrist* is a submission signal used exclusively by women and gay men. In a similar way, a bird feigns a damaged wing to distract prey away from its nest. In other words, it's a great

Birds will feign an injured wing to get attention; women use a Limp Wrist attention getter. It's very attractive to men because it makes them feel as if they can dominate. In business situations, however, a Limp Wrist seriously detracts from a woman's credibility and others will fail to take her seriously, although some men will probably ask her for a date.

The stem of the wine glass suggesting things that may yet come

5. Fondling a Cylindrical Object

Fondling cigarettes, a finger, the stem of a wine glass, a dangling earring or any phallic-shaped object is an unconscious indication of what may be in the mind. Taking a ring off and on the finger can also be a mental representation of having sex. When a woman does these things, a man is likely to symbolically try to possess her by fondling her cigarette lighter, car keys or any personal item she has nearby.

6. Exposed Wrists

An interested woman will gradually expose the smooth, soft underside skin of her wrists to the potential male partner and will increase the rate she flashes her wrists as her interest grows. The wrist area has long been considered one of the highly erotic areas of the female body because it is one of the

Exposing the soft under side of the wrists is a powerful attraction signal

more delicate skin areas; it's uncertain whether this is a learned behaviour or is innate but it certainly operates on an unconscious level. The palms are also usually made visible to the man while she's speaking. Women who smoke cigarettes find this wrist/palm exposure simple to do while smoking by simply holding the palm up beside the shoulder. The *Exposed Wrist* and head toss gestures are often mimicked by homosexual males who want to take on a feminine appearance.

Women put perfume on the underside of the wrist believing it has something to do with the wrist pulse distributing the perfume. But its real purpose is to thrust the wrist forward towards a potential partner. The perfume simply draws attention to the woman and lets the man see her under-wrists.

7. Sideways Glance Over Raised Shoulder

The Raised Shoulder is self-mimicry of the rounded female breasts. With partially drooped eyelids, the woman holds the man's gaze just long enough for him to notice, then she quickly looks away. This action produces the feeling of peeping in the woman who does it and being peeped at by the man who receives it.

Raising the shoulder highlights the femaleness
of roundness and curves

8. Rolling Hips

For childbearing reasons, women have wider hips than men and have a wider crotch gap between the legs. This means that when a woman walks she has an accentuated roll which highlights her pelvic region. Men can't walk like this, so it becomes a powerful sex difference signal. It also explains why few women are good runners because their wider hips make their legs splay out to the side when they run. Rolling of the hips is one of the subtle female courtship gestures that has been used for centuries in advertising to sell goods and services. Women who see these advertisements have the desire to be like the model depicted, which results in an increased awareness of the product being promoted.

Wiggling when you walk highlights the
differences between men and women

9. The Pelvic Tilt

Medical evidence shows that a woman in excellent health and
most capable of successfully bearing children has a waist-to-
hips ratio of 70%, that is, her waist is 70% the size of her hips.
This gives her what's known as an hourglass figure. Throughout recorded history this is the body ratio that has proved the
most dramatic male attention-grabber. Men begin to lose
interest when the ratio exceeds 80% and, for most men, the
greater or lesser the ratio the less attentive he will be. He completely loses interest when her ratio reaches 100% but still
maintains a level of interest even when it drops below 70%,
but 70% still remains the perfect ratio for reproductive
success. The way a woman highlights this ratio is simple – she
simply tilts her pelvis when she stands.

*Tilting the pelvis while standing highlights a
woman's ability to bear children successfully.*

Professor Devendra Singh, an evolutionary psychologist at the University of Texas, studied the physical attractiveness of Miss America beauty contestants and *Playboy* centrefolds over a period of 50 years and found that the hips-to-waist ratio that holds the greatest appeal for men is between 67% and 80%.

Professor Singh conducted a test using images of women who were underweight, overweight and of average weight and showed them to groups of men who were asked to rate them in terms of their attractiveness. Women of average weight with a hips-to-waist ratio of around 70% were found to be the most alluring. In the overweight and underweight groups, the women with the narrowest

Kylie Minogue with a cocktail of the things all men love – long hair, neck display, 70% hips-to-waist ratio, open wet mouth, pouting, drooping eyelids, protruding breasts and rounded buttocks, self-touching and Hand-on-Hip gestures

waist got the vote. The experiment's remarkable finding was that men gave the 70% hips-to-waist ratio the highest rating even when the woman's weight was quite heavy. This means a woman can be physically larger but will still turn male heads if she has this ratio.

10. Handbag in Close Proximity

Most men have never seen the contents of a woman's handbag and studies show that most men are afraid even to touch her handbag, let alone open it. A woman's handbag is a personal item that's treated by her almost as if it's an extension of her body and so it becomes a strong signal of intimacy when she puts it close to a man. If she finds him particularly attractive, she may slowly fondle and caress her handbag. She can ask him to pass the handbag or to even retrieve something from it.

Placing the handbag near him so he can see it or touch it is a strong signal she's interested; keeping it away from him indicates emotional distance.

Placing her handbag close to a man is a sign of acceptance

11. The Knee Point

One leg is tucked under the other and points to the person she finds the most interesting. This is a relaxed position, which also takes the formality out of a conversation and gives the opportunity for a fleeting exposure of the thighs.

Pointing her knee at the most interesting person

12. The Shoe Fondle

Dangling the shoe on the end of the foot also indicates a relaxed attitude and has the phallic effect of thrusting the foot in and out of the shoe. This action unsettles many men without them knowing what is happening.

The shoe gives a clue

The Leg-Twine: men's number
one female sitting position

13. The Leg Twine

Most men agree that the *Leg Twine* is the most appealing sitting position a woman can take. It's a gesture that women consciously use to draw attention to their legs. Albert Scheflen states that one leg is pressed firmly against the other to give the appearance of high muscle tone, which, as previously mentioned, is a condition that the body takes when a person is ready for sexual performance.

Other leg signals used by women include crossing and uncrossing the legs slowly in front of the man and gently stroking the thighs with her hand, indicating a desire to be touched.

Without referring back to what you have just read,
how many courting signals and gestures can you see?

What Men Look At in Women's Bodies

In *Why Men Lie & Women Cry* (Orion) we summarised the research about which body parts men and women look at on each other. The research was clear – men's brains are wired to be attracted to women who show the most healthy reproductive ability and sexual availability. When it comes to body shape, both men and women prefer someone with an athletic body shape. To men, this signals high levels of health and a woman's ability to successfully reproduce his genes.

Evidence shows that men are more attracted to women with a child-like face – large eyes, small noses, full lips and cheeks – because these signals evoke paternal, protective feelings in most men. This is why most advertising for cosmetic surgery places so much emphasis on these features. Women, conversely, prefer men with adult faces that show the ability to defend – strong jaws, larger brows and strong nose.

Women with child-like faces cause the release of hormones in men that make them want to protect females.

The good news is that a woman doesn't need to be naturally beautiful to attract a man – beauty certainly gives her an initial edge over competitors – she mainly needs to be able to display the signs that she *could* be available. This is why some women who are not particularly physically attractive always seem to have plenty of suitors. Overall, a man is more attracted to a woman by the signs of her availability than by her physical attractiveness, and you can learn and practise availability signals. Some women are appalled at the idea of modern men being initially attracted to a woman based on her appearance and availability instead of wanting her for her ability to nurture, communicate, be a domestic goddess or play the piano. They see discussions on this subject as degrading to modern women.

But almost every study into attraction conducted over the last 60 years reached the same conclusions as the painters, poets and writers over the past 6000 years – a woman's appearance and body and what she can do with it is more attractive to men than her intelligence or assets, even in the politically correct twenty-first century. The twenty-first-century man wants the same immediate things in a woman as his forefathers did at first sight, but, as we said in *Why Men Lie & Women Cry*, he has different criteria for a long-term partner.

The reality is that you need to attract a man first before he can find out about all your inner virtues. When you go fishing you bait the hook with what the fish likes, not with what you like. Have you ever tasted a worm? You might be repulsed by the thought but, for a fish, it's his favourite dish.

How Beautiful People Miss Out

Most people are tempted to believe that physical appearance is the key to attracting a potential partner, but this is largely an idea promoted by television, films and the media. Extremely attractive people are rare, and are erroneously promoted as the standard to which we should all aspire, but studies show that most of us are sceptical about beautiful people. The studies found that we prefer to find mates who are roughly as attractive as we are, which means they are more likely to stay and not look for a better offer. This preference appears to be inborn, as babies show a preference for looking at average faces rather than at beautiful ones.

Is He a Bum, Boobs or Leg Man?

When it comes to a man's favourite female body part, men are universally split into three fairly even groups – boobs, bums and legs.

In this section, we will be analysing only the physical characteristics of the female body and why each part has such an impact on the male senses. A woman's body has evolved as a permanent, portable sexual signalling system which is purpose-built to attract male attention for reproduction and bums, breasts and legs play the most significant part in this process. This may not be politically correct, but it is biologically correct.

1. Bums

Men find rounded, peach-shaped buttocks the most attractive. Female human buttocks differ from other primates in that other primate females display enlarged, protruding buttocks only when they are ready for mating. Human females display enlarged buttocks permanently and are almost always sexually available to males. This is because one of the main purposes of regular human sexual activity is to encourage long-term pair-bonding for the successful rearing of children.

Female humans are the only primates with permanently enlarged buttocks

Humans are the only primates that mate face-to-face – in other primate species, the males approach females from the rear and use her swollen red buttocks as a signal that she's ready for mating. And therein lies the key to men's attraction to women's bums – they always give the impression that she's available for him. Women's buttocks also have two other purposes: they store fat for breastfeeding and act as an emergency food storage in lean times, similar to a camel's hump.

Wearing designer jeans has also become popular because they highlight the buttocks and give them a firm, rounded look. High-heeled shoes make the wearer arch her back, push out her buttocks, and make her wiggle when she walks, which invariably draws male attention. Marilyn Monroe reputedly chopped three-quarters of an inch (2cm) off the heel of her left shoe to emphasise her wiggle. The females of several species of beetle also wiggle their rears in front of potential mates to attract attention.

2. The Breasts

Most of the world has developed an obsession with breasts in recent years and cleavage and cosmetic breast enhancement is now a multi-billion dollar business. This is remarkable considering that human breasts are little more than enlarged sweat glands.

Most of the breast consists of fat tissue. This gives them their rounded shape and most of this tissue is not involved in milk production.

Overall, breasts serve one clear purpose – sexual signalling. Breasts mimic a woman's rear view – a relic from the days when humans walked on all fours. If a monkey or chimp walked towards you on two legs you'd be unable to tell whether it was male or female. Humans walk upright on two legs and enlarged female breasts evolved as a mimic of the female rear. Tests conducted with pictures of bum cracks and breast cleavage convincingly show that most men are unable to differentiate one crack from the other.

Tests show that most men can't tell the difference between a bum crack and cleavage

Low-cut dresses and push-up bras emphasise this signal by creating cleavage. Fortunately, nearly all sex research surveys show that men love breasts in most shapes and sizes – it's the cleavage that stimulates men the most. It doesn't matter whether a woman's breasts are the size of a small lemon or look like watermelons – most men are keenly interested in them all and love a cleavage. A woman who is attracted to a man is likely to lean forward and bring her arms closer to her body, which presses her breasts together and makes a cleavage.

BEFORE   AFTER

Mona Lisa after two weeks in the USA

Men's favourite breasts are those of a woman at her sexual and reproductive peak – in her late teens and early twenties. These are typical of the breasts seen in men's magazine centrefolds, on erotic dancers and in advertisements that trade on sex appeal.

Researchers at Purdue University in America found that a woman hitchhiker can double the number of lifts she is offered by increasing her bust size by adding 2 inches (5cm) of padding.

When Someone is 'Hot Stuff'

The core temperature for the human body is 98.6 degrees Fahrenheit but the skin temperature varies depending on our emotional state. As mentioned earlier, people who are described as 'cold' and 'stand-offish' are usually also physically cooler people because their blood is drawn into the leg and arm muscles for the 'fight or flight' response created by tension. So when you call someone a 'cold fish' you are correct on both the emotional and physical levels. Conversely, when one person is attracted to another, their blood rises to the surface of the skin, making them warmer. This is why lovers who are in the 'heat of passion', give a 'warm embrace', have 'steamy encounters' and can be 'hot stuff'. In many women, this increase in body temperature can be seen as their chests will become flushed or covered in red blotches and their cheeks also flush.

If you're a man, you just got your money's worth in the last section.

3. The Lure of Long Legs

There is a biological reason why men love women's long legs. When a girl reaches puberty, her legs undergo rapid lengthening as hormones flood her body and change her into a woman. Her extra long legs become a powerful non-verbal signal telling males she is sexually maturing and is now capable of childbearing. This is why long legs have always been associated with potent female sexuality.

Supermodels and filmstars have disproportionate bodies that have retained their pubescent long legs

Men love high heels on a woman because it gives her the illusion of having fertile-looking legs. High heels enhance a woman's sexual shape by lengthening her legs, arching her back, forcing her buttocks to protrude, making her feet appear smaller and thrusting her pelvis forward. This is why the shoe with the highest heel – the stiletto – with its bondage straps, is by far the most efficient sex aide on the market.

> *High heels lengthen a woman's legs, make her buttocks sway and her breasts protrude.*

Most men also prefer a woman with shapely, thicker legs over those with thinner, spindly legs, because additional fat in the legs highlights the sex difference between male and female legs and is an indicator of better lactation. Men like women's legs to look athletic but will be turned off if she looks like she could play football for England.

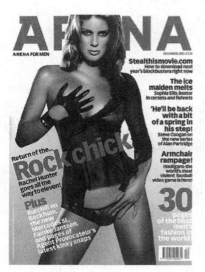

Models such as Elle MacPherson and Rachel Hunter turned female attraction signals into a multi-million dollar business

Male Courtship Signals and Gestures

Male displays involve the show of power, wealth and status. If you're a woman, you'll probably be disappointed with our summary of male courtship signals because, compared to those of women, there aren't too many. While a woman will dress sensually, wear make-up and use a wide range of courtship gestures, men rev their car engines, brag about how much they earn and challenge other men. When it comes to courtship rituals, most men are as effective as someone standing in a river trying to catch fish by hitting them on the head with a big stick. Women have more lures and fishing skills to land their fish than any male could ever hope to acquire.

In this section we'll cover the most common male body language signals you're likely to see, much of which is focused around his crotch. Men are generally not good at sending or receiving the signals used in the mating game and, as we mentioned earlier, women not only control the game and make the rules, they own the scoreboard. Most of the time, men simply react to signals they see.

Some magazines try to convince readers that men's courtship skills are improving because of the increase in the numbers of men who are paying more attention to their appearance. Men now have facials, do their nails and toenails, tint their hair, straighten their teeth, use hair conditioner and face creams and wear face powder. In the UK in 2004, a study by Gillette showed that Scotsmen were Britain's most vain men, spending an average of 16 minutes a day in front of a mirror preening themselves. But most of this behaviour is an increase in male vanity levels – not in men's ability to read women's courtship signals.

An American survey found the three words women
would most like to hear from their male partner were
not 'I love you'. They were 'you've lost weight'

As with most male animals, the human male displays preening behaviour as a potential partner arrives on the scene. In addition to the automatic physiological reactions already mentioned, he will straighten his tie, smooth his collar, brush imaginary dust from his shoulder and touch his cufflinks or watch, and rearrange his shirt, coat and other clothing.

Male tie-preening gesture

Why Men Talk to Women at the Beginning of a Relationship

Many men understand that talking at length to a woman about the personal intimate details of his or her life wins points and can open her mind – and more – to him. At the beginning of a new relationship a man will often use the talking strategy but after the honeymoon period he's likely to go back to his stereotypical behaviour of not talking – sticking only to facts, information and solutions to problems when he does talk.

The Male Crotch Obsession

The most direct sexual display a man can make towards a woman is the aggressive thumbs-in-belt gesture that highlights his crotch. He may also turn his body towards her and point his foot at her, use an intimate gaze and hold her gaze for longer than usual. When he's seated or leaning against a wall, he may also spread his legs to display his crotch.

In troops of baboons, and with several other primates, males display their dominance by using a penis display. By spreading their legs to give others a full view of the size of their wedding tackle and giving it the occasional adjustment from time to time, they can constantly assert and reassert their dominant status. This same display is used by human males to assert their manhood, though it is more subtle than the baboons, mainly because of the hefty prison sentence the baboon display would carry.

The fifteenth century saw the introduction of the not-so-subtle codpiece, which purported to display the size of a man's masculinity and therefore his social status. In the twenty-first century, New Guinea natives still employ penis displays, while Western men can achieve the same effect with tight-fitting pants, small-size Speedo swimming trunks or dangling a large bunch of keys or the long end of a belt in front of his crotch.

These hanging objects give a man the opportunity to reach down from time to time for any necessary adjustments. Most women can't imagine being in a public place and reaching down to scratch their crotch and are amazed that men will do this nonchalantly and with regularity. It's the same message for all male primates, they just use different approaches.

Belt and crotch-grabbing while dancing are some of the less subtle forms of crotch display.

This Mek warrior from Irian Jaya with his traditional penis sheath leaves no one confused about the message

The Crotch Adjust

The most common form of public male sexual display is the *Crotch Adjust*. Women everywhere complain that they will be talking with a man and suddenly, for no apparent reason, he will begin adjusting or handling his crotch. The inference is that his genitalia are so large and cumbersome that they need constant attention to prevent the cut-off of blood circulation.

The great thing about being a man is you don't have to leave the room to adjust yourself.

Watch any group of young males together, especially where macho attitudes are encouraged, such as in sporting teams, and you will see continual crotch adjustment as each male unconsciously tries to assert his masculinity in front of the others. Women are horrified when a man then proceeds to get her a drink using the same hand he just used for his adjustments and he then greets people with a handshake.

Wearing a Tie to One Side

If you're a man and you want to find out which women like you, wear a neatly pressed suit and tie, but wear the tie slightly off to one side and put a little lint on one shoulder. Any women who find you attractive can't resist brushing the lint off and straightening your tie so that you look just right.

Wearing the tie slightly off-centre gives interested women the opportunity to straighten it

Men's Bodies – What Turns Women On the Most

Surveys show that women continually express a preference for men with deeper, smoother voices because deep tones are directly linked to testosterone levels. The change in voice tone is noticeable in boys because, when they reach puberty, their bodies flood with male hormones as they begin to change into men and their voices 'crack' virtually overnight. When a man is around a woman he fancies he's likely to start speaking in deeper tones to highlight his masculinity while a responsive woman is likely to start talking in higher pitched tones to contrast her femaleness. Since the feminist movement began in the 1960s, women have taken on male job roles and tasks that require the production of testosterone, the hormone that drives us to achieve and that has been described as the 'success hormone'. Research now shows that in countries such as the USA, United Kingdom, Australia and New Zealand where feminism has been more influential, women's voices have become deeper because women have become more assertive and authoritative. Hopefully, the hairy chest won't follow.

Is She a Chest, Legs or Bum Gal?

Women's sexual responses to men are triggered visually by

certain aspects of the male body. When it comes to a woman's favourite male body parts, women are also universally split into three groups – legs, bums and chests/arms with bums taking 40% of the votes for first prize. In this section, we will be analysing only the physical characteristics of the male body and why each part has such an impact on the female senses.

Overall, women also look for athletic body shape, broad shoulders, muscular chest and arms and a tight butt. Even in the twenty-first century, surveys overwhelmingly show women still want a man who looks as if he can wrestle animals and fight off invaders.

> *Male bodies are purpose built to chase, catch and wrestle animals, carry heavy things and kill spiders.*

1. Broad Shoulders, Chest and Muscular Arms

The upper torso of the hunting male is wide and tapers to narrow hips, whereas a woman's body is narrower at the shoulders and widens at the hips. Men evolved these features

Women are attracted to a well-defined male upper body, but most dislike the 'muscle man' body-builder look; a woman feels he is likely to be more interested in his own beauty than in hers.

to allow them to lug heavy weapons over long distances and carry home their kills.

The male chest developed to house large lungs enabling more effective distribution of oxygen and allowing him to breathe more efficiently when running and chasing. In past generations, the bigger his chest, the more respect and power a man commanded, and this is still the case with most surviving primitive tribes.

2. The Small, Tight Bum

A small, compact bum is the favourite of women everywhere but few understand its magnetic attraction. The secret is that a tight, muscular rear is necessary to make the strong forward thrusting motion needed for successful sperm transfer during sex. A man with a fat or flabby *derrière* has difficulty with this forward movement and has a tendency to throw his entire body weight into the thrust. For women, this isn't ideal, as the man's weight can be uncomfortable on her and make it difficult to breathe. By contrast, the small, tight rear promises a greater chance of doing an effective job.

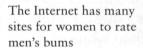
The Internet has many sites for women to rate men's bums

3. Narrow Hips and Muscular Legs

Men's legs are attractive to women only insofar as they are symbols of masculine power and endurance. The powerful, angular legs of the human male are the longest of all primates and his narrow hips allow him to run swiftly over long distances to chase and hunt. Women's wide hips cause many women to have difficulty running, as their lower legs and feet often flay out to the side to balance body weight. Leading US neuropsychology professor Dr Devendra Singh discovered that women find male hips with a 90% waist-to-hips ratio the most appealing.

Summary

The world is in the grip of a singles epidemic. In all Western countries, marriage rates are the lowest they've been in 100 years – half the rate of 25 years ago. In places such as Australia, 28% of adults have never married.

The fact that men and women are initially motivated by body features may be disheartening to some but, on the plus side, everyone has the chance to improve their appearance and make a conscious decision to increase their attractiveness to the opposite sex. For those who choose to stay as they are, online dating, IT matchmaking, flirt-a-thons and speed-dating events are booming everywhere and the *New York Times* estimated that it had an annual turnover of 3 billion dollars worldwide in 2003. And because men have more difficulty than women in meeting the opposite sex, most flirting classes worldwide have more male attendees than women.

Chapter 16

OWNERSHIP, TERRITORY AND HEIGHT SIGNALS

We stake a physical claim on what we believe is ours

We lean against other people or objects to show a territorial claim to that person or object. Leaning against something can also be used as a method of dominance or intimidation if the object being leaned on belongs to someone else. For example, if you are going to take a photograph of a friend and his new car, boat or personal belonging, it's likely that he'd lean against his new possession, put his foot on it or place his arm around it. When he touches the property, it becomes an extension of his body and this is how he shows others that it belongs to him. Lovers hold hands or put their arms around each other in public to show competitors they have a claim over that person. The business executive puts his feet on his desk or leans against his office doorway to show his claim to that office and its furnishings. A woman dusts imaginary pieces of lint from the shoulder of her husband to tell other women he's taken.

People showing ownership by connecting
the item to their body

Victoria Beckham confirms her claim to David Beckham by imprinting her hand on his chest

An easy way to intimidate someone is to lean against, sit on or use their possessions without their permission. In addition to the obvious abuse of another's territory or possessions, such as sitting at his desk or borrowing his car without asking, there are many other subtle intimidation techniques. One is to lean against the doorway in another person's office or to sit in his chair.

A salesperson calling on a customer at his home should ask, 'Which chair is yours?' before he sits, because sitting in the wrong chair intimidates its owner and puts him offside.

The doorway intimidator

Some people are habitual doorway leaners and go through life intimidating everyone from first introduction. These people are well advised to practise an upright stance with palms visible to create a favourable impression on others. Others form up to 90% of their opinion about us in the first four minutes and you never get a second chance to make a first impression.

Michael Jackson's purpose in his infamous 'baby dangling' incident was to close the distance between the baby and the fans so that they could experience temporary 'ownership' of the baby. He just overlooked the distance between the baby and the ground.

If the boss's chair has no arms – which is unlikely as this is usually a feature of the visitor's chair – he may be seen with one or both feet on the desk. If his superior enters the office, it is unlikely that the boss – who is now the subordinate – would continue to use such an obvious territorial/ownership gesture, but instead would resort to more subtle versions such as putting his foot on the bottom drawer of his desk, or, if there

319

are no drawers in the desk, placing his foot hard against the leg of the desk to stake his claim to it.

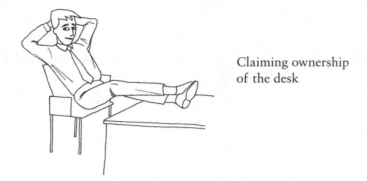

Claiming ownership of the desk

Body Lowering and Status

Historically, raising or lowering the height of your body in front of another person has been used as a means of establishing superior–subordinate relationships. We refer to a member of royalty as 'Your Highness', whereas individuals who commit unsavoury acts are called 'low', 'low down' and 'low lifes'. No one wants to be described as 'short-sighted', be 'looked down on' or 'fall short' of their targets. The protest rally speaker stands on a soapbox to be higher than everyone else, the judge sits higher than the rest of the court, the Olympic gold medal winner stands higher than the other medal winners, those who live in a penthouse command more authority than those who live at ground level, some cultures divide their social classes into the 'upper class' and 'lower class' and pharmacists stand 18 inches above everyone else.

Superior people can sometimes get on their 'high horses', 'rise to the occasion', 'put themselves on a pedestal' or become 'high and mighty'. And no self-respecting God would ever live down in the boondocks, on the salt flats or in the valley. They live in Valhalla, on Mount Olympus or in Heaven above. And everyone understands the significance of standing to speak to a meeting to gain control.

We reduce our height to show subordination to
others and increase height to gain status

Most women curtsey when they meet royalty and men incline
their heads or remove their hats, making themselves appear
smaller than the royal person. The modern salute is a relic of
the act of removing a hat to make oneself appear shorter. The
person symbolically goes to remove their hat and the salute is
the modern result. Today's hatless man can still be seen giving
a simple tap to his forehead when he meets a woman as a relic
of his hat-doffing ancestors' habit. The more humble or subordinate an individual feels towards another, the lower he
stoops his body.

*Some people described Roger as the backbone
of the organisation. Others didn't go that high.*

Some Japanese businesses have reintroduced the 'bowing
machine', which teaches staff the exact angle to bow to a customer, usually 15 degrees for a customer who is 'just looking'
and up to 45 degrees for a purchaser. In business, the people

who continually 'bow' to the management are labelled with derogatory name-tags such as 'bootlickers', 'crawlers' and 'brown-nosers'.

He's a Big Man Around Town

Despite what it may be politically correct to believe about height, studies convincingly show that taller people are more successful, healthier and live longer than short people. Dr Bruce Ellis, Head of Experimental Psychology at the University of Canterbury in New Zealand, found that taller men also have greater reproductive success than shorter men, not only because increased testosterone levels are linked to tallness but also because women choose men who are taller than they are as partners. Taller men are seen as more protective and can pass this advantage on through their genes. Men prefer shorter women because it gives men the apparent height advantage.

The shorter you are the more likely it is that you will be interrupted by men. One of our clients, a 5 feet 1 inch (1.55m) female senior manager in a predominately male accounting firm, complained that she was continually being interrupted by her peers at management meetings and it was rare for her to present her ideas fully or even finish her sentences. We devised a strategy that required her to stand and go to the coffee table and, when she returned to her seat, remain standing as she spoke and presented her thoughts. She was amazed at the difference it made to how she was received. While she can't use the coffee routine every time, it allowed her to see how, by simply adjusting her height perspective, she could gain more authority.

You always see taller men with shorter women but rarely the reverse.

In our seminars, we constantly observe how top-level managers are significantly taller than everyone else. Through the Institutes of Management, we recorded the height and salaries of 2565 managers at company director level and found that every inch of height above the company norm added almost £400 to that person's salary package, regardless of whether the person was a man or a woman. Research in the USA showed that height is also linked to financial success: on Wall Street every inch of height added £340 to each person's bottom line. The same correlation has even been found in government departments and universities, who supposedly promote people based on their competence level and equality, not their height. One American study showed that tall people not only got the best jobs in American firms, they received higher starting salaries. Those over 6 feet 2 inches (1.9m) got 12% more than those under 6 feet (1.85m).

Why Some People Seem Taller on TV

People who are 'perceived' as tall also do better in politics on television: on-screen people are only six inches tall (15cm) so we are left subconsciously to decide how tall the person really is. The height we decide they are and the amount of power we give them is directly related to the power and authority of their presentation. This is why so many short actors, politicians and personalities do so well on television – they simply act tall. For example, Australian Prime Minister John Howard became stuck with the nickname 'Little Johnny' because, on television, his approach was softer and quiet. Our surveys found that the voting electorate perceived him as 5 feet 6 inches (1.67m) – reasonably short for a man – whereas in fact he was 5 feet 9 inches (1.75m). One of his adversaries, former Prime Minister Bob Hawke, was constantly seen as over 6 feet (1.85m) tall as he always gave a 'big' performance. In fact, he was 5 feet 7 inches (1.7m) tall.

---

*On television, a strong performance
makes you seem taller.*

Pioneering research by Wilson (1968) found that when a student addressed other students, he would be seen as 5 feet 8 1/2 inches (1.75m) tall by the other students. When the same student was introduced as a professor, the audience perceived him as 6 feet 3 inches (1.9m) tall. A powerful performance or an impressive title both lead to you being perceived as taller.

Try the Floor Test

If you want to test the authority that goes with height, try this exercise with a friend. First, lie on the floor and get your friend to stand over you to maximise the height difference. Next, ask your friend to reprimand you as loudly and forcefully as he can. Then change positions – you stand, he lies down – and ask him to repeat his reprimand. You'll find that not only does he find it nearly impossible to do, his voice will sound different and he'll lack any authority while trying.

The Downsides of Height

Being tall, however, is not always a bonus. While tall people often command more respect than short people, height can also be detrimental to some aspects of one-to-one communication, for instance where you need to 'talk on the same level' or have an 'eye-to-eye' discussion with another person and do not want to be perceived as 'too big for your boots'.

In Britain, Philip Heinricy, a 6 feet 8 inches (2m) tall chemical salesperson, formed the Tall Person's Club to promote the practical, medical and social needs of the taller members of society. He found that his height was threatening to his customers; they felt imposed upon and could not concentrate on what he had to say. He discovered that when he gave a sales presentation in a seated position, not only did the atmosphere become more conducive to good communication, the removal of his physical threat also increased his bottom line sales by a whopping 62%.

How Body Lowering Can Sometimes Raise Status

There are some circumstances in which lowering your body can be a dominance signal. This happens when you slouch down and make yourself comfortable in an easy chair in another person's home while the owner is standing. It's the complete informality on the other person's territory that communicates the dominant or aggressive attitude.

A person will always be superior and protective on his own territory, especially in his own home, and so practising submissive gestures and behaviour is effective for getting the person on side with you.

How TV Politicians Can Win Votes

For over three decades, we have advised people who appear in the public eye on how to be seen as credible and believable. They have ranged from rock stars and politicians to weather forecasters and Prime Ministers. On one occasion, two political leaders were invited to give two television debates about how they would run the country. One candidate – call him candidate A – was 5 feet 9 inches (1.75m) and was seen by voters as shorter due to his milder, quieter approach, while his competitor – candidate B – was 6 feet 2 inches (1.9m) and perceived by the electorate as even taller due to his assertive, authoritative attitude. After the first TV debate, the shorter candidate was seen as having lost badly to the taller one. Candidate A called us for advice and we suggested a number of strategies including cutting 4 inches (10cm) off his lectern, which would give the same visible distance between the top of the lectern and his chin as candidate B had. We also suggested that A should arrange for his TV camera to be slightly lowered to shoot upwards, giving him a taller appearance. We told him to pitch his message directly to the camera so that each voter felt as if they were being addressed personally. It worked. After the next debate, candidate A was seen as being the clear winner and the media reported that he 'had a new sense of authority and leadership'. After the election that followed, candidate A became leader of the country. The lessons here were that voters generally aren't deeply interested and don't remember much of what politicians say in election debates. Voters cast their final vote based on the belief that the winner is best suited to be the leader.

How to Placate Angry People

It's possible to avoid intimidating others by consciously making yourself appear smaller in relation to them. Let's examine the body language of the situation in which you have committed a minor driving offence, such as failing to stop at a stop sign, not giving way or speeding, and you are pulled over by the police. In these circumstances, the officer may regard you as an adversary as he approaches your vehicle, and most drivers' reaction is to remain in the car, wind the window down and make excuses or deny the offence. The body language negatives of this are:

1. The officer is forced to leave his territory (the patrol car) and come across to your territory (your vehicle).
2. Assuming that you are in fact guilty, your excuses may represent an attack to the officer.
3. By remaining in your car, you create a barrier between yourself and the police officer.

Considering that under these circumstances the police officer is in the superior position to you, this behaviour serves only to make things go from bad to worse and your chances of getting a ticket are increased. Instead, try this if you are pulled over:

1. Immediately get out of your car (your territory) and go fowards to the police officer's car (his territory). In this way he is not inconvenienced by having to leave his space. (Don't try this approach in the USA where getting out of your car and rushing towards an officer may result in sudden lead poisoning.)
2. Stoop your body over so that you are smaller than him.
3. Lower your own status by telling the officer how irresponsible you've been and raise his status by thanking him for pointing out your mistake and telling him that you realise how difficult his job must be, having to deal with fools like you.
4. With your palms out, in a trembling voice, ask him not to give you a ticket. If you're female and the officer is male, smile a lot, blink your eyes repeatedly and talk in a higher pitched voice. If you're a man, just take the ticket and pay it.

'Please don't book me!'

This behaviour shows the police officer that you are not a threat and encourages him to take the role of a reprimanding parent, in which case he may decide to give you a stern warning and tell you to be on your way – without a ticket! When this technique is used as directed, it can save you from being booked in up to 50% of instances where a police car pulls you over.

The same technique can be used to calm an irate customer who is returning faulty goods to a retail store or wants to complain about something. In this case, a store counter represents a barrier between the store staff and the customer. Control of an irate customer would be difficult if the staff remained on their side of the counter, and creates a 'you-versus-me' approach which can make the customer even angrier. If the staff member moves around to the customer's side of the counter with his body stooped over and palms visible and uses the same technique we used with the police officer, it can usually placate an angry person. Staying behind a desk or counter can raise anger levels.

What's Love Got to Do With It?

Polish anthropologist, Dr Boguslaw Pawlowski, found that – in an ideal relationship – trust, money and respect are less important than the height difference ratio 1 to 1.09. His study in 2004 found that, to ensure marital bliss, a man needs to be 1.09 times taller than his partner. This formula fits in the case of failed romances, for instance Nicole Kidman (5 feet 11 inches, 1.8m) and Tom Cruise (5 feet 7 inches, 1.7m).

Couples who fit this success ratio include the following:

Cherie Blair and Tony Blair = 1.10
Jennifer Anniston and Brad Pitt = 1.11
Victoria Beckham and David Beckham = 1.09

Those who technically fail the test ratio include:

Camilla Parker-Bowles and Prince Charles = 1.01
Penny Lancaster and Rod Stewart = 0.97

Some Strategies For Gaining Perceived Height

If you are a shorter person, there are several strategies you can employ to neutralise the power of taller people who set out to intimidate you. This is important if you are a woman because women are, on average, 2 inches (5cm) shorter than men. Set up a space where you can control the environment by having chairs of varying heights and ask tall people to sit on the lower chairs. Sitting neutralises height and sitting the Incredible Hulk on a low sofa diminishes his perceived power. Sitting at opposite ends of a table also evens things up, as does leaning in someone's office doorway to talk while they are seated. Talking in a public place, such as a bar or in a crowd, or in a car or plane, also limits the tactics of taller associates. If someone is overbearing or standing over you while you are sitting, get up and walk over to a window and gaze outside as you discuss an issue. You will look as if you are giving deep consideration to the discussion and the bigger person can't have a height advantage when you aren't looking at them. Finally, acting assertively can also minimise height differences. These strategies will put you 'head and shoulders' above the height intimidators and let you 'stand tall' among those who try to 'get one up' over you.

Summary

Height differences have a significant impact on relationships but height and power are often just perceptions. Shorter people can increase their perceived height and are more likely to be remembered as taller when they wear dark-coloured clothing, pin-striped suits or trouser suits, softer, more muted make-up (for women) and full-size chronograph watches. The smaller the watch size, the less clout a person is perceived to have. Standing erect, sitting up straight and 'walking tall' are ways of giving yourself a confident appearance and, because of the law of cause and effect, you will feel more confident when you do these things.

Chapter 17

SEATING ARRANGEMENTS – WHERE TO SIT, AND WHY

'Just feel at home and tell me all about it!'

Where you sit in relation to other people is an effective way of obtaining co-operation from them. Aspects of their attitude towards you can also be revealed in the seating position they take relative to you.

We conducted surveys with seminar delegates during the 1970s, 1980s and 1990s to determine which positions at a table they felt gave the best result for communicating specific attitudes. We did this by delegate involvement at seminars and by using survey questionnaires from our database. The first major study in seating positions was conducted by psychologist Robert Sommer from the University of California, who analysed a cross-section of students and children in public and social situations such as bars and restaurants. We applied Sommer's findings to seating positions in business and negotiation situations. While there are marginal differences between cultures and the relationships between people, we have summarised here the seating positions you will encounter most of the time in most situations.

In his book *Non-Verbal Communication in Human*

Interaction, Mark Knapp from the University of Vermont noted that, although there is a general formula for interpretation of seating positions, the environment may have an effect on the position chosen. Research conducted with middle-class people showed that seating positions in public bars can vary from the seating positions taken in a high-class restaurant. The direction the seats are facing and the distance between tables can also have a distorting influence on seating behaviour. For example, intimate couples prefer to sit side by side wherever possible, but in a crowded restaurant where the tables are close together this is not possible and the couples are forced to sit opposite each other in what is normally a defensive position.

Keeping that in mind, we'll now present the main seating choices we have in a variety of circumstances at work and socially.

Take the Table Test

Let's assume that you are going to sit at a rectangular table with person A and that you are person B. Which seating position would you choose in the following circumstances:

- You will interview someone for a job in a small, friendly company.
- You are going to help someone complete a crossword puzzle.
- You are going to play chess against someone.
- You are in a public library and don't want any involvement.

Look at the next illustration and make your choices.

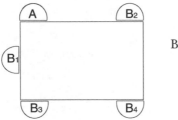

Basic seating positions

Here are your most likely answers:

- You took, B1, the Corner Position, to conduct the interview, as this allows you to see the person clearly without seeming competitive or aggressive, as you might in B3, or too familiar as in B2.
- You sat in position B2, the Co-operative Position, to help with the crossword puzzle, because this is where we sit to give help or build rapport.
- You chose position B3 to play chess against the person. This is called the Competitive/Defensive Position and is the one we choose to compete against an adversary because it lets us have a full view of their face and what they're doing.
- Finally, you used the Diagonal Position, B4, in the library to communicate your independence or non-involvement.

The Corner Position (B1)

This position is used by people who are engaged in friendly, casual conversation. It allows for good eye contact and the opportunity to use numerous gestures and to observe the gestures of the other person. The corner of the desk provides a partial barrier in case one person begins to feel threatened, and this position avoids territorial division of the table. This is the most successful strategic position from which person B can deliver a presentation, assuming that person A is the audience. By simply moving the chair to position B1 you can relieve a tense atmosphere and increase the chances of a positive outcome.

The Corner Position

The Co-operative Position (B2)

When two people are thinking alike or both working on a task together, this position often occurs. We found that 55% of people chose this position as the most co-operative, or intuitively took it when asked to work jointly with another person.

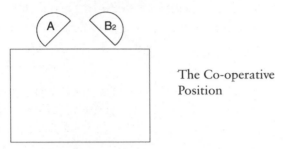

The Co-operative
Position

It is one of the best positions for presenting your case and having it accepted because it allows good eye contact and the opportunity for mirroring. The trick is, however, for B to be able to move into this position without A feeling as if his territory has been invaded. This is also a successful position to take when a third party is introduced into the negotiation by B. Say, for example, that a salesperson was having a second interview with a client and the salesperson introduces a technical expert. The following strategy will work well:

The technical expert is seated at position C opposite customer A. The salesperson sits at either position B2 (Co-operative) or B1 (Corner). This allows the salesperson to be 'on the client's side' and to ask the technician questions on behalf of the client. This position is known as 'siding with the opposition'.

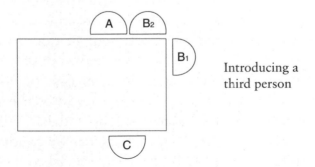

Introducing a
third person

The Competitive/Defensive Position (B3)

In this arrangement, competitors face each other, just like Western gunslingers. Sitting across the table from a person can create a defensive, competitive atmosphere and can lead to each party taking a firm stand on his point of view because the table becomes a solid barrier between both parties.

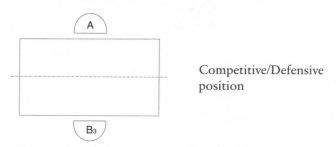

Competitive/Defensive position

In business scenarios, 56% of respondents saw this as a competitive position but in social situations, such as a restaurant, 35% saw it as conversational. It's the most commonly observed restaurant sitting position on the dating scene, but this is mainly because waiters seat people at tables this way. It works with a couple in a restaurant because it allows good eye contact while subtly highlighting gender differences by being 'opposite'. In a work environment, however, this position is taken by people who are either competing with each other or if one is reprimanding the other. It can also be used by A to establish a superior/subordinate role when it's used on A's territory.

Why Some Bosses Are Disliked

We found that, in business scenarios, people speak in shorter sentences from the Competitive/Defensive Position, can recall less of what was said and are more likely to argue.

A. G. White conducted an experiment in doctors' offices that showed that the presence or absence of a desk had a significant effect on whether a patient was at ease or not. Only 10% of patients were perceived to be at ease when the doctor's desk was present and the doctor sat behind it. This figure increased to 55% when the desk was absent. We conducted an experiment (Pease & Pease, 1990) where we asked 244 senior managers and 127 lower/middle managers to sketch the furniture arrangement they preferred to have in their offices when relocating to a new building. A full 76% of the senior managers (185) drew a sketch placing their desks between themselves and their subordinates. Only 50% of the lower managers (64) did this and male managers were twice as likely as females to put the desk between them and others.

The most interesting finding was how other staff members perceived the managers who did not have their desks placed like a barrier. These managers were described by their staff as more fair-minded, more prepared to listen to their ideas without criticism and less likely to show favouritism to others.

Sitting directly opposite others creates bad vibes.

If B is seeking to persuade A, the Competitive Position reduces the chance of a successful negotiation, unless B is deliberately sitting opposite as part of a pre-planned strategy. For example, it may be that A is a manager who has to reprimand employee B, and the Competitive Position can add weight to the reprimand. On the other hand, if B wants to make A feel superior, B can deliberately sit directly opposite A.

Whatever business you're in, if it involves dealing with people you are in the influencing business and your objective should always be to see the other person's point of view, to put him at ease and to make him feel right about dealing with you; the Competitive Position does not lead to that end. More co-operation will be gained from the Corner and Co-operative Positions than will ever be achieved from the Competitive Position. Conversations are significantly shorter and more pointed in the Competitive Position.

The Independent Position (B4)

This is taken by people when they don't want to interact with each other. It occurs between strangers in places such as libraries, park benches or restaurants and is the position we refer to when we say we are 'diametrically opposite' to an idea. To 42% of our respondents, the message it conveyed was a lack of interest and it was read by some as showing indifference or hostility. This position should be avoided where open discussions between people are your goal.

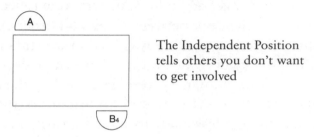

The Independent Position tells others you don't want to get involved

It's Not What You Say, It's Where You Sit

As we've said, rectangular tables create a competitive or defensive relationship between people because each person has equal space, equal frontage and separate edges. It lets everyone take a 'position' on a given subject and allows more direct eye contact across the table. Square tables are ideal for having short, to-the-point conversations or for creating superior or subordinate relationships. Most co-operation comes from the person seated beside you, and the one on the right tends to be more co-operative than the one on the left.

Historically, the person on the right is less likely to be able to successfully stab you with their left hand, hence the 'right-hand man' is more favoured and others subconsciously credit the right-hand person with having more power than the one on the left side. Most resistance comes from the person seated directly opposite in the 'gunslinger' position and, when four people are seated, everyone has someone sitting opposite.

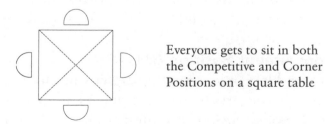

Everyone gets to sit in both the Competitive and Corner Positions on a square table

King Arthur's Concept

King Arthur used the Round Table as an attempt to give each of his knights an equal amount of authority and status. A round table creates an atmosphere of relaxed informality and is ideal for promoting discussion among people who are of equal status, as each person can claim the same amount of table territory. The circle itself has become a worldwide symbol of unity and strength and simply sitting in a circle promotes the same effect. Unfortunately, King Arthur was unaware that if the status of one person is higher than the others in the group it completely alters the dynamics of group power. The king held the most power and this meant that the knights seated on either side of him were silently granted the next highest amount of power, the one on his right having more than the one on his left. The power then diminished relative to the distance that each knight was seated away from the king.

A high status person at a round table distorts the power distribution

The knight seated directly opposite King Arthur was, in effect, in the Competitive/Defensive position and was likely to be the one to give the most trouble. Sixty-eight per cent of respondents saw the person sitting directly opposite them on a round table as the one most likely to argue or be competitive. Fifty-six per cent also said that sitting opposite could be used to show non-involvement or lack of interest, as in a public library. When sitting directly beside another person, 71% said they were either having a friendly conversation or co-operating.

Many of today's business executives use rectangular, square and round tables. The rectangular desk, which is usually the work desk, is used for business activity, brief conversations, reprimands and so on. The round table, often a coffee table

337

with wrap-around seating or lower chairs, is used to create an informal relaxed atmosphere or to persuade. It is also often found in families that practise democracy or don't have a dominant parent. Square tables belong in a canteen.

Keeping Two People Involved

Let's assume that you, person C, are going to talk with persons A and B, and that you are all sitting in a triangular position at a round table. Assume that person A is talkative and asks many questions and that person B remains silent throughout. When A asks you a question, how can you answer him and carry on a conversation without making B feel excluded? Use this simple but effective inclusion technique: when A asks a question, look at him as you begin to answer, then turn your head towards B, then back to A, then to B again until you make your final statement, looking finally at A again as you finish your sentence.

This technique lets B feel involved in the conversation and is particularly useful if you need to have B on side with you.

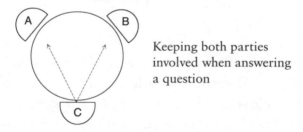

Keeping both parties involved when answering a question

Rectangular Board Tables

On a rectangular table, it seems to be a cross-cultural norm that position A has always commanded the most influence, even when all people at the table are of equal status. In a meeting of people of equal status the person sitting at position A will have the most influence, assuming that he doesn't have his back to the door.

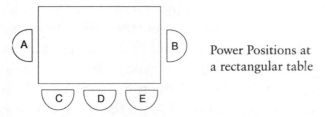

Power Positions at
a rectangular table

If A's back was facing the door, the person seated at B would be the most influential and would be strong competition for A. Strodtbeck and Hook set up some experimental jury deliberations which revealed that the person sitting at the head position was chosen significantly more often as the leader, particularly if that person was perceived as being from a high economic class. Assuming that A was in the best power position, person B has the next most authority, then D, then C. Positions A and B are perceived as being task-oriented while position D is seen as being occupied by an emotional leader, often a woman, who is concerned about group relationships and getting people to participate. This information makes it possible to influence power plays at meetings by placing name badges on the seats stating where you want each person to sit. This gives you a degree of control over what happens in the meeting.

Why Teacher's Pet Sits On the Left

Researchers at the University of Oregon determined that people can retain up to three times more information about things they see in their right visual field than they do in their left. Their study suggests that you are likely to have a 'better side' to your face when you are presenting information to others. According to this research your better side is your left because it's in the other person's right visual field.

Studies show that the left side of your face is the best side for giving a presentation.

Dr John Kershner of Ontario Institute for Studies in Education studied teachers and recorded where they were looking every 30 seconds for 15 minutes. He found that teachers almost ignore the pupils on their right. The study showed that teachers looked straight ahead 44% of the time, to the left 39% of the time and to their right only 17% of the time. He also found that pupils who sat on the left performed better in spelling tests than those on the right and those on the left were picked on less than those on the right. Our research found that more business deals are made when a salesperson sits to the customer's left than to their right. So, when you send a child to school, teach them to jockey for the teacher's left side but, when they become adults and attend meetings, tell them to go for the extra perceived power given to the person on their boss's right.

Power Plays at Home

The shape of a family dining-room table can give a clue to the power distribution in that family, assuming that the dining-room could have accommodated a table of any shape and that the table shape was selected after considerable thought. 'Open' families go for round tables, 'closed' families select square tables and 'authoritative' types select rectangular tables.

Next time you have a dinner party, try this experiment: place the shyest, most introverted guest at the head of the table, furthest from the door with their back to a wall. You will be amazed to see how simply placing a person in a powerful seating position encourages them to begin to talk more often and with more authority and how others will also pay more attention to them.

How to Make an Audience Cry

The Book of Lists – a volume that lists each year all sorts of information about human behaviour – shows public speaking as our number one fear, with fear of death ranking, on average, at number seven. Does this mean that, if you're at a funeral, you're better off being in the coffin than reading the eulogy?

If you are asked to address an audience at any time, it's important to understand how an audience receives and retains information. First, never tell the audience you feel nervous or overawed – they'll start looking for nervous body language and will be sure to find it. They'll never suspect you're nervous unless you tell them. Second, use confidence gestures as you speak, even if you're feeling terrified. Use Steeple gestures, open and closed palm positions, occasional Protruding Thumbs and keep your arms unfolded. Avoid pointing at the audience, arm crossing, face touching and lectern gripping. Studies show that people who sit in the front row learn and retain more than others in the audience, partially because those in the front row are keener than others to learn and they show more attention to the speaker in order to avoid being picked on.

> **People who sit in the front rows learn more, participate more and are more enthusiastic.**

Those in the middle sections are the next most attentive and ask the most questions, as the middle section is considered a safe area, surrounded by others. The side areas and back are the least responsive and attentive. When you stand to the audience's left – the right side of the stage – your information will have a stronger effect on the right brain hemisphere of your audience's brains, which is the emotional side in most people. Standing to the audience's right – the left side of stage – impacts the audience's left brain hemisphere. This is why an audience will laugh more and laugh longer when you use humour and stand to the left side of the stage, and they respond better to emotional pleas and stories when you deliver them from the right side of the stage. Comedians have known this for decades – make them laugh from the left and cry from the right.

The Attention Zone

Using parameters by researchers Robert Sommer and Adams and Biddle, we conducted a study of audiences to estimate how much participation was given by delegates based on where they were sitting in a seminar room and how much they could recall of what the presenter was saying. Our results were remarkably similar to the original Robert Sommer study, even though our participants were adults and Sommer's were students. We also found few cultural differences between Australians, Singaporeans, South Africans, Germans, Brits, French or Finns. High-status individuals sit in the front row in most places – most notably in Japan – and they participate the least, so we recorded audience data only where delegates were generally of equal status. The result was what we call the '*Funnel Effect*'.

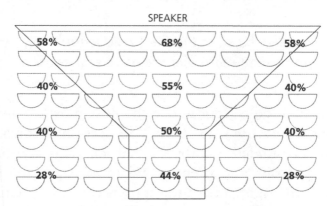

Retention of information and participation by attendees based on their choice of seat (Pease, 1986)

As you can see, when participants are sitting in classroom style, there is a 'learning zone' shaped like a funnel, which extends directly down the centre of an audience and across the front row. Those sitting in the 'funnel' gave the most amount of participation, interacted most with the presenter and had the highest recall about what was being discussed. Those who participated the least sat in the back or to the sides, tended to be more negative or confrontational and had the lowest recall. The rear positions also allow a delegate a greater opportunity to doodle, sleep or escape.

An Experiment in Learning

We know that people who are most enthusiastic to learn choose to sit closest to the front and those who are least enthusiastic sit in the back or to the sides. We conducted a further experiment to determine whether the Funnel Effect was a result of where people chose to sit, based on their interest in the topic, or whether the seat a person sat in affected their participation and retention. We did this by placing name cards on delegates' seats so they could not take their usual positions. We intentionally sat enthusiastic people to the sides and back of the room and well-known back-row hermits in the front. We found that this strategy not only increased the participation and recall of the normally negative delegates who sat up front, it *decreased* the participation and recall of the usually positive delegates who had been relegated to the back. This highlights a clear teaching strategy – if you want someone really to get the message, put them in the front row. Some presenters and trainers have abandoned the 'classroom style' meeting concept for training smaller groups and replaced it with the 'horseshoe' or 'open-square' arrangement because evidence suggests that this produces more participation and better recall as a result of the increased eye contact between all attendees and the speaker.

Getting a Decision Over Dinner

Bearing in mind what has already been said about human territories and the use of square, rectangular and round tables, let's consider the dynamics of going to a restaurant for a meal, but where your objective is to get a favourable response to a proposition.

If you are going to do business over dinner, it's a wise strategy to complete most of the conversation before the food arrives. Once everyone starts eating the conversation can come to a standstill and alcohol dulls the brain. After you've eaten, the stomach takes blood away from the brain to help digestion, making it harder for people to think clearly. While some men hope to achieve these types of effects with a woman on a date, it can be disastrous in business. Present your proposals while everyone is mentally alert.

No one ever makes a decision with their mouth full.

A hundred thousand years ago, ancestral man would return with his kill at the end of a hunting day and he and his group would share it inside a communal cave. A fire was lit at the entrance to the cave to ward off predators and to provide warmth. Each caveman sat with his back against the wall of the cave to avoid the possibility of being attacked from behind while he was engrossed in eating his meal. The only sounds that were heard were the gnashing and gnawing of teeth and the crackle of the fire. This ancient process of food sharing around an open fire at dusk was the beginning of a social event that modern man re-enacts at barbecues, cookouts and dinner parties. Modern man also reacts and behaves at these events in much the same way as he did over a hundred thousand years ago.

Now to our restaurant or dinner party: getting a decision in your favour is easier when the other person is relaxed and his defensive barriers have been lowered. To achieve this end, and keeping in mind what has already been said about our ancestors, a few simple rules need to be followed.

First, whether you are dining at home or at a restaurant, have the other person sitting with his back to a solid wall or screen. Research shows that respiration, heart rate, brainwave frequencies and blood pressure rapidly increase when a person sits with his back to an open space, particularly where others are moving about. Tension is further increased if the person's back is towards an open door or a window at ground level. So this a good position to seat someone when you want to unnerve or rattle. Next, the lights should be dimmed and muffled background music should be played to relax the senses. Many top restaurants have an open fireplace or fire facsimile near the entrance of the restaurant to recreate the effects of the fire that burned at the ancient cave feasts. It would be best to use a round table and to have the other person's view of other people obscured by a screen or large green plant if you want a captive audience.

Top restaurants use these relaxation techniques to extract large amounts of money from their customers' wallets for ordinary food, and men have been using them for thousands of years to create a romantic atmosphere for their women. It's far easier to obtain a favourable decision under these circumstances than it will ever be in restaurants that have bright lighting, tables and chairs placed in open areas and the banging of plates, knives and forks.

Summary

Seating positions should not be accidental; placing certain people in specific positions can affect the outcome of a meeting. The next time you go to a meeting with anyone, ask yourself: who is the person you want to influence most and where is the best position to sit to achieve this? Who is likely to want to argue or oppose? If there is no appointed leader, who has claimed a seating position to give themselves the most power? If you want to control, where should you sit? The answers to these questions will not only give you a powerful edge, they will prevent others from trying to dominate or control the meeting.

Chapter 18

INTERVIEWS, POWER PLAYS AND OFFICE POLITICS

Adam left the interview suspecting he'd done badly. Was it what he'd said that blew it? Or perhaps his chocolate brown suit, goatee beard, earring and overstuffed briefcase turned them off? Or had he simply sat in the wrong chair?

Most job interviews are non-productive because studies show a strong correlation between how much the interviewer likes the interviewee and whether or not they get the job. In the end, most of the factual information that comes from the curriculum vitae – the real stuff about the candidate that is a good indicator of performance – is forgotten. What is remembered is the impression the candidate made on the interviewer.

....

First impressions are the 'love-at-first-sight'
of the business world.

....

Professor Frank Bernieri of the University of Toledo analysed the performances of job applicants of various ages and backgrounds during 20-minute interviews in which the interviewers were asked to rate each candidate on attributes such as ambition, intelligence and competence. Then a group of observers was asked to watch video footage of just the first 15 seconds of each interview. The results showed that the observers' first impressions in 15 seconds almost paralleled the impressions of the interviewers. This study gives us further convincing evidence that you definitely don't get a second chance to make a first impression and that your approach, handshake and overall body language are the key factors in deciding the outcome.

Why James Bond Looked Cool, Calm and Collected

Research in the field of linguistics has shown a direct relationship between the amount of status, power or prestige a person commands, and their vocabulary range. The higher up the social or management ladder a person is, the better he is likely to be able to communicate in words and phrases. Body language research has revealed a correlation between a person's command of the spoken word and the number of gestures they use to communicate their message. The person at the top end of the status scale can use his range of vocabulary to communicate his meaning, whereas the less educated, less skilled lower-status person will rely more on gestures than words to communicate his message. He doesn't have the words so he substitutes gestures for words. As a general rule, the higher up the person is on the socio-economic scale, the less gesticulation and body movement they are likely to use.

Special Agent James Bond used these principles to great effect by having minimal body gestures, especially when he was under pressure. When he was being intimidated by the baddies, being insulted or shot at, he remained relatively motionless and spoke in short, monotone sentences.

---

*James Bond was so cool he could even make
love immediately after killing ten villains.*

High status people always 'keep their cool', which means revealing as little of their emotions as possible. Actors such as Jim Carrey are the opposite – they often play highly animated roles, emphasising a lack of power; and usually plays power-less, intimidated men.

The Nine Golden Keys to Making Great First Impressions

Let's assume you're going to an interview and you want to make the best first impression. Keep in mind that others form up to 90% of their opinion about you in the first four minutes and that 60 to 80% of the impact you will make is non-verbal.

Here are nine Golden Keys to getting it right first time in an interview:

1. In the Reception Area

Remove your outerwear and give it to the receptionist if possi-ble. Avoid entering an office with your arms full of clutter that can make you fumble and look inept. Always *stand* in a recep-tion area – never sit. Receptionists will insist you 'take a seat' because when you do, you're out of sight and they no longer have to deal with you. Stand with Hand-in-Hand behind your back (confidence) and slowly rock back and forth on your feet (confident, controlled) or use the Steeple gesture. This body language is a constant reminder that you are still there and waiting. But never do this at the Tax Office.

2. The Entry

Your entry tells others how you expect to be treated. When the receptionist has given you the green light to enter, walk in without hesitation. Do not stand in the doorway like a naughty schoolchild waiting to see the headmaster. When you walk through the door of the person's office, maintain the same speed. People who lack confidence change gears and perform a small shuffle as they enter.

3. The Approach

Even if the person is on the phone, rummaging through a drawer or tying his shoelaces, walk in directly and confidently with a smooth motion. Put down your briefcase, folder or whatever is in your hands, shake the person's hand and immediately take a seat. Let the other person see that you are accustomed to walking confidently into offices and that you don't expect to be kept waiting. People who walk slowly or take long strides convey that they have plenty of time on their hands, are not interested in what they are doing or have nothing else to do. This is fine for retired millionaires and those who live in Florida and Queensland, but not for anyone who wants to convey power, authority or capability or that they are a healthy, potential mate. Influential people and those who command attention walk briskly at a medium pace with medium length strides.

4. The Handshake

Keep your palm straight and return the pressure you receive. Let the other person decide when to end the handshake. Step to the left of a rectangular desk as you approach to avoid being given a Palm-Down handshake. Never shake directly across a desk. Use a person's name twice in the first 15 seconds and never talk for more than 30 seconds at a time.

5. When You Sit

If you are compelled to sit in a low chair directly facing the other person, turn it away 45 degrees from the person to avoid being stuck in the 'reprimand' position. If you can't angle the chair, angle your body instead.

6. Seating Areas

If you're invited to sit in an informal area of the person's office, such as at an informal coffee table, this is a positive sign because 95% of business rejections are delivered from behind a desk. Never sit on a low sofa that sinks so low it makes you look like a giant pair of legs topped by a small head – if necessary, sit upright on the edge so you can control your body language and gestures, and angle your body to 45 degrees away from the person.

7. Your Gestures

People who are cool, calm, collected and in control of their emotions use clear, uncomplicated, deliberate movements. High-status individuals use fewer gestures than low-status individuals. This is an ancient negotiating ploy – people with power don't have to move much. Keep in mind that Eastern Europeans gesture more from the elbow down than Westerners, and Southern Europeans gesture more with their entire arms and shoulders. Mirror the other person's gestures and expressions when appropriate.

8. Distance

Respect the other person's Personal Space, which will be largest in the opening minutes of the meeting. If you move too close, the person will respond by sitting back, leaning away or using repetitive gestures such as drumming the fingers. As a rule, you can move closer to familiar people but further back from new ones. Men generally move closer to women they work with while women generally move further back when they work with men. Work closer to those of similar age and further back from significantly older or younger ones.

9. Your Exit

Pack your things calmly and deliberately – not in a frenzy – shake hands if possible, turn and walk out. If the door was closed when you entered, close it behind you as you leave. People always watch you from behind as you leave so, if you're a man, make sure you have shined the back of your shoes. This is an area many men neglect and women are critical of this.

When a woman decides to leave she will point her foot towards the door and begin to adjust the back of her clothing and hair so that she makes a good rear-view impression as she departs. As mentioned earlier, hidden cameras show that, if you're a woman, others study your rear as you depart – whether you like it or not. When you get to the door turn around slowly and smile. It's far better that they recall your smiling face than your rear end.

When Someone Keeps You Waiting

If someone keeps you waiting for more than 20 minutes it shows either they're disorganised or it could be a form of power play. Keeping someone waiting is an effective way of reducing their status and enhancing the status of the person who is making them wait. This same effect can be seen when people are waiting in line at a restaurant or cinema – everyone assumes that the wait is going to be worthwhile, otherwise why would we all be waiting?

Always take a book, PDA, laptop or office work, which shows that you too are busy and are not prepared to be inconvenienced. When the person who has kept you waiting comes out to meet you let them speak first, lift your head slowly from your work and greet them, then pack up smoothly and confidently. Another good strategy when made to wait is to take out some financial papers and a calculator and do calculations. When they call for you say, 'I'll be ready in a moment – I'll just finish these calculations.' Or you could make all your mobile phone calls. The clear message you are sending is that you're a very busy person and are not being inconvenienced by their disorganisation. And if you suspect the other person is playing a power game, arrange for an urgent call to be put through to you during your meeting. Take the call, loudly mention large amounts of money, drop in a well-known name or two, tell the caller you never settle for second best and that they are to report back to you as soon as possible. Hang up the phone, apologise for the interruption and continue as if nothing had happened. Hey, it works for James Bond...it'll work for you.

If the other person takes a phone call during the meeting or a third person enters and begins what seems like a long conversation, take out your book or homework and begin to read. This gives them privacy and demonstrates that you don't waste your time. If you feel the person is doing these things intentionally, take out your own mobile phone and make several important follow-up calls about the important ventures you were discussing earlier.

Fake It Till You Make It?

If you avoid Hand-to-Face gestures and always talk using openness signals, does this mean you can tell some real whoppers and get away with it? Well...not necessarily, because if you use open positions when you *know* you're lying, your palms are likely to sweat, your cheeks may twitch and your pupils constrict. The most competent liars are those who can go into their acting role and act as if they actually believe the lie. A professional actor who can do this better than anyone else is presented with an Oscar. While we are not suggesting you tell lies, there is powerful evidence that if you practise the positive skills we've mentioned throughout this book, they will become second nature to you and serve you well for the rest of your life.

Scientists proved the 'fake it till you make it' concept using tests on birds. In many bird species, the more dominant a bird is, the darker its plumage will be. Darker coloured birds are first in line for food and mates. Researchers took a number of lighter, weaker birds and dyed their plumage dark so that these birds would be 'lying' to the other birds that they were dominant. But the result was that the 'liar' birds were attacked by the *real* dominant birds because the 'liars' were still displaying weak and submissive body language. In the next tests the weaker birds, both male and female, were not only dyed but also injected with testosterone hormones to make them act dominantly. This time the 'liars' succeeded as they began strutting around acting in confident, superior ways, which completely fooled the real dominant birds. This demonstrates that you need to cast yourself into a believable role in an interview and mentally practise in advance how you will behave if you want others to take you seriously.

Seven Simple Strategies for Giving You the Extra Edge

1. Stand up for Meetings

Conduct all short-term decision-making meetings standing up. Studies show that standing conversations are significantly shorter than sitting ones and the person who conducts a standing meeting is perceived as having higher status than those who sit. Standing whenever others enter your workspace is also an excellent timesaver, so consider having no visitors' chairs in your own work area. Standing decisions are quick and to the point and others don't waste your time with social chatter or questions such as 'How's the family?'

2. Sit Competitors with Their Backs to the Door

As discussed, studies reveal that when our backs are towards an open space we become stressed, blood pressure increases, our heart beats faster, our brainwave output increases and we breathe more quickly as our body readies itself for a possible rear attack. This is an excellent position in which to place your opponents.

3. Keep Your Fingers Together

People who keep their fingers closed when they talk with their hands and keep their hands below chin level, command the most attention. Using open fingers or having your hands held above the chin is perceived as less powerful.

4. Keep Your Elbows Out

When you sit on a chair, keep your elbows out or on the arms of the chair. Submissive, timid individuals keep their elbows in to protect themselves and are perceived as fearful.

5. Use Power Words

A study at the University of California showed that the most persuasive words in spoken language are: *discovery, guarantee, love, proven, results, save, easy, health, money, new, safety* and *you*. Practise using these words. The new results you'll get from the discovery of these proven words will guarantee you more love, better health and will save you money. And they're completely safe, and easy to use.

6. Carry a Slim Briefcase

A slim briefcase with a combination lock is carried by an important person who is concerned only with the bottom-line details; large, bulky briefcases are carried by those who do all the work and are perceived as not being sufficiently organised to get things done on time.

7. Watch Their Coat Buttons

Analysis of videotaped confrontations, for example, between unions and corporations, show a higher frequency of agreement is reached when people have their coats unbuttoned. People who cross their arms on their chest often do it with their jacket buttoned and are more negative. When a person suddenly unbuttons their jacket in a meeting, you can reasonably assume that they have also just opened their mind.

Summary

Before you go to an important interview or meeting, sit quietly for five minutes and mentally practise seeing yourself doing these things and doing them well. When your mind sees them clearly, your body will be able to carry them out and others will react accordingly.

Office Power Politics

Have you ever been for a job interview and felt overwhelmed or helpless when you sat in the visitor's chair? Where the interviewer seemed so big and overwhelming and you felt small and insignificant? It is likely that the interviewer had cunningly arranged his office furnishings to raise his own status and power and, in so doing, lower yours. Certain strategies using chairs and seating arrangements can create this atmosphere in an office.

There are three factors in raising perceived status and power using chairs: the size of the chair and its accessories, the height of the chair from the floor and the location of the chair relative to the other person.

1. Chair Size and Accessories

The height of the back of the chair raises or lowers a person's status. The higher the back of the chair, the more power and status the person sitting in it is perceived to have. Kings, queens, popes and other high-status people may have the back of their throne or official chair as high as 8 feet or more (2.5m) to show their status relative to everyone else; the senior executive has a high-backed leather chair and his visitor's chair has a low back. How much power would the Queen or the Pope have if they were always sitting on a small piano stool?

Swivel chairs have more power and status than fixed chairs, allowing the user freedom of movement when he is placed under pressure. Fixed chairs allow little or no movement and this lack of movement is compensated for by the sitter's use of body gestures that reveal their attitudes and feelings. Chairs with armrests, those that lean back and those that have wheels have more power.

2. Chair Height

The acquisition of power using height was covered in Chapter 16 but it is worth noting that status is gained if your chair is adjusted higher off the floor than the other person's. Some advertising executives are known for sitting on high-backed chairs that are adjusted for maximum height while their visitors sit opposite, in the defensive position, on a sofa or chair that is so low that their eyes are level with the executive's desk.

3. Chair Location

As mentioned in the chapter on seating arrangements, most power is exerted on a visitor when his chair is placed directly opposite in the Competitive Position. A common power play is to place the visitor's chair as far away as possible from the executive's desk into the social or public territory zone, which further reduces the visitor's status.

How to Switch Table Territories

When two people sit directly opposite each other across a table, they unconsciously divide it into two equal territories. Each claims half as his own territory and will reject the other encroaching upon it.

There will be occasions, however, when it may be difficult or inappropriate to take the corner position to present your case. Let's assume that you have a folder, book, quotation or sample to present to another person who is sitting behind a rectangular desk and your objective is to get into the best position for presenting. First, place the article on the table and he'll either lean forward and look at it, take it over to his side, or push it back into your territory.

Paper placed on territorial line

If he leans forward to look at it but doesn't pick it up, you're compelled to deliver your presentation from where you sit because he doesn't want you on his side of the desk. If this happens, angle your body away at 45 degrees to present your case. If he takes it onto his side, however, this gives you the opportunity to ask permission to enter his territory and take either the Corner or Co-operative Position.

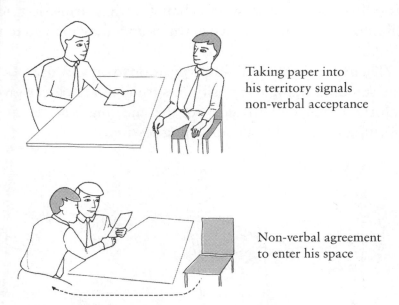

Taking paper into his territory signals non-verbal acceptance

Non-verbal agreement to enter his space

If, however, he pushes it back towards you, stay on your side. Never encroach on the other person's territory unless you have been given verbal or non-verbal permission to do so or you will put them offside.

Seated Body Pointing

Take the following situation: you're a supervisor and are about to counsel a subordinate whose work performance is not up to scratch. You feel that you will need to use direct questions that require direct answers and this may put the subordinate under pressure. At times you will also need to show the subordinate compassion and, from time to time, that you agree with his thoughts or actions.

Leaving aside interview and questioning techniques for these illustrations, consider the following points: (1) The counselling session will be in your office; (2) The subordinate will be seated on a chair with fixed legs and no arms, one that causes him to use body gestures and postures that will give you an understanding of his attitudes; and (3) You'll be sitting on a swivel chair that has arms, letting you eliminate some of your own gestures and allowing you to move around.

There are three main angle positions you can use. As with the standing triangular position, sitting at 45 degrees gives an informal, relaxed attitude to the meeting and is a good opening position for a counselling session.

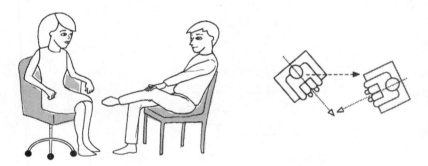

Opening a session using a 45 degree angle
keeps things relaxed

You can show non-verbal agreement with the subordinate from this position by mirroring his movements and gestures. As in the open standing position, their bodies point to a third point to form a triangle, which can show agreement.

By turning your chair to point your body directly at someone you non-verbally tell them that you want direct answers to your direct questions.

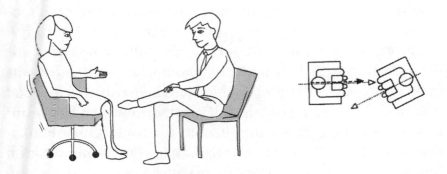

Direct body pointing keeps things serious

When you position your body 45 degrees away from the other person, you take the pressure off the interview. This is an excellent position from which to ask delicate or embarrassing questions, encouraging more open answers to your questions without them feeling as if they are being pressured.

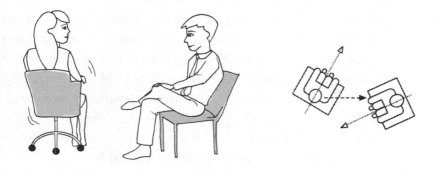

The right 45 degrees away position

How to Re-arrange an Office

Having read this far in the book, you should now be able to work out how to arrange an office to have as much power, influence or control as you want or to make it as relaxed, friendly and informal as you want. Here now is a case study showing how we rearranged someone's office to help solve some of his personal manager/employee relationship problems.

John worked for a large finance company. He had been promoted to a manager's position and given an office. After a few months in the role, John found that the other employees disliked dealing with him and his relationship with them was often tense, particularly when they were in his office. He found it difficult to get them to follow his instructions and had heard they were talking about him behind his back. Our observations of John's dilemma revealed that the communication breakdowns were at their worst when the employees were in his office.

For the purposes of this exercise, we'll ignore any of John's management skills and concentrate on the non-verbal aspects of the problem. Here's a summary of our observations and conclusions about John's office set-up:

1. The visitor's chair was placed in the competitive position in relation to John.
2. The walls of the office were solid panels except for an outside window and a clear glass partition where John could look into the general office area and be seen by the rest of the staff. His visibility reduced John's status and could increase the power of any subordinate who was sitting in the visitor's chair because the other employees were located directly behind the visitor and were, in effect, on the subordinate's side of the table
3. John's desk had a solid front that hid his lower body and prevented the subordinates observing his lower gestures to evaluate how he felt.
4. The visitor's chair was placed so that the visitor's back was to the open door.
5. John often sat using the Catapult or Leg-Over-Arm-of-Chair gestures or both whenever a subordinate was in his office.
6. John had a swivel chair with a high back, armrests and wheels. The visitor's chair was a plain low-backed chair with fixed legs and no armrests.

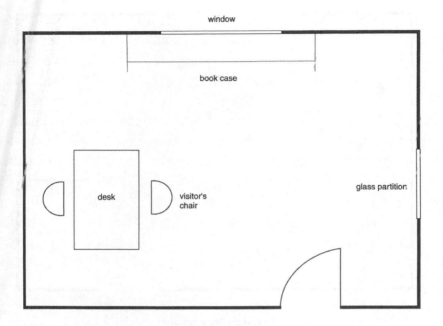

John's initial office layout

From a user-friendly, non-verbal standpoint, his office was a disaster area. It felt unfriendly to anyone who entered. The following rearrangements were made to help encourage John's management style to become more friendly:

1. John's desk was placed in front of the glass partition, making his office appear bigger and allowing him to be visible to those who entered. In this way, visitors were greeted by John personally, not by his desk.
2. The 'hot seat' was placed in the Corner Position, making communication more open and allowing the corner to act as a partial barrier for staff who felt insecure.
3. The glass partition was coated with a mirror finish, allowing John to see out, but not permitting others to see in. This raised John's status by securing his territory and creating a more intimate atmosphere inside his office.

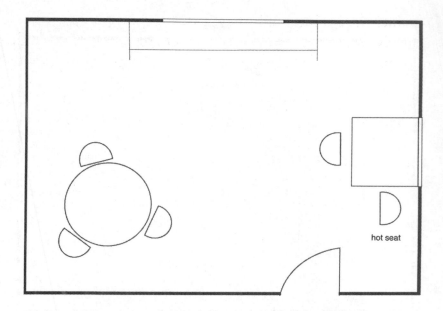

Revised office layout

4. A low round table with three identical swivel chairs were placed at the other end of the office so informal meetings could take place.
5. In the original layout, John's desk could give half the desktop space to the visitor but the revised layout gave John back the entire desktop.
6. John practised sitting in open positions, used subtle Steeple gestures and consciously used his palms whenever he spoke with others.

The results? Significantly improved manager/staff relationships and some staff began describing John as 'easygoing' and as a relaxed person to work with.

All that is needed to raise your status, and increase your power and effectiveness with others, is a little thought given to non-verbal gymnastics in your office or home. Unfortunately, most executive offices are arranged as John's was initially set out, because offices are designed by office designers, not by those who understand interaction between people. Rarely is consideration given to the negative non-verbal signals that can be unwittingly communicated to others.

Study your own workplace layout and use the preceding information to make the positive changes needed.

Summary

The thing about power plays and office politics is that you can anticipate them and even plan your own in advance. Adam never knew that, in Western cultures, men wearing chocolate coloured suits turn women off, or that a goatee beard, while it may be a fashion statement, subconsciously repels older people because of its association with Satan. And the earring and the overstuffed briefcase...well, these items are taken to interviews by the non-verbally uninformed.

CHAPTER 19

PUTTING IT ALL TOGETHER

When you look quickly at this image, you'll see an elephant. It's only when you examine it closely that you see that things are not what they appear to be. When most people look at others they see the person, but they miss revealing details that are obvious when pointed out. And so it is with body language. Communication through body language has been going on for over a million years but has only been scientifically studied to any extent since the end of the twentieth century. Body language is finally being 'discovered' by people throughout the world and is now a part of formal education and business training everywhere.

This final chapter is devoted to social and business scenarios and will give you the opportunity to see how well you can now read body signals. Before you read the notes, however, study each picture sequence and see how many body language signals you can see from what you've read in this book. Score one point for every major signal you can spot and you will receive an overall rating assessment at the end. You will be amazed to find how much your 'perceptiveness' has improved. Keep in mind that while we are analysing frozen gestures here, it all needs to be read in clusters of gestures, in context, and with allowance for cultural differences.

How Well Can You Read Between the Lines?

1. What Are the Three Main Signals in this illustration?

Answers ....

This is a good example of an openness cluster. The palms are fully exposed in the submissive position and the fingers are spread to give more impact to the gesture and to signal non-aggressiveness. His entire body is open showing that nothing is being concealed. This man is communicating an open, non-threatening attitude.

2. What Are the Five Main Signals?

Answers..

This is a classic deceit cluster. As he rubs his eye he looks away and both eyebrows are raised to the disbelief position. His head is turned away and slightly down, showing a negative attitude. He also has an insincere, tight-lipped smile.

3. What Are the Three Main Signals?

Answers ....

The incongruency of gestures is obvious here. The man is pretending to smile confidently as he crosses the room but one hand has crossed his body to adjust his watch and form a partial arm barrier. His smile is a basic fear-face. This shows that he is unsure of himself or his circumstances.

4. What Are the Five Main Signals?

Answers ....

This woman disapproves of the person at whom she's looking. She has turned neither her head nor body towards him but is giving him a sideways glance with her head slightly down (disapproval), eyebrows slightly turned down (anger), a full arm-cross gesture (defensive) and the corners of her mouth are turned down.

5. What Are the Four Main Signals?

Answers ....

Dominance, superiority and territoriality are evident here. The Catapult shows a superior 'know-it-all' attitude and feet-on-desk shows a territorial claim to it. To further highlight his ego he has a high-status chair with wheels, arms and other accessories. He is also sitting in the defensive/competitive position.

6. What Are the Three Main Signals?

Answers ....

The hands-on-hips gesture is used by the child to make himself appear larger and more threatening. The chin is jutting forward to show defiance and the mouth is opened wide to expose the teeth, just as animals do before they attack.

7. What Are the Five Main Signals?

Answers ....

This cluster can be summed up in one word – negative. The folder is used as a barrier and the arms and legs are folded due to nervousness or defensiveness. His coat is buttoned and his sunglasses hide any eye or pupil signals. Considering that people form 90 per cent of their opinion of someone in the first four minutes, it's unlikely that this man will ever get to first base with another person.

8. What Are the Six Main Signals?

Answers ....

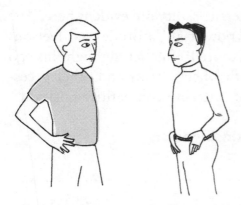

Both men are using aggressive and readiness gestures, the man on the left using the Hands-on-Hips gesture and the man on the right, the Thumbs-in-Belt. The man on the left is less aggressive than the man on the right as he is leaning backwards and his body is pointing slightly away from the man on the right. The man on the right, however, has assumed an intimidating pose by pointing his body directly at the other man and taking an erect stance. His facial expression is also consistent with his body gestures and his mouth is turned down.

9. What Are the Thirteen Main Signals?

Answers ....
....

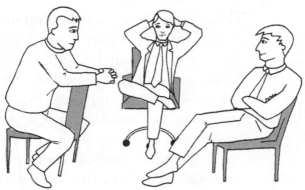

The man on the left is straddling his chair in an attempt to take control of the discussion or to dominate the man on the right. He is also pointing his body directly at the man on the right. He has clenched fingers and his feet are locked together under his chair, showing a frustrated attitude, which means that he's probably having difficulty getting his point across.

The man in the centre feels superior to the other two because of the Catapult gesture he is using. He also has the Figure 4 leg position, indicating that he could be competitive or argumentative. He has a high-status chair that swivels, leans back and has wheels and armrests. The man on the right is seated on a low-status chair that has fixed legs and no accessories. His arms and legs are tightly crossed (defensive) and his head is down (hostile), body pointing away (disinterest), indicating that he doesn't like what he hears.

10. What Are the Fourteen Main Signals?

Answers ....
....

The woman is displaying classic courtship gestures. She has one foot forward, pointing towards the man on the far left (interest), a combination of Hand-on-Hip and Thumb-in-Belt (assertive, readiness), her left wrist is being flashed (sensual) and she is blowing cigarette smoke upwards (confident, positive). She is also giving a sideways glance to the man on the far left and he is responding to her courtship gestures by adjusting his tie (preening) and pointing his foot at her. His head is up (interested). The man in the centre is clearly unimpressed with the other man as he has his body pointing away and is giving him an aggressive sideways glance. He has his palms out of sight and is blowing his cigarette smoke down (negative). He is also leaning against the wall (territorial aggression).

11. What Are the Twelve Main Signals?

Answers ....
....

The man on the left is using superiority gestures and has an arrogant attitude towards the man sitting opposite. He is using eye block signals to block the other man from sight and his head is tilted back to 'look down his nose' at him. Defensiveness is also evident because his knees are held tightly together and he is holding his wine glass with both hands to form a barrier. The man in the middle has been excluded from the conversation by the two other men not forming a triangle to include him. He does, however, seem aloof, as shown by his Thumbs-in-Waistcoat gesture (superiority), leaning back on his chair and is using a Crotch Display (macho). The man on the right has heard enough and has taken the starter's position (ready to leave) and his foot and body are pointed towards the nearest exit. His eyebrows and the corners of his mouth are turned down, and his head is slightly down, revealing disapproval.

12. What Are the Eleven Main Signals?

Answers ....

The man on the left and the man on the right have taken closed body positions. The central man's attitude shows superiority and sarcasm and he is using the Lapel-Grasping gesture with a thumb-up (superiority) plus a thumb-point gesture towards the man on his left (ridicule). The man on the right has responded defensively with crossed legs, and aggressively with the Upper-Arm Grip gesture (self-control) and sideways glance. The man on the left of this sequence is also unimpressed with the central man's attitude. He has crossed legs (defensive), Palm-in-Pocket (unwilling to participate) and is looking at the floor while using the Pain-in-Neck gesture.

13. What Are the Twelve Main Signals?

Answers ....
....

This sequence also shows a tense atmosphere. All three men are sitting back in their chairs to keep the maximum distance from each other. The man on the right is probably causing the problem because of his negative gesture cluster. As

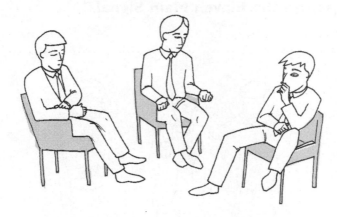

he is speaking he is using the nose touch gesture (deceit) and his right arm has crossed his body to make a partial arm barrier (defensive). His lack of concern about the other men's opinions is shown by the Leg-over-Chair gesture, Crotch Display and his body is pointed away from them. The man on the left disapproves of what the man on the right has to say and is using the Lint-Picking gesture (disapproval), his legs are crossed (defensive) and pointed away (uninterested). The man in the middle would like to say something but is holding back his opinion, shown by his self-restraint gesture of gripping the arms of the chair and his locked ankles. He has also issued a non-verbal challenge to the man on the right by pointing his body at him.

14. What Are the Eight Main Signals?

Answers ....

In this scene the man on the left and the woman have mirrored each other's gestures to form 'bookends' on the couch. The couple are very interested in each other and have positioned their hands in such a way that they can expose their wrists, and they have crossed their legs towards one another. The man in the middle has a Tight-Lipped Smile in an attempt to look interested in what the other man has to say but this is incongruent with his other facial and body gestures. His head is down (disapproval), the corner of his mouth turned down, his eyebrows are also down (anger) and he is giving the other man a sideways glance. His arms and legs are tightly crossed (defensive) – all indicating that he has a very negative attitude.

15. What Are the Fifteen Main Signals?

Answers ....
.. ..

The man on the left is using a cluster to convey openness and honesty – exposed palms, foot forward, head up, coat unbuttoned, arms and legs apart, leaning forward and smiling gestures. Unfortunately for him, however, his story is not getting across. The woman is sitting back in her chair with her legs crossed away (defensive), she has a partial arm-barrier (defensive), a clenched fist (tension), her head down and is using a critical evaluation gesture (hand to face). The man in the middle has a raised Steeple gesture, indicating that he feels confident or smug and he is sitting in the Figure 4 leg position, showing that his attitude is competitive or argumentative. We can assume that his overall attitude is negative as he is sitting back, his head down.

16.a What Are the Nine Main Signals?
The following three scenes demonstrate typical defence, aggression and courtship clusters.

Answers ....

The beginning of the conversation

In the first scene, all three people have their arms folded, two have their legs crossed (defensive) and all have their bodies oriented away from each other, all indicating that they may have just met for the first time. The man on the right appears interested in the woman as he has his right foot twisted around to point at her and he is giving her a sideways glance, combined with raised eyebrows (interest) and a smile; he is leaning towards her with the upper part of his body. She is closed off to both men at this point.

16b. What Are the Eleven Main Signals?

Answers ....

....

Five minutes later

The woman has now uncrossed her legs and is standing in the Attention position, while the man on the left has uncrossed his legs and is pointing one foot at her (interest) and leaning towards her. He is using the Thumbs-in-Belt gesture, which is either intended as a competitive display towards the other man, in which case the attitude is aggression, or is directed towards the woman, making it a sexual display. He is also standing straighter to make himself appear bigger. The man on the right seems intimidated by the other man, as seen by his now more erect stance, his crossed arms and the fact that he is giving the other man a sideways glance combined with eyebrows down (disapproval) and his smile has gone.

16c. What Are the Fifteen Main Signals?

Answers ....

....

Fifteen minutes later

The attitudes and emotions of these people are now clearly shown by their body language. The man on the left has kept his Thumbs-in-Belt, Foot-Forward position and has turned his body more towards the woman, making it a complete courtship display. His thumbs are also gripping his belt much tighter to make the gesture more noticeable and his body has become even more erect. The woman is responding to this courtship display with her own, showing that she is interested in being involved with him. She has uncrossed her arms, turned her body towards him and is pointing one foot at him. Her courtship gestures include hair touching, exposed wrists, chest forward to show cleavage and positive facial expression, and she is blowing her cigarette smoke upwards (confidence). The man on the right is unhappy about being excluded and is using the Hands-on-Hips gesture (aggressive readiness) and standing Crotch Display to show his displeasure.

In summary, the man on the left has won the woman's attentions and the other man should take a hike in the Himalayas.

How Did You Rate?

130 – 150 points
Holy intuition Batman! You are an extremely effective communicator who is sensitive to other people's feelings most of the time. Go to the top of the class!

100 – 130 points
You are very good with people and generally have a 'feel' about what's going on. With perseverance and practice you can become a top-notch communicator.

70 – 100 points
Sometimes you twig to how people are feeling about things or about each other, at other times you find out several days later. You need diligent body language practice.

70 or fewer
You've read this book and still not even scored 70? We suggest you search for a career in computing, accounting or as a medical receptionist where people skills are not a requirement. Go back to the start of this book and read it again. Meanwhile, do not leave home or even answer a telephone.

Summary

Research has now shown convincingly that if you change your body language, you can change many things about your approach to life. You can alter your mood before going out, feel more confident at work, become more likeable and be more persuasive or convincing. When you change your body language you interact differently with people around you and they, in turn, will respond differently to you.

When you first start increasing your awareness of body language you'll probably feel uncomfortable and self-conscious. You will be aware of practically every expression you make, surprised at how many gestures you make and how often you fiddle with things and you'll feel as if everyone around is seeing it all too. Remember that most people are completely unaware of what their bodies are doing and they're so busy trying to make an impression on you that they are not consciously noticing what you are doing. It may seem strange at first to consciously have your palms open and keep steady eye contact if you've spent your life keeping your hands in your pockets or holding hands with yourself and looking away.

You may ask, 'How do I watch someone's body language while thinking about my own body language and trying to concentrate on what we're talking about?' Remember that your brain is already programmed to read many body language signals so all you are doing is learning consciously to read the signals and messages. It's like riding a bicycle for the first time – it feels a little scary at the start and you might take an occasional tumble but before long you'll be riding like a pro.

Some people may feel that learning body language skills is manipulative or insincere, but learning to be proficient at reading it and using it is no different to wearing certain types of clothes, using certain language or telling stories that put you in the best light. The difference here is that it won't happen unconsciously and you'll make a better impression on others. If you're a man, remember that women are reading and decoding your body language whether you realise it or not, so learning how it's done can give you an equal footing. Without effective body language you can be like a spaghetti Western – the lips don't match the words and the viewers are constantly confused or switch channels.

Finally, here is a summary of the keys points for making a positive body language impression on others.

The Six Secrets of Attractive Body Language

Face: Have an animated face and make smiling a part of your regular repertoire. Make sure you flash your teeth.

Gestures: Be expressive but don't overdo it. Keep your fingers closed when you gesture, your hands below chin level and avoid arm or feet crossing.

Head Movement: Use Triple Nods when talking and Head Tilt when listening. Keep your chin up.

Eye Contact: Give the amount of eye contact that makes everyone feel comfortable. Unless looking at others is a cultural no-no, lookers gain more credibility than non-lookers.

Posture: Lean forward when listening, stand straight when speaking.

Territory: Stand as close as you feel comfortable. If the other person moves back, don't step forward again.

Mirror: Subtly mirror the body language of others.

REFERENCES

Acredolo, L. and Goodwin, S., *Baby Signs: How to Talk with your Baby Before your Baby Can Talk*, Vermilion (2000)

Acton, G. S., 'Measurement of impulsivity in a hierarchical model of personality traits: implications for substance use', *Substance Use and Abuse*, in press (2003)

Adams, R. S., Biddle, B. and Holt, *Realities of Teaching: Exploration with Video Tape*, Rinehart & Winston (1970)

Andreas, S. and Faulkner, C., *NLP: The New Technology of Achievement*, Nicholas Brealey Publishing (1996)

Ardrey, R., *The Territorial Imperative*, Collins (1967)

Argyle, M. and Cook, M., *Gaze and Mutual Gaze*, Cambridge University Press (1976)

Argyle, M. and Ingham, R., 'Gaze, mutual gaze, and proximity', *Semiotica*, 6, 32-49 (1972)

Argyle, M., *Bodily Communication*, Methuen (1975)

Argyle, M., 'Gestures and bodily movements' in *Bodily Communication* (151-271), International Universities Press, Inc. (1975)

Argyle, M., *Skills with People: A Guide for Managers*, Hutchinson (1973)

Argyle, M., *Social Interaction*, Methuen (1968)

Argyle, M., *The Psychology of Interpersonal Behaviour*, Penguin Books (1967)

Argyle, M., 'The syntax of bodily communication', *Linguistics*, 112, 71-91 (1973)

Argyle, M., *Training Manager*, The Acton Society Trust, London (1962)

Asher, M., *Body Language*, Carlton, 1999

Axtell, R. E., *Gestures*, John Wiley & Sons (1991)

Bacon, A. M., *A Manual of Gestures*, Griggs, Chicago (1875)

Bandler, R. and Grinder, J., *Patterns of the Hypnotic Techniques of Milton H. Erickson, MD: Volume 1*, Metamorphous Press (1997)

Bandler, R. and Grinder, J., *The Structure of Magic: A Book About Language and Therapy*, Science and Behavior Books (1976)

Bandler, R., *Insider's Guide to Sub-modalities*, Meta Publications (1993)

Barkow, J., Cossmides, L. and Tooby, J., *The Adapted Mind: Evolutionary Psychology and the Generation of Culture*, Oxford University Press (1992)

Beattie, G., *The Candarel Guide to Beach Watching*, Hove, Rambletree (1988)

Beattie, G., *Visible Thought: The New Psychology of Body Language* (2003)

Beattie, G., *All Talk: Why It's Important to Watch your Words and Everything Else you Say* Weidenfeld and Nicolson, London (1988)

Benthall, J. and Polhemus, T., *The Body as a Medium of Expression*, Allen Lane, London (1975)

Berne, E., *Games People Play*, Grove Press, New York (1964)

Birdwhistell, R. L., 'The language of the body: the natural environment of words' in A. Silverstein, (ed.), *Human Communication: Theoretical Explorations* (203-220), Lawrence, Hillsdale, NJ (1974)

Birdwhistell, R. L., *Kinesics and Context*, University of Pennsylvania Press (1970)

Birdwhistell, R. L., *Introduction to Kinesics*, University of Louisville Press (1952)

Birdwhistell, R. L., *Kinesics and Context*, Allen Lane, London (1971)

Blacking, J., *Anthropology of the Body*, Academic Press, London/New York, (1977)

Botting, K. & D., *Sex Appeal*, Macmillan (1995)

Bottomley, M., *Executive Image*, Penguin (1988)

Brun, T., *The International Dictionary of Sign Language*, Wolfe Publishing, London (1969)

Bryan, W. J., *The Psychology of Jury Selection*, Vantage Press, New York (1971)

Burton, S., *Impostors: Six Kinds of Liar*, Viking (2000)

Buss, D., *The Evolution of Desire*, Basic

Books (1994)

Calero, H., *Winning the Negotiation*, Hawthorn Books, New York (1979)

Camras, L. A., Oster, H., Campos, J. J., Miyake, K. and Bradshaw, D., 'Japanese and American infants, response to arm restraint', *Development Psychology*, 28, 578-583 (1992)

Cappella, J. N., 'The facial feedback hypothesis in human interaction: review and speculation', *Journal of Language and Social Psychology*, 12 (1993)

Carnegie, D., *How to Win Friends and Influence People*, Angus and Robertson, Sydney (1965)

Caro, M., *Caro's Book of Poker Tells*, Cardoza Publishing (2003)

Caro, M., *The Body Language of Poker*, Carol Publishing (1994)

Cashdan, E., 'Smiles, speech and body posture: how women and men display sociometric status and power', *Journal of Nonverbal Behavior*, 22 (4) (1998)

Cassidy, C. M., 'The Good Body: when big is better', *Medical Anthropology*, (1991)

Chaplin, W. F., Phillips, J. B., Brown, J. D. and Clanton, N. R., 'Handshaking, gender, personality, and first impressions', *Journal of Personality and Social Psychology*, 79 (1)

Chapman, A. J., 'Humor and laughter in social interaction and some implications for humor research' in P. McGhee and J. H. Goldstein (eds), *Handbook of humor research. Volume 1*, basic issues (135-157), Springer-Verlag (1983)

Clayton, P., *Body Language at Work*, Hamlyn (2003)

Collett, P., *Foreign Bodies: A Guide to European Mannerisms*, Simon & Schuster (1993)

Collett, P., *Social Rules and Social Behaviour*, Blackwell, Oxford (1977)

Collett, P., *The Book of Tells*, Doubleday (2003)

Colton, H., *The Gift of Touch*, Seaview/Putnam (1996)

Cook, M., 'Experiments on Orientation and Proxemics', *Human Relations* (1970)

Cooper, K., *Bodybusiness*, AMA Com (1979)

Creagan, M., *Surfing Your Horizons*, Angus and Robertson (1996)

Critchley, M., *Silent Language*, Butterworth, London (1975)

Critchley, M., *The Language of Gesture*, Arnold, London (1939)

Cundiff, M., *Kinesics*, Parker Publishing, New York (1972)

Dabbs, J. M., 'Testosterone, smiling and facial appearance', *Journal of Nonverbal Behavior*, 21 (1992)

Dale-Guthrie, R., *Body Hot-Spots*, Van Nostrand Reinhold, New York (1976)

Dalgleish, T. and Power, M., *Handbook of Cognition and Emotion*, John Wiley & Sons Ltd (1999)

Danesi, M., *Of Cigarettes, High Heels, and Other Interesting Things*, Macmillan (1999)

Darwin, C., *The Expression of Emotion in Man and Animals*, Appleton-Century-Crofts, New York (1872)

Darwin. C., *The Expression of the Emotions in Man and Animals*, Philosophical Library (1872)

Darwin, C., with Introduction, Afterword and Commentary by Paul Ekman, HarperCollins; New York, Oxford University Press (1998)

Davies, P., *Your Total Image*, Piatkus (1990)

Davis, K., 'Clinton and the truth: on the nose', *USA Today* (19 May 1999)

Davitz, J. R., *The Communication of Emotional Meaning*, McGraw-Hill, New York (1964)

Dimberg, U. and Ohman, A., 'Behold the wrath: psychophysiological responses to facial stimuli', *Motivation and Emotion*, 20, 149-182 (1996)

Dimberg, U., Thunberg, M. and Elmehed, K., 'Unconscious facial reactions to emotional facial expressions', *Psychological Science*, 11 (2000)

Dixon, N. F., *Our Own Worst Enemy*, Ebury (1987)

Doran, G. D., 'Shake on it', *Entrepreneur Magazine* (July 1998)

Duchenne de Boulogne, 'Recherches faites à l'aide du galvanisme sur l'état de la contractilité et de la sensibilité électro-musculaires dans les paralysies des membres supérieures', *Comptes rendus de l'Académie des sciences*, 29: 667-670 (1849)

Duncan, S. and Fiske, D. W., *Face-to-Face Interaction*, Erlbaum, Hillsdale, New Jersey (1977)

Dunkell, S., *Sleep Positions*, Heinemann, London (1977)

Effron, D., *Gesture, Race and Culture*, Mouton, The Hague (1972)

Eibl-Eibesfeldt, I., *Ethology: The Biology of Behaviour*, Holt, Rinehart & Winston (1970)

Eibl-Eibesfeldt, I., *Love and Hate: The*

Natural History of Behaviour Patterns, Holt, Rinehart & Winston (1971)

Ekman, P. and Friesen, W. V., *Pictures of Facial Affect,* Consulting Psychologists Press (1976)

Ekman, P. and Heider, K. O., 'The universality of contempt expression: a replication', *Motivation and Emotion,* 12, 303-308 (1988)

Ekman, P. and Friesen, W., *Unmasking the Face,* Prentice-Hall, London (1975)

Ekman, P., 'Cross-cultural studies of facial expression' in P. Ekman (ed.), *Darwin and Facial Expression: A Century of Research in Review,* Academic Press, 169-222 (1973)

Ekman, P., *Darwin and Facial Expression,* Academic Press (1973)

Ekman, P., 'Facial expression of emotion', *American Psychologist,* 48, 384-392 (1993)

Ekman, P., Friesen, W. and Ellsworth, P., *Emotion in the Human Face,* Pergamon Press, New York (1972)

Ekman, P., Friesen, W. V. and Tomkins. S. S., 'Facial affect scoring technique: a first validity study', *Semiotica,* 3, 37-58 (1971)

Ekman, P., Levenson, R. W. and Friesen, W. V., 'Autonomic nervous system activity distinguishes between emotions', *Science,* 221, 1208-1210 (1983)

Ekman, P., Sorenson, E. R. and Friesen, W. V., 'Pan-cultural elements in facial displays of emotions', *Science,* 164 (3875), 86-88 (1969)

Ekman, P., 'Strong evidence for universals in facial expressions: a reply to Russell's mistaken critique', *Psychological Bulletin,* 115, 268-287 (1994)

Ekman, P., *Telling Lies,* W. W. Norton (2001)

Ekman, P., 'Universals and cultural differences in facial expressions of emotion', in J. Cole (ed.), *Nebraska Symposium on Motivation, 1971,* University of Nebraska Press, 207-283 (1972)

Ekman, P. and Davidson, R. J., 'Voluntary smiling changes regional brain activity', *Psychological Science,* 4, 342-345 (1993)

Ekman, P. and Friesen, W. V., 'Constants across cultures in the face and emotion', *Journal of Personality and Social Psychology,* 17, 124-129 (1971)

Ekman, P. and Friesen, W. V., 'The repertoire of nonverbal behavior: categories, origins, usage, and coding', *Semiotica,* 1, 49-98 (1969)

Ekman, P. and Friesen, W. V., 'A new pan-cultural expression of emotion', *Motivation and Emotion,* 10, 159-168 (1986)

Ekman, P., 'About brows: emotional and conversational signals', in M. von Cranach, K. Foppa, W. Lepenies and D. Ploog, *Human Ethology,* Cambridge University Press, 169-248 (1979)

Ekman, P., 'Biological and cultural contributions to body and facial movement', in J. Blacking (ed), *Anthropology of the Body,* Academic Press, 34-84 London(1977)

Ekman, P., Davidson. R. J. and Friesen, W. V., 'The Duchenne smile: emotional expression and brain physiology II', *Journal of Personality and Social Psychology,* 58, 342-353 (1990)

Ekman, P., 'Expression or communication about emotion', in N. Segal, G. E. Weisfeld and C. C. Weisfeld (eds), *Genetic, Ethological and Evolutionary Perspectives on Human Development: Essays in Honor of Dr. Daniel G. Freedman,* American Psychiatric Association, Washington, DC (1997)

Ekman, P., 'Facial expression of emotion: new findings, new questions', *Psychological Science,* 3, 34-38 (1992)

Ekman. P., Friesen, W. V., O'Sullivan, M., Chan, A., Diacoyanni-Tarlatzis. I., Heider, K., Krause, R., LeCompte, W. A., Pitcairn, T., Ricci-Bitti, P. E., Scherer, K. R., Tomita, M. and Tzavaras, A., 'Universals and cultural differences in the judgments of facial expressions of emotion', *Journal of Personality and Social Psychology,* 53, 712-717 (1987)

Elliot, A. J., *Child Language,* Cambridge University Press (1981)

Ellis, A. and Beattie, G., *The Psychology of Language and Communication,* Weidenfeld and Nicolson, London (1985)

Ellis, B. J., 'The Evolution of Sexual Attraction: Evaluative Mechanisms in Women', in J. H. Cosmides and J. Tooby, *The Adapted Mind: Evolutionary Psychology and the Generation of Culture,* Oxford University Press (1992)

Ellis, B. J., *The Evolution of Sexual Attraction: Evaluative Mechanisms in Women* (1992)

Ellis, B. J. and Malamuth, N., 'Love and anger in romantic relationships: A discrete systems model', *Journal of Personality,* 68: 525-556 (2000)

Ellyson, S. L. and Dovidio J. F., *Power, Dominance and Nonverbal Behaviour,* Springer-Verlag (1985)

Elsea, J. G., *First Impression Best Impression,* Simon & Schuster (1984)

Fast, J. and B., *Reading Between the Lines*, Viking, New York (1979)

Fast, J., *Body Language*, Pan Books, London and Sydney (1970)

Feldman, R. R., and Rime, B., *Fundamentals of Nonverbal Behaviour*, Cambridge University Press (1991)

Feldman, R. S., Forrest, J. A. and Happ, R. R., 'Self-presentation and verbal deception: do self-presenters lie more?', *Basic and Applied Social Psychology*, 24(2) (2002)

Feldman, S., *Mannerisms of Speech and Gesture in Everyday Life*, International University Press (1959)

Foot, H. C. and Chapman, A. J., 'The social responsiveness of young children in humorous situations', in A. J. Chapman and H. C. Foot (eds), *Humour and Laughter: Theory, Research, and Applications* (187-214) Wiley, London (1976)

Furnham, A., Dias, M. and McClelland, A., 'The role of body weight, waist-to-hip ratio, and breast size in judgements of female attractiveness', *Sex Roles*, 3/4 (1998)

Gayle, W., *Power Selling*, Prentice Hall, New York (1959)

Glass, L., *I Know What You're Thinking: Using the Four Codes of Reading People to Improve Your Life*, John Wiley & Sons Inc. (2002)

Goffman, E., *Behaviour in Public Places*, Free Press, Illinois (1963)

Goffman, E., *Interaction Ritual*, Allen Lane, London (1972)

Goffman, E., *The Presentation of Self in Everyday Life*, Edinburgh University Press (1956)

Goodall, J., *The Chimpanzees of Gombe*, Harvard University Press (1986)

Goodheart, A., *Laughter Therapy: How to Laugh About Everything In Your Life That Isn't Really Funny*

Gordon, R. L., *Interviewing Strategy, Techniques and Tactics*, Dorsey, Homewood, Illinois (1976)

Gottman, J. M., Murray, J. D., Swanson, C. C., Tyson, R. and Swanson, K. R., *The Mathematics of Marriage: Dynamics Nonlinear Models*, MIT Press (Bradford Books), Cambridge, MA (2003)

Gottman, J. M. and Silver, N., *The Seven Principles for Making Marriage Work*, Crown Publishers (1999)

Grammer, K., 'Strangers meet: Laughter and nonverbal signs of interest in opposite-sex encounters', *Journal of Nonverbal Behavior*, 14, 209-236 (1990)

Grammer, K., Kruck, K. B. and Magnusson, M. S., 'The courtship dance: patterns of nonverbal synchronization in opposite-sex encounters', *Journal of Nonverbal Behavior*, 22, 3-29 (1998)

Griffin, J., *How to Say It at Work: Putting Yourself Across with Power Words, Phrases, Convincing Body Language, and Communication Secrets*, NYIF (1998)

Gschwandtner, G., with Garnett, P., *Non Verbal Selling Power*, Prentice Hall (1985)

Hall, E. T., *Silent Language*, Doubleday & Co., New York (1959)

Hall, E. T., *The Hidden Dimension*, Doubleday & Co., New York (1966)

Harper, R. G., *Non-Verbal Communication; the State of the Art*, John Wiley, New York (1978)

Hecht, M. A. and LaFrance, M., 'License or obligation to smile: The effect of power and gender on amount and type of smiling', *Personality and Social Psychology Bulletin*, 24, 1326-1336 (1988)

Henley, N., 'Body politics', in A. Branaman, *Self and Society*, Blackwell (2001)

Henley, N. M., *Body Politics: Power, Sex and Non-Verbal Communication*, Prentice-Hall (1977)

Hess, E., *The Tell-Tale Eye*, Van Nostrand Reinhold, New York (1975)

Heyes, C. M. and Galef, B. G., *Social Learning in Animals: The Roots of Culture*, Academic Press,

Hillary, E., *View from the Summit*, Doubleday (1999)

Hind, R., *Non-Verbal Communication*, Cambridge University Press (1972)

Hopkins, W. D., Bales, S. A. and Bennett, A. J., 'Heritability of hand preferences in chimpanzees', *International Journal of Neuroscience*, 74 (1994)

Hore, T., *Non-Verbal Behaviour*, Australian Council for Educational Research (1976)

James, W., *Principles of Psychology*, Holt, Rinehart, New York (1892)

Jung, C., *Man and his Symbols*, Aldus, London (1964)

Kahn and Rudnitsky, *Love Codes*, Piatkus (1989)

Kahn, R. I. and Cannell, C. F., *The Dynamics of Interviewing*, Wiley, New York (1957)

Keating, C. F., 'Human dominance signals: the primate in us', in S. L. Ellyson and J. F. Dovidio, *Power, Dominance, and Non-verbal Behaviour*, Springer, Verlag (1985)

Keating, C. F. and Keating, E. G., 'Visual

scan patterns of rhesus monkeys viewing faces', *Perception*, 11: 211-219 (1982)

Kendon, A., *Organisation of Behaviour in Face-to-Face Interaction*, Mouton, The Hague (1975)

Kendon, A., 'Some relationships between body motion and speech: An analysis of an example', in A. W. Siegman and B. Pope (eds), *Studies in Dyadic Communication*, Pergamon Press (1994)

Key, M. R., *Non-Verbal Communication: A Research Guide and Bibliography*, Scarecrow Press, Metuchen, New Jersey (1977)

Key, M. R., *Paralinguistics and Kinesics; Non-Verbal Communication*, Scarecrow Press, Metuchen, New Jersey (1975)

King, N., *The First Five Minutes*, Simon & Schuster (1988)

Klein, R., *Cigarettes Are Sublime*, Picador (1995)

Knapp, M., *Non-Verbal Communication in Human Interaction* (2nd edition), Holt, Rinehart and Winston, New York (1978)

Knight, S., *NLP at Work: The Difference that Makes a Difference in Business*, Nicholas Brealey Publishing (2002)

Korda, M., *Power in the Office*, Weidenfeld and Nicolson, London (1976)

Korda, M., *Power! How To Get It, How To Use It*, Weidenfeld and Nicolson, London (1975)

Korman, B., *Hands: The Power of Awareness*, Sunridge Press, New York (1978)

LaFrance, M. and Hecht, M. A., 'A meta-analysis of sex differences in smiling', in A. Fischer (ed.), *Nonverbal Communication and Gender*, Cambridge University Press (1999)

LaFrance, M. and Hecht, M. A., 'Why smiles generate leniency', *Personality and Social Psychology Bulletin*, 21, 207-214 (1995)

LaFrance, M. and Hecht, M.A., 'Option or obligation to smile: the effect of power and gender on facial expression', in P. Philippot, R. S. Feldman and E. J. Coats (eds), *The Social Context of Nonverbal Behaviour*, Cambridge University Press (1999)

LaFrance, M. and Hecht, M. A., 'Why do women smile more than men?', in A. Fischer (ed.), *Gender and Emotions*, (118-142), Cambridge University Press (2000)

Lamb, W., *Body Code*, Routledge and Kegan Paul, London (1979)

Lamb, W., *Posture and Gesture*, Duckworth, London (1965)

Lambert, D., *Body Language*, HarperCollins (1996)

Lewis, D., *The Secret Language of Success*, Carroll and Graf (1989)

Lewis, D., *The Secret Language of Your Child*, Souvenir Press, London (1978)

Lewis, M. and Sarrni, C., *Lying and Deception in Everyday Life*, Guilford Press (1993)

Liggett, J., *The Human Face*, Constable, London (1974)

Lloyd-Elliott, M., *Secrets of Sexual Body Language*, Hamlyn (1995)

Lorenz, K., *King Solomon's Ring*, London Reprint Society (1953)

Lorenz, K., *On Aggression*, Methuen, London (1967)

Lowndes, L., *How to Talk to Anyone: 101 Little Communication Tricks for Big Success in Relationships*, Contemporary Books (2003)

Lyle, J., *Understanding Body Language*, Hamlyn (1989)

MacHovec, F. J., *Body Talk*, Peter Pauper Press, New York (1975)

McCormack, S. A. and Parks, M. R., 'What women know that men don't: sex differences in determining the truth behind deceptive messages', *Journal of Social and Personal Relationships*, 7 (1990)

McCroskey, Larson and Knapp, *An Introduction to Interpersonal Behaviour*, Prentice-Hall, Englewood Cliffs, New Jersey (1971)

McIntosh, D. N., 'Facial feedback hypothesis: evidence, implications, and directions', *Motivation and Emotion*, 20 (1996)

Malandro, L. A. and Barker, L., *Nonverbal Communication*, Addison-Wesley (1983)

Mallery, G., *The Gesture Speech of Man*, Salem (1881)

Masters, W. H. and Johnson, V. E., *Human Sexual Response*, Little, Brown, Boston (1966)

Mehrabian, A., *Silent Messages*, Wadsworth, Belmont, California (1971)

Mehrabian, A., *Tactics in Social Influence*, Prentice-Hall, Englewood Cliffs, New Jersey (1969)

Millar, M. G. and Millar, K., 'Detection of deception in familiar and unfamiliar persons: the effects of information restriction', *Journal of Nonverbal Behavior*, 19(2) (1995)

Miller, A., 'Re-dressing classical statuary: The eighteenth-century "Hand-in-Waistcoat" portrait', *Art Bulletin* (College Art Association of America), Vol. 77, No2,

45-64 (March 1995)

Mitchell, M. E., *How to Read the Language of the Face*, Macmillan, New York (1968)

Montagu, A., *Touching: The Human Significance of the Skin*, Columbia University Press (1971)

Morris, D. and Marsh, P., *Tribes*, Pyramid (1988)

Morris, D. with Collett, Marsh and O'Shaughnessy, *Gestures, Their Origins and Distribution*, Cape, London (1979)

Morris, D., *Babywatching*, Jonathan Cape (1991)

Morris, D., *Bodywatching*, Jonathan Cape (1985)

Morris, D., *Initmate Behaviour*, Cape, London (1971)

Morris, D., *Manwatching*, Jonathan Cape, London (1977)

Morris, D., *The Human Zoo*, Cape, London (1969)

Morris, D., *The Naked Ape*, Cape, London (1967)

Morris, D., *Bodytalk*, Jonathan Cape (1994)

Morris, D., *Manwatching*, Jonathan Cape (1977)

Morris, D., *People Watching*, Vintage (1977)

Nierenberg, G. and Calero, H., *How to Read a Person like a Book*, Hawthorn Books, New York (1971)

Nierenberg, G., *The Art of Negotiating*, Hawthorn Books, New York (1968)

O'Connell, S., *Mindreading: An Investigation into How We Learn to Love and Lie*, Doubleday (1998)

O'Connor, J. and Seymour, J., *Introducing NLP Neuro-Linguistic Programming*, HarperCollins (1993)

O'Connor, J., *NLP: A Practical Guide to Achieving the Results You Want: Workbook*, HarperCollins (2001)

Patterson, J., *The Day America Told the Truth*, Plume (1992)

Pease, A., *Body Language*, Sheldon Press (1997)

Pease, A. V., *The Hot Button Selling System*, Elvic & Co., Sydney (1976)

Pease, Allan & Barbara, *Why Men Don't Listen & Women Can't Read Maps*, Orion, 2001

Pease, Allan & Barbara, *Why Men Lie & Women Cry*, Orion, 2003

Pease, Allan & Barbara, *Why Men Can Only Do One Thing at a Time & Women Won't Stop Talking*, Orion, 2003

Pease, R. V. and Dr Ruth, *My Secret Life as a Porn Star*, Camel Publishing (2004)

Perper, T., *Sex Signals: The Biology of Love*, ISI Press (1985)

Pinker, S., *How the Mind Works*, W. W. Norton (1997)

Place, U. T., 'The role of the hand in the evolution of language', Psycoloquy 11 (2000)

Pliner, O., Kramer, L. and Alloway, T., *Non-Verbal Communication*, Plenum Press, New York (1973)

Provine, R. R. and Fischer, K. R., 'Laughing, smiling, and talking: Relation to sleeping and social context in humans', *Ethology*, 83(4), 295-305 (1989)

Provine, R. R. and Yong, Y. L., 'Laughter: A stereotyped human vocalization', *Ethology*, 89(2), 115-124 (1991)

Provine, R. R., *Laughter: A Scientific Investigation*, Penguin (2000)

Provine, R. R., 'Contagious yawning and laughter: Significance for sensory features, and the evolution of social behaviour'

Provine, R. R., *Yawns, Laughs, Smiles, and Talking: Naturalistic and Laboratory Studies of Facial Action and Social Communication*, (1997)

Provine, R. R., *Laughter: A Scientific Investigation*, Viking Press (2000)

Pujol, J., Deus, J., Losilla, J. M. and Capdevila, A., 'Cerebral lateralization of language in normal left-handed people studied by functional MRI', *Neurology 52* (1999)

Quilliam, S., *Sexual Body Talk*, Headline (1992)

Quilliam, S., *Your Child's Body Language*, Angus and Robertson (1994)

Quilliam, S., *Body Language*, Carlton Books (1995)

Quilliam, S., *Body Language Secrets*, Thorsons (1996)

Reik, T., *Listening with the Third Ear*, Farrar, Straus and Giroux, New York (1948)

Robinson, J., *Body Packaging*, Watermark Press (1988)

Russell, J. A., 'Facial expressions of emotion: what lies beyond minimal universality?' *Psychological Bulletin*, 118, 379-391 (1995)

Russell, J. A., 'Is there universal recognition of emotion from facial expression? A review of cross-cultural studies', *Psychological Bulletin*, 115, 102-141 (1994)

Russell, J. A., Suzuki, N. and Ishida, N., 'Canadian, Greek, and Japanese freely produced emotion labels for facial expression', *Motivation and Emotion*, 17, 337-351 (1993)

Russell, J. A. and Fernandez-Dols, J. M. (eds), *The Psychology of Facial Expression*, (158-175), Cambridge University Press,

Russo, N., 'Connotation of seating arrangement', *Cornell Journal of Social Relations* (1967)

Saitz, R. L. and Cervenka, E. C., *Handbook of Gestures: Columbia and the United States*, Mouton, The Hague (1972)

Sathre, F., Olson, R. and Whitney, C., *Let's Talk*, Scott Foresman, Glenview Illinois (1973)

Scheflen, A. E., *Body Language and the Social Order*, Prentice Hall, New Jersey (1972)

Scheflen, A. E., 'Quasi-courtship behavior', in S. Weitz (ed.), *Nonverbal communication* (182-198), Oxford University Press (1974)

Scheflen, A. E., *How Behavior Means*, Garden City, Anchor (1975)

Scheflen, A. E., *Human Territories*, Prentice-Hall, New Jersey (1976)

Scheflen, A. E., 'On communicational processes', in A. Wolfgang (ed.), *Nonverbal Behavior: Applications and Cultural Implications* (1-16), Academic Press (1979)

Scheflen, A. E., *Body Language and the Social Order*, Prentice Hall (1981)

Schultz, A. H., 'Proportions, variability and asymmetries of the fones of the limbs and the clavicles in man and apes', *Human Biology*, 9 (1937)

Schutz, W. C., *A Three-Dimensional Theory of Interpersonal Behaviour*, Holt, Rinehart and Winston, New York (1958)

Siddons, H., *Practical Illustration of Rhetorical Gestures*, London (1822)

Singh, D. and Young, R. K., 'Body weight, waist-to-hip ratio, breasts, and hips: role in judgements of female attractiveness and desirability for relationships', *Ethology and Sociobiology*, 16 (1995)

Sommer, R., *Personal Space: The Behavioural Basis of Design*, Prentice Hall, Englewood Cliffs, New Jersey (1969)

Steel, J. and Mays, S., 'Handedness and directional asymmetry in the long bones of the human upper limb', *International Journal of Osteoarchaeology*, 5 (1995)

Steele, D., *Body Language Secrets: A Guide During Courtship and Dating*, SBP (1999)

Strack, F., Martin, L. and Stepper, S., 'Inhibiting and facial conditions of the human smile: a nonobtrusive test of the facial feedback hypothesis', *Journal of Personality and Social Psychology*, 54 (1988)

Strodtbeck, F. and Hook, L., 'The Social Dimensions of a Twelve Man Jury Table', *Sociometry* (1961)

Suter, W. A., *My Life as a She-Man*, Camel Publishing (2004)

Szasz, S., *Body Language of Children*, Norton, New York (1978)

Von Cranach, M., *Social Communication and Movement: Studies of Interaction and Expression in Man and Chimpanzee*, Academic Press, London (1973)

Vrij, A. S., Vrij, G. R. and Bull, R., 'Insight into behavior displayed during deception', *Human Communication Research*, 22(4), 544-562 (1996)

Vrij, A., 'Credibility judgments of detectives: The impact of nonverbal behavior, social skills, and physical characteristics on impression formation', *The Journal of Social Psychology*, 133, 601-610 (1993)

Vrij, A., *Detecting Lies and Deceit*, John Wiley (2001)

Wainwright, G. R., *Teach Yourself Body Language*, Hodder & Stoughton (1985)

Weisfeld, G. E. and Beresford, J. M., 'Erectness of posture as an indicator of dominance or success in humans', *Motivation and Emotion*, Vol 6(2)

Weisfeld, G. E. and Linkey, H. E., 'Dominance displays as indicators of social success motive', *Motivation and Emotion*

White, A. G., 'The Patient Sits Down: A Clinical Note', *Psychosomatic Medicine* (1953)

Whiteside, R. L., *Face Language*, Pocket Books, New York (1975)

Whitney, Hubin and Murphy, *The New Psychology of Persuasion and Motivation in Selling*, Prentice Hall, New Jersey (1978)

Wilson, P. R., 'Perceptual Distortion of Height as a Function of Ascribed Academic Status', *Journal of Social Psychology* (1968)

Wolfe, C., *A Psychology of Gesture*, Methuen, London (1948)